Leabharlann Chontae Luimní

BUYING & SELLING
ANTIQUES

Some other related titles from How To Books

Your Own Business
The complete guide to succeeding with a small business

Book-keeping & Accounting for the Small Business
How to keep the books and maintain financial control over your business

Starting Your Own Business
How to plan, build and manage a successful enterprise

The Ultimate Business Plan
Secure financial backing and support for a successful business

howtobooks

Please send for a free copy of the latest catalogue:

How To Books
3 Newtec Place, Magdalen Road,
Oxford OX4 1RE, United Kingdom
email: info@howtobooks.co.uk
http://www.howtobooks.co.uk

SUCCESSFUL BUSINESS
START-UPS

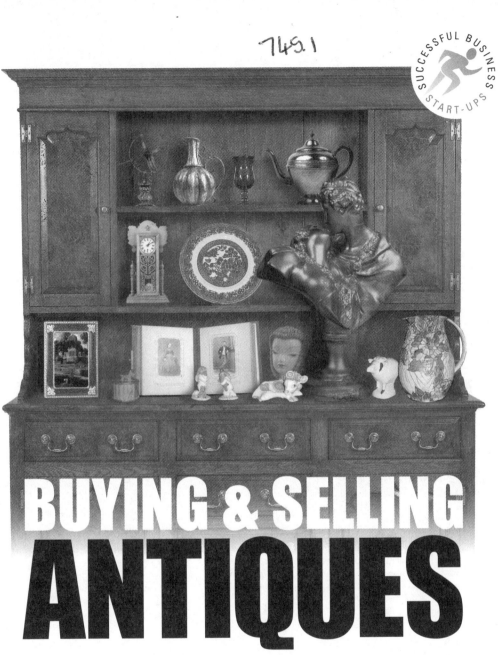

BUYING & SELLING
ANTIQUES

INSIDER KNOWLEDGE AND TRADE TIPS TO
HELP YOU MAKE MONEY FROM YOUR HOBBY

FIONA SHOOP

·REVISED AND UPDATED·
2ND
·SECOND EDITION·

how tobooks

Published by How To Books Ltd,
3 Newtec Place, Magdalen Road,
Oxford OX4 1RE. United Kingdom.
Tel: (01865) 793806. Fax: (01865) 248780.
email: info@howtobooks.co.uk
http://www.howtobooks.co.uk

First edition 2002
Second edition 2004

British Library Cataloguing in Publication Data
A catalogue record for this book is available from the British Library

Cover design by Baseline Arts Ltd, Oxford
Produced for How To Books by Deer Park Productions
Typeset by PDQ Typesetting, Newcastle-under-Lyme, Staffs.
Printed and bound by Bell & Bain Ltd, Glasgow.

NOTE: The material contained in this book is set out in good faith for general
guidance and no liability can be accepted for loss or expense incurred as a result of
relying in particular circumstances on statements made in the book. The laws and
regulations are complex and liable to change, and readers should check the current
position with the relevant authorities before making personal arrangements.

Contents

Preface

If you've picked up this book, then you must be one of two things – a dealer or a would-be dealer. Either way, I can help you to be a successful one, no matter what you're selling or where you intend to sell it. This book was written for you to help you to fulfil your potential and enjoy doing so.

In this simple, step-by-step guide, I will show you how to save money when you buy and, even more vitally, make a profit when you sell. Not only will you be introduced to different types of dealing from fairs to the Internet, but I'll also warn you about the tricks of the trade and help you to avoid the most common mistakes made by new (and even old) dealers – and some of the costlier ones as well.

But who am I to tell you all this? My name is Fiona Shoop, I've been a dealer for over twenty years, starting at the age of ten with a corner of my father's stall at a north London antiques fair. Since then, I've bought and sold through fairs, auctions, antiques centres and the Internet. I know how to avoid being caught out – and I'm going to teach you the same. I'm also a TV expert, broadcaster and journalist. You might know my name from the by-lines of some of the most talked about articles in recent years. If there's a con going on, I'll let you know about it. I've also written over 700 articles on antiques from furniture to jewellery and just about everything in between, including dirty toilets.

Twenty years ago, I sat in a café in London's Portobello Road, an area famous for its antiques, and read *The Antiques Trade Gazette*. I knew then that I was where I belonged but I didn't realise that, all these years on, I'd still be a dealer and a columnist for the same paper. And that's the thing about antiques, you never know where they'll take you. It's an exciting life and I love sharing it with people.

Dealing offers so many rewards, whether you do it once or all the time. It's unlike any other job, you'll be surrounded by beautiful things and meet fascinating people. It's a strange but exciting world where no two days are ever the same and you never know what you'll find.

One last comment – when your alarm wakes you up at 4 am for your next fair, don't blame me, I did tell you that Internet dealing might offer an easier way of making money. Or did I? Read on to find out – and good luck, a dealer's life is not always an easy one but it is always fulfilling,

Fiona Shoop

PART ONE
Establishing the Basics

CHAPTER ONE

Why Do You Want to Become an Antiques Dealer?

There are three basic reasons for becoming an antiques dealer: love, money and need. The first of these is probably the easiest to understand and the reason why most people consider antiques as a potential career, second job or hobby. If you love antiques, sooner or later you acquire too many of them – if there can be such a thing. The reason people love antiques is easy to understand. Quite simply, what's not to love? They are attractive, many of them are practical, there is joy in their acquisition and, with the exception of 'fads' (see Section Five, Chapter 21), they are a sound investment.

The trouble with loving antiques is that you can overspend but the good news is that they are relatively easy to sell and a very easy way of raising money. At some time in your lives, most of you will have a bill to pay or want something which could be considered a luxury – a holiday, a better computer or even a new outfit. By selling an antique or collectable, something which has appeal to others, you can realise your goal without running up dangerous debts.

> **You don't need a loan if:**
> **1. You have something to sell.**
> **2. You have enough knowledge to buy low and sell high.**

This book is your starting block. By following its simple guidelines, you can make money – the second most popular reason why people become antiques dealers.

And then there is need. It's possibly the hardest of the three factors to define but it is the need for something that could change your life. If you need a job, a career or a change in lifestyle, if you want to get out of the 9–5 grind and become your own boss, then you're not alone. To become an antiques dealer you do not need qualifications, you do not necessarily need experience or knowledge (but they help) and, most of all, you don't need to impress anyone to get the position. The only person who needs convincing that you're good enough to be a dealer is yourself because *you* are the only person who matters.

What makes it so exciting is that you're investing in yourself with minimal risk. *The only requirement that you need to become a dealer is to have some antiques or collectables. In the trade, we call that 'stock'.*

What Are the Advantages of Being a Dealer?

Some of these points will only concern full-time or part-time dealers but even if you only stall out a few times a year, there are huge advantages over virtually any other money-making hobby or career.

1. A huge sense of freedom – you are your own boss – you can't get sacked, made redundant or passed over for promotion.

2. You decide when or even *if* you're going to work.

3. You may have extra money for luxuries such as a holiday, eating out or even something previously thought unattainable.

4. You decide how often you have to work per month.

5. You can go on holiday whenever and for as long as you want without having to get permission first or having to count how much holiday leave you have left.

6. You are free to make your own decisions without having to defer to someone else.

7. Whatever you make is yours – you don't just get a cut of your own hard work.

8. You get to meet new people and not just the same dull ones every day!

9. You get to travel.

10. You can make new friends wherever you go.

11. It's a friendly trade with little or no competitive streaks because no one's competing for the same job or bonus.

12. No more commuting so no more getting stuck on broken down trains or hot, overcrowded tubes or buses – if they're even running, that is.

13. Complete privacy – no one else needs to know how much you've earned. No one else reads your post or e-mails. You can't get sacked or reprimanded for speaking to your friends and family during the day.

14. You can even take as much time off as you need to be with your family without risking losing your job.

15. Unlike many jobs, you're dealing in something viable, you can see it, appreciate it and, when you want, you just sell it on for a profit.

16. You're surrounded by beautiful things and, for the time being, they're all yours.

17. It's both interesting and enjoyable with a fresh challenge every day.

Are There Disadvantages As Well?

As with any job, there are negative aspects of dealing but these are far outweighed by the freedom of the trade. For some people, the lack of restrictions usually imposed by office hours is unsettling. However, most people I have met find it invigorating and use that time to do other things such as staying in bed late, shopping, reading, travelling, starting a new hobby or going to the gym, going on courses or just catching up with the family. But it isn't always perfect and you have to consider all of the disadvantages if you're thinking about dealing professionally or even as a hobby (the distinctions will be outlined in the next chapter).

Most dealers will, at some time or other, find the following a disadvantage but some are more applicable to full-time dealers than anyone else.

1. Early hours – you will get to see the wrong side of dawn at least once a month. 4am is the time to get up and go to work, not to bed after a good night out.

2. You have to remember to put aside enough money for your tax bill every year as it won't be done automatically under PAYE, but if you become a full-time dealer, you will pay less tax and less National Insurance than someone who's employed (see Section Six, Chapter 1 for all tax matters).

The next disadvantages really only concern full-time dealers, although all dealers should be aware of them:

3. Uncertain finances: if you decide to become a full-time dealer it can be difficult not having a regular income.

4. Irregular finances: might mean that you're earning more than you ever did, just not on set days of the month. But try explaining that to a mortgage provider. Not as bad as it sounds, as there are reputable companies such as The Mortgage Business (part of The Bank of Scotland, now partnered with The Halifax) who cater for the self-employed, but it can make life awkward at times, even when applying for store or credit cards or car finance.

5. You'll need to take out a private pension and pay for it all yourself.

6. You don't get holiday pay or sick leave (but can take as many days off a year as you want).

The disadvantages mainly concern financial matters, but they are not all as significant as they might appear at first glance. Dealers enjoy earning their living this way. They enjoy the challenge of working as much or as little as they want, without having to worry about redundancy or getting sacked. Unlike most people in 'regular' employment, you won't wake up one morning to find yourself without a job. *As a dealer, your job is your own and that is one of the most attractive aspects of dealing. That, and one very basic fact: it's enjoyable.*

CHAPTER TWO

What Type of Dealer Do You Want To Be?

When you apply for a job or consider starting a career, the one thing you normally don't get asked is 'how many hours do you really want to work?' With antiques, it's different: you can be full-time, part-time or just work when you want to, what's known as a 'hobby dealer' in the trade. The only person who can decide this is you, and it doesn't matter what you choose because there are good and bad dealers in all of these categories and the only person who really matters is you.

◆ If antiques provide your entire income, you're a full-timer.

◆ If you have another job but sell antiques on a regular basis (at least three fairs a month), you're a part-timer.

◆ If, however, you only indulge for fun or when you need a bit of cash for a holiday or to pay off a large bill, you're what's classified as a hobby dealer.

Full-time

The title itself is very misleading. This is not a 9–5 job and it also depends on where you live. To work five days a week or more depends on the markets and fairs around you if, that is, you want to sell full-time at antiques fairs. As you will discover when reading this book, there are many types of dealing, but the hardest – and often the most rewarding – is dealing at antiques fairs and markets. Most dealers work virtually every Sunday in the year, as this is the main day for fairs and can be the most lucrative, especially in quieter cities when not all shops are open.

> ### Keyword
> **Full-time does not refer to the hours worked but your source of income.**
> **Full-time dealers depend solely on antiques for their living.**

The antiques business is not a Monday–Friday job. Many dealers will take the entire summer off as this is traditionally a quieter time of the year, whilst others work throughout the year. There is no such thing as a typical dealer. So, where does that leave you? *Quite simply, you choose when you want to work*. If you live in London, have a shop or a unit in an antiques centre, you can work seven days a week. Why especially if you live in London? It's one of the busiest areas for antiques markets but also has the most competition so London dealers, contrary to popular opinion, also have to be the most competitively priced. In theory, at least!

Becoming a Full-time Dealer

Most full-timers who do not have shops or their own units in centres sell around three-four days a week, depending on fairs. The rest of the time is spent buying. To be a successful dealer, you need to buy at the lowest possible price and that is why many dealers attend auctions. Whilst people who work 9–5, five days a week rest in the evenings, some dealers work until 9 or 10 at night buying at auction, with one dealer known to attend three auctions a day. That is excessive but it does show that full-time is a comparative term. For dealers, the word full-time does not reflect the days or hours worked but the source of income.

The advantage of dealing full-time is that you don't have to depend on anyone else for an income. You can work as hard or as easily as you like, go on holiday without permission and never have to answer to anyone but yourself.

The main disadvantage is that you are not guaranteed a regular income. Hard work is not always rewarded with a healthy bank balance, but it can be and that is the joy of the trade – it's entirely unpredictable.

Becoming a Part-time Dealer

Why do you need to become a part-time dealer? You might fancy some extra cash for savings, a holiday or other unexpected needs or you might just want to get out of the house, mix with people and enjoy the trade without having to depend on it for your financial security. There are many reasons why people choose to deal part-time. Many dealers start out as full-timers but discover other interests or careers and don't want to have to give up dealing. Some hobby dealers start dealing more often and became part-timers, whilst other people deal part-time because they don't *need* to deal full-time or just don't want to. It really doesn't matter and that's why it's such a tempting trade. *It's entirely up to you when, where and how you work.*

If you have a regular job but don't want to give it up, part-time dealing is a great way to trade. You might take a few days off work now and then to stall out at the big, midweek two or three day fairs but it's up to you if you do that. As with everything in the trade, it is not compulsory to attend these fairs but it can be useful and most dealers have, at some time or other, gone to Newark[1], the bimonthly, two-day fair which is the largest in Europe. If you are thinking of dealing, on whatever level, you will find this fair fascinating, useful and rather awe-inspiring although it is not grand at all. There are around 4,000 stallholders at the event, many of whom are part-timers.

There is a certain snobbishness in the trade which sees full-time dealing as the only option but that, in many ways, is jealousy. All dealers dream of being able to combine the best of both worlds (clichéd but true), of paying bills, having holidays and enjoying the freedom of running their own business with minimal work. Part-time dealing gives you this option. I've given several career talks and my advice has always been simple – do what you enjoy and, if necessary, do something else as well to pay the bills. By dealing part-time you really can have the best of everything.

> ### Useful tip
> As with all dealing, full-time, part-time or hobby, do things properly. Register for tax and keep accurate records – save yourself the expense and embarrassment of being caught out.

Dealing as a Hobby

Let's start by defining hobby dealing. It means that you enjoy dealing but don't want or

---

[1] Newark is run by DMG, one of the largest fairs' organisers. Tel: 01636 702326.

need to do it very often. You could have a unit in an antiques centre (see Section Three, Chapter 5 for details) which will enable you to earn a bit of extra money with minimal work, or you could do a fair every month, if that regularly. The whole point is that, to you, antiques are enjoyable, they are not a career (although they may become so if you so choose) and you've probably started by selling off the extra pieces in your collection or excess belongings to clear some space. Whichever way you start, your view of the antiques world is different from that of a full-time dealer. To put it at its most basic level, you enjoy it and that's as far as it goes.

And that's great. Hobby dealers tend to work on some (but not all) Sundays and the odd Bank Holiday only, they don't need the money so find it a very relaxing pursuit. They tend not to do the bigger fairs or the weekday ones, many finding them too much like hard work although some hobby dealers do enjoy the extra challenge which they represent.

There is no set type of hobby dealer but they tend to be collectors, many of them are retired but not willing to stop work entirely and why should they? If you want to carry on working when your company deems that you're only fit for redundancy or retirement, why not do what thousands of other people have done and set yourself up in business – but as a hobby only? It will not only give you a chance to earn some extra money but introduce you to new people and a new way of life. If you enjoy it, do some more – but only if you want to.

Whatever type of dealer you decide to be, enjoy it and be as good as you can.

CHAPTER THREE

To Specialise or Not

If you go round any antiques fair or centre, you'll notice that there are, essentially, two types of dealers – the general and the specialist. Some will deal in anything which brings a profit, whilst others go for a 'theme' – Art Deco, a specific make of china such as Sylvac or Masons, tins or toys – anything as long as it's the same 'type' as their other stock. Actually, it isn't that simple because some dealers do both. Look more closely at the general dealer and you might start spotting patterns – do they specialise in something as well as seeming to sell everything? I think you'll find that many of them do. I know that I do.

Let's start with something very basic. You're probably just starting out or thinking about being a dealer. You're probably a bit confused about what sort of things you want to sell. I'll be covering that in much more detail in Section Five but you need to think of something very basic before you start to spend any money and decide whether you want to specialise or not. What sort of dealer do you want to be? I'm not talking full-time, part-time or hobby but what *sort* of things do you want to sell – not in great detail. But, for now, do you want to sell:

◆ smalls (eg china and glass)
◆ or larger pieces such as furniture?

Furniture is very attractive, often has very good profit margins but it is not always practical for all people. If you're not very strong, you can still deal in furniture but you might need to hire someone (or several people) to help you to move the goods which will cut down on your profits. You'll need to own a van in the long-run as hire costs are often too high to be practical on a regular basis. Some general dealers have the odd piece of furniture with their normal stock, which can be a good idea if your car is big enough to hold it all. Don't even think about furniture if you only drive a motorbike or a small car such as a Smart car and have no intention of changing or just can't afford to – it just won't work.

Furniture takes up far more room than a standard stock of smalls (if there is such a thing). If you live in a flat without a lift or a small house, it is not practical to be a furniture dealer unless you have separate storage, and not just storage but secure storage –

there's no point paying for it, otherwise. Your local telephone directory will list storage facilities as will the classifieds section of some of the antiques publications such as *The Antiques Trade Gazette*. (Subscriptions for this are available on 020 7420 6600, via their website on *www.atg-online.com* or buy copies from the larger antiques fairs.) If you have enough money and room, it might be worth considering hiring or building a garage instead, but furniture must be kept in a dry environment to prevent costly warping.

Useful tip

To be a furniture dealer you must:

+ **Be strong or have someone to lift and display the goods for you.**

+ **Have a large van or be able to hire one on a regular basis at a reasonable cost (not always practicable).**

+ **Be able to drive and manoeuvre a large vehicle or hire someone to do so (often the same person who can lift the furniture for or with you).**

+ **Know how to polish without causing ugly smudges – a simple way to increase sales.**

+ **Have sufficient storage space or enough money to hire secure space.**

+ **Have sufficient money to deal in either top or middle of the range, not low end furniture – better profits and easier to sell than cheaper, less attractive and poorer quality pieces.**

If you decide that furniture is not for you, then you're a 'smalls', art, scientific instruments or book dealer (amongst others). It doesn't matter what you do as long as it's practical. Antiques should all be about beauty but the practicalities have got to be considered. If you live in a city, don't drive and don't want to learn or even think about getting a car, then you're restricted, but not as much as you would be without transport in the country. In a city you have access to public transport but you wouldn't be able to deal in furniture or anything too bulky that way. However, if you're a jewellery dealer, all you need is a bag containing your stock and, if you want, a jewellery case as well. With that sort of stock, it's practical to work anywhere. The same goes for someone who deals in paper goods such as autographs or postcards, but you really will need access to a car (or a cheap taxi firm) if you want to deal in bulkier and heavier goods and go to fairs anywhere in the country, not just local ones.

How Do You Find Out About the Different Types of Specialisation?

That's easy. Take the time to go looking round fairs, auctions and centres before spending any money at all. You might find that you love everything you see, you might quite like some bits or you might be drawn to others. If you find that you're drawn to the same type of goods over and over again, then you're a specialist.

Useful tip
People don't *decide* to specialise, they need to.

That might be over-simplified but a lot of the dealers who are specialists didn't necessarily start out that way. Most people start off by buying what they like – it's a very sensible way to do business. If you like something, there's a strong possibility that someone else will like it as well. They then realised that they started buying the same type of stock, not just because they liked it but because they had established regular buyers who also liked it. *The basic rule of dealing is that if something works, stick with it – that's how to specialise.*

The word 'specialise' should not be taken too literally. Some china dealers claim they specialise in china but to 'specialist' china dealers (eg who only sell Art Deco or a specific make), that's not specialising at all. One of the simplest ways to work it out is to go through a fair guide (available from most fairs and antiques centres) and see what sort of fairs are advertised. If you have sufficient stock to do a clock and watch fair, you're a specialist but if, like most general dealers, you only have one or two bits or none at all, you're not that type of specialist. But that's assuming that you have stock. Look at what draws you. If you keep looking at brightly coloured, geometric pieces from the 1920–30s, you should think about dealing in Art Deco, but good Deco does require a lot of money. That is the main disadvantage of being a specialist, if you want to be a good one, depending on your specialisation you need good funding to match. By being a general dealer you have the option of having a specialist section (eg a couple of shelves' worth) but you don't have to have a lot of money to do so.

You'll notice that a few of the pros and cons on page 14, conflict and that's because dealing is not always logical. There is no Recommended Retail Price (RRP) when it comes to antiques and collectables – which is why it's such an exciting business. Specialist fairs attract not only specialist buyers but also specialist sellers. That might seem obvious to you but there's an inherent problem with too many specialists stalling together

Specialise – Pros	Specialise – Cons
It looks attractive which attracts buyers	It can be expensive
You don't waste time and money by trying to sell at unsuitable venues	Stall rent is generally more expensive than at general fairs
Your buyers know what they're talking about (well, most of the time) and are prepared to pay more than those without a specialist knowledge/collection	You could restrict the number of buyers – if people don't buy your type of stock, they won't even stop to see if anything appeals at general fairs
You can focus your knowledge without having to learn something about everything	You don't have a broad enough knowledge, allowing you to expand when the market changes
You can pick up bargains from non-specialists	You could miss out on bargain stock because it doesn't match your criteria
You can command a higher price than a general dealer because people assume that it's worth it	People can think that you're over-charging because you're a specialist
You can do specialist fairs which attract people wanting to buy your type of stock	You're at the mercy of the market. If interest in that area dies, you're in trouble

– they often sell the same goods. I know that seems obvious but I mean it literally – effectively, the same pieces. What's rare in the antiques world at large becomes common at specialist fairs and that means that your buyers have too good a choice – which could mean that you lose out. Imagine if you've been searching everywhere for a Silver Crane Dodgem Car novelty teapot. You go to a specialist teapot fair and you see, not one of these hard-to-find teapots, but three. What are you going to do? Are you going to buy the first one that you see because you're surrounded by hundreds of other would-be buyers or are you going to race around the fair and see if you can find it more cheaply elsewhere? With experience, it will probably be the latter and the stallholders – that will be you soon – will know it.

A few years ago, when specialist china fairs (eg only selling Wade china) were new, some of the stallholders were known to raise their prices according to the length of the queue, but not any longer.

If you want to specialise or do a specialist fair, you have to be competitive because you want to be the one whose rare teapot gets sold, not left on the shelf at the end of the day because of an overly-ambitious price label. Take the same teapot with the same price to a non-specialist fair and, ironically, it will probably sell. Why? Because it becomes rare again.

That said, specialist fairs are very successful if you price accordingly. The buyers are often more serious than those at general fairs, whilst a lot of trading goes on before the fair even opens with stallholders buying from each other. That is not the case at all fairs and buyers can find bargains no matter what time they visit. *Remember, not everyone wants the same pieces so it's worth visiting specialist (and general) fairs at all times of the day, not just the beginning.*

Do Specialist Goods Sell at General Fairs As Well?

Never underestimate appearances. There is something very attractive about seeing a stall full of the same type of stock if it is well presented – Art Deco or novelty teapots *en masse* will immediately attract interested buyers but could alienate those who don't want that type of stock. There is a danger of becoming too specialist. Those who only deal in chintz (flowery goods, generally china), will be ignored by anyone who doesn't buy that type of stock whereas a general dealer tends to appeal to most would-be buyers unless they, too, are very specialist. Someone who only buys jewellery is going to ignore china and furniture pitches whilst those looking for presents and people who aren't very comfortable at fairs will bypass any stall which looks 'too expensive'. It can be a no-win situation.

Some dealers start life as specialist dealers but change – either they get bored or move with the market. Just because you start out as one thing doesn't mean that you have to stay the same for all of your dealing life.

Case Study

I'm a specialist turned general dealer. I started out selling Wade china at the age of 10. I sold 'doubles' from my own collection which enabled me to buy the bigger and better pieces. Over a decade on, when the market changed and prices of Wade dipped, I risked going under so I changed. I was also a bit bored with Wade by that time and wanted a fresh challenge. I thought about changing to the very marketable area of dog and cat items (ornaments, jewellery, pictures etc) but managed to get hooked on costume jewellery instead. I went to buy a dog brooch and ended up with stylish plastic brooches by the 1950's

French designer, Lea Stein. From there, I bought more and more designer jewellery which worked very well in London but struggled away from the knowledgeable specialist buyers. I still had a lot of Wade so mixed it with the costume jewellery, effectively specialising in both and that was much more successful at general fairs. I stalled out with Art Deco china and jewellery at Art Deco fairs but these were very expensive and I didn't *need* to do them because my stock was varied enough to sell at general fairs and didn't only appeal to one type of buyer.

I think of myself as a general dealer with specialist areas. Whilst I am a known expert on Wade china, contributing to books and valuing goods for auctioneers and insurance companies, I no longer specialise in it but I still retain the knowledge. I have small areas of specialisation, including some of the English figural (ladies, animals etc) studio potters and Carlton Ware but I rarely do specialist fairs. It's my choice and some dealers might not consider it the right one, but I enjoy my lifestyle and the variety of my stock ensures that I am never bored, complacent or at the mercy of market forces.

By being a specialist, you are confining the scope of your stock and knowledge but you will be surrounded by goods which you love and can usually still do general fairs as well as specialist ones. There is more competition within specialist areas but, conversely, you can also make friends with similar interests. As with all aspects of dealing, look around and judge for yourself whether you want to specialise and whether you want to do specialist fairs if you do. It is advisable to do at least one specialist fair to get a look from the inside and pick up handy tips from your fellow dealers. Likewise, general dealers can benefit from visiting the specialist fairs as buyers or just browsers – you can't really decide what to do until you know what to expect.

> *Keyword*
> **Specialist fairs can sound too upmarket or specialist for the novice or general dealer.**
> **But there are lots of different types of fair from specific makes (eg Royal Doulton, Beswick and**
> **Wade or just Carlton Ware) through to groups such as Art Deco and Art Nouveau, teapots, glass**
> **or scientific instruments.**

There is no hurry. You don't have to decide right now what you want to be. Start out small and build up when you get a better idea of the market and what you enjoy buying and selling. There's no point being a specialist dealer in militaria if you can't sell military goods in your area or you don't like them – or just can't get to the specialist militaria fairs. Book dealers can sell at any fair, including book fairs, but there are specialist areas within specialist areas with some book dealers selling scientific books only, others military history and still more with mass appeal children's fiction. Look around and see what works for you.

Useful tip

To specialise isn't to confine. Instead, it can bring you extensive knowledge of one area and the opportunity to be surrounded by goods which you – and your buyers – really appreciate.

CHAPTER FOUR

Can You Afford to Be a Dealer?

Most people outside the trade think that you have to be rich to be a dealer. The truth is that you don't – unless you decide to sell high-end goods or top-of-the-range furniture. There are basic costs to cover, not just stock, but one of the cheapest ways to start dealing is to turn your own, unwanted belongings or tired collections into stock. As you become more experienced, you'll find it easier to part with your own goods or separate stock from personal belongings. Dealers buy pieces for their own collections with the knowledge that they can always sell them on (generally for a healthy profit) if they need either stock or money, but this is a very hard concept for novice dealers. Until you get more experience, don't sell anything which you'll regret later.

Obviously, there is no set monetary figure for buying stock. It varies from area to area and you can't compare all types of stock – expect to pay more for real jewellery than most costume jewellery while Art Deco costs more than most other periods of china – but not always. There is no set rule and you can often get higher profits from cheaper goods than more expensive ones.

> **Useful tip**
> You can become a dealer by spending less than £500 on stock, or even nothing at all if you 'raid' your own house or sell unwanted inherited goods, but it's better to spend more if you want to make more money. You have to spend money to make money.

Start off small – it's not a good idea to spend all of your redundancy, retirement, inheritance or savings before you have even tried dealing, but you can't deal properly without stock. Sit down and work out what you can afford, maybe just buy goods which you'd be happy to have at home if it doesn't work out – you can always sell them at auction if you decide that fairs – or the antiques trade generally – is not for you.

Realistically, if you're intending to be a mid-range (i.e. not too highbrow, not too car boot sale) dealer, you'll need around £5,000–10,000 worth of stock *but* you don't have to buy it all at once. You can build up your stock over the course of a few weeks, using your initial outlay over and over again when you sell the goods for a profit and then invest that profit as well.

> *Confused? Don't be.* Imagine that you buy something for £100 and sell it for £150. You don't just have £50 to spend on more stock but get the £100 back again – and again and again.

You might choose to set up a bank account just for your business. Not a business account at this stage but just something to separate your household and everyday account from the money which you'll be investing in your business. I say 'investing' wisely because this is money which will regenerate itself and generally far more quickly than playing the stock exchange – with no costly middleman. Unless you're very, very lucky, it won't make you a fortune overnight but, whatever type of dealing you do, it will give you a comfortable existence with a good lifestyle, but only if you remember those little extra costs.

I've Put Money Aside for Stock – What Else Do I Need?

This will be covered in more detail in Section Three, but there are obvious outlays which you need to take into account before going any further.

Rent

This will be covered in more detail in Section Three but you have got to consider rent before you can start dealing. Your first fair should cost you around £30–35, hopefully less. This sounds very cheap, and it is, but stall rent soon adds up.

> **Keyword**
> Pcm stands for per calendar month and not per cubic metre – a popular misconception. It's used when renting space (a unit), shelves or a cabinet in an antiques centre. Pcm means that you pay rent from the first to the last day in a month – which can make the shorter February a bad month to start trading.

If you're thinking about selling in an antiques centre, costs vary hugely and a higher rent is not always indicative of a better centre. You are normally expected to sign up for three months at a cost of around £35–90+ pcm (per calendar month) for a locked cabinet and about £150–250+ pcm for a unit. This means that your first three months will cost you £105–270+ per locked cabinet and £450–750+ for a unit.

> *Keyword*
> **Unit – a space at an antiques centre, where dealers sell furniture and other items. Unit sizes vary greatly with one dealer assigned per unit – although some share with friends/fellow dealers. You can use your own locked cabinets in a unit, which is often a very cost-effective way for large-scale smalls dealers to have more room but pay less rent than they would for several cabinets.**

Petrol

This is the forgotten cost of dealing and it will take a huge chunk out of your expenditure. If you don't drive it isn't relevant, but think of transport costs when budgeting to see if you can afford to be a dealer. The price of petrol varies, almost from day to day at times, but you will be doing a lot of driving, not just to sell stock but to buy it. Every time you drive to a centre, an auction or a fair, you are using petrol. There is no such thing as an average dealer and you might choose to stay close to home, but it is not uncommon for dealers to drive over 1,000 miles a week. The average driver, according to car insurance firms, drives up to 1,000 miles a month – if that.

The more you drive, the higher the wear and tear on your car so be prepared to take more expensive servicing and quicker tyre replacements into account. It's not as bad as it sounds but the cost of car maintenance should certainly be considered and never done too cheaply. For many dealers, their car is their livelihood. If you skimp on servicing, you could make a costly mistake.

> *Useful tip*
> **Look after your car and it will look after both you and your business/hobby.**

Budgeting

You would never start any business without sitting down and writing at least a basic budget. So take some time – it doesn't have to be a lot – to write down expenses and make sure that you have enough money to start dealing. When you're starting out you can initially skimp on some of the basics but you do need to be aware that they exist so that, if you decide to continue dealing or wish to expand, you're not caught out by unexpected demands.

Starting Out on a Small Budget

- **Stock** – some of your own goods (or raid your local car boot sale for decent quality but very cheap stock if you can find it) and at least two boxes of decent auction or fair-bought stock – £500–1,000.

- **Rent** – depends on how active you wish to be but minimum of £105 for the first three months in a cabinet and around £30–35 per fair, becoming more costly with experience (eg some of the bigger or better fairs cost £65+ per day with two-day fairs generally charging £85+ for the two days). Many full-time dealers spend at least £200 p/m on fairs, more if there are two-day fairs. Hobby dealers can spend as little as £30 a month on fairs – less if they stick to small, village hall ones.

- **Car** – budget it in if you don't already have one and add 'petrol' to the list regardless.

- **Accessories for record keeping** – notebooks, stockbook, pens, labels etc – £100 p/a.

- **Food and drink** – it soon adds up, even on buying trips. £2–10+ a day per person.

- **Time** – your time costs, remember that. Dealers do not get the minimum wage on bad days or buying days – take that into account when tempted to discount goods.

Average Budget

If you're going to deal more often, you'll need a larger budget. Many of the points will be the same but just a bit more costly – stall rent will be more than £30 a month because you'll be doing more fairs, stock will cost you more and you'll need a mobile phone – not to mention its bills. Phones will be covered in more detail in the next chapter but you do have to be aware of them when sitting down and working out your *minimum* budget.

- **Stock** – you'll really need about £5,000 to start dealing fully – less if you're lucky or more (around £10–25,000) if you want to deal at a slightly higher level such as Art Deco china. If you're thinking of dealing at the top end of the spectrum (or near there) where a single item can cost at least £10,000, budget accordingly.

- **Rent** – set aside £120–150+ for your first month's rent if you're planning to do antiques fairs and £105–270+ for the first three months in an antiques centre with medium to large cabinets or £450–750+ for the first three months in a larger unit (see Section Three, Chapter 5 for more details).

- **Petrol** – allow at least £100 before you've even started trading. Depending where you live, this will allow you to drive around to buy stock, looking at centres and fairs as a potential seller. Petrol is one of the biggest and most frequently forgotten costs of dealing. After that, count on spending at least £60 a week on petrol if you're dealing full or part-time, especially if you're not working locally.

- **Stockbooks, notebooks, receipt books, pens and labels** – it soon adds up, budget around £100 p/a. More if you're turning over a lot of stock. Labels cost around £1.50 for 100 which might sound cheap but 100 labels don't last long.

- **Food and drink** – keep costs down by making your own sandwiches, or spend a bit more by buying them from supermarkets before you arrive at a fair, but try not to buy them at the venue – a roast beef sandwich made at home will cost you about 50–70p, £1.50–2.00 from a supermarket and £2.50–3.50 from most fair venues – that can be £3 extra per sandwich! Drinks can cost up to £3 at fairs during the summer months so use tap water from home or buy your own drinks from a supermarket at around 45p per can – a worst case scenario saving of around £2.55 and that's just for one drink.

- **Reference books** – all dealers, at some time or other, have spent money on books. They are often cheaper to buy at fairs[2] than in the shops but expect to spend £5–50 on most antiques books.

---

[2] Two of the best and friendliest of the bookdealers are Bobby's Books who also offer a mail order service – Tel: 01474 823388 or *e-mail bobbysbooks@aol.com* and Books for Collectors (Frank and Shirley). Tel: 01525 875100.

♦ **Fair guides** – an essential tool of dealing which cost around £6–15 p/a. A small cost but useful to include in any budget. If you rely on more than one publication, don't forget to allow extra. The Weekly *Antiques Trade Gazette*, the main antiques newspaper, costs £1.80 per issue (at the time of writing) from larger fairs or save 10% by subscribing to the 50 issues a year (ring 020 7420 6601 for more details). The ATG (as it's popularly known) contains details of auctions and fairs as well as news and is an essential guide for middle- to top-end dealers. Its sister paper, *The Antique Dealer Newspaper*, is aimed at lower- to middle-end dealers, contains fair listings and news and is either free from fairs or costs £1.50 from some antiques centres (not all centres charge). The three-monthly, *The Antiques Trade Calendar* (from most fairs or ring 020 8446 3604 to subscribe) costs £1.50 per issue and is an essential buy for all dealers and buyers.

♦ **Mobile phone and phone bills** – essential for dealers, phones can either be free or cost between £50–250. Bills obviously vary according to your contract and frequency of use.

♦ **Calculator** – £5 +. They get lost and broken very easily in the trade so budget for more than one per year.

♦ **Business cards** – from £3 for 50.

♦ **Tax** – remember to keep some money aside as you'll pay your tax bill in one go, unlike regular wages which are taxed throughout the year. Even hobby dealers need to take this into account and set money aside after each profitable fair for tax purposes.

♦ **Car servicing** – £180 + p/a. Public transport is wonderful when it works but won't always get you where you need to go, when you need to get there. You might have to budget for a car (and even driving lessons) if applicable. Long-term, it might be worth saving up for an estate car – the more stock you have, the greater your potential profit. You'll also have more room for your purchases, even when stalling – something which most smaller car drivers find problematic.

♦ **An accountant** – someone who can help save you money by showing you what's taxable and what's not.

◆ Insurance – not all dealers take out insurance as it can be costly and not necessarily beneficial but it's worth looking into. You might also choose to increase your household insurance if you're storing antiques there, but check first as some insurers might charge you extra for business use – or refuse to insure you at all. Don't forget to change your car insurance to cover business use as an antiques dealer as you can be fined otherwise.

> **Just because something is cheap, it doesn't necessarily mean that it's a good buy.**
> **Think in terms of quality and style, no matter what your budget.**

Long-term Needs

On top of these very basic budgets, there are the one-off costs needed by most (but not all) fair-selling dealers, but not essential at your first ever fair – with the exception of the cloth which is used to cover the tables supplied by the fair organisers and an alarm clock.

◆ Cloth £6+

◆ Alarm clock – essential for those early starts – £4+

◆ Lights with extension leads for fairs £20–30+

◆ Two to three sets of shelves £30–35+ per set

◆ Sturdy paste table £30

◆ Trolley £25+

◆ Display stands – useful for plates, cups and saucers, tea services, jewellery etc £1–15+ per stand

◆ Jewellery cases for jewellery and also smaller items such as tiny Toby jugs and other costly, easy-to-steal/fragile items – £50–150 +

◆ Free-standing cabinets for larger fairs or in antiques centre units (if applicable) £150 +

◆ Walkie-talkies – very useful equipment if you're stalling with someone else (a friend or partner). They save money on phone costs and are a cost-effective way of keeping in touch after the initial outlay of £75–100 for the pair. Particularly useful at the larger fairs where it's easy to get lost – whether you're buying or selling

◆ Flask £7 +

◆ More stock – £500–3,000 + pm depending on your needs and turnover – most of this will be paid for out of profit but not always, especially if you wish to expand or have separate centre and fair stock, like most professional dealers who do both types of dealing.

Whatever your initial budget, allow extra for those unexpected extras and those must-buy bargains. This is especially important if you're thinking about becoming a full-time dealer or money is tight. Car boot sales can be the perfect place to pick up those high-profit pieces (if you're lucky) but you'll also need money to tide you over during the wet winter and spring months before the car boot sales start and for those surprisingly good local auctions which offer more than you expected. Budget accordingly and carry cash – it's more acceptable than anything else.

CHAPTER FIVE

Communications

Unless you have a shop of your own, or a fully equipped unit in an antiques centre, you won't always be near a telephone and, like most businesses, you need a phone to communicate. For a dealer, it is an essential expense.

Love Them or Hate Them, You'll Need a Mobile Phone

No antiques dealer should be without a mobile phone. You might hate them or relish the opportunity to be somewhere where you can't be reached but you do need one. There are several reasons for this. As a dealer, you should expect to travel to buy stock – some dealers will go further than others but, even if you stick to a thirty-mile radius, you will still need a phone. Why? Because you might break down, get lost, need help carrying goods or just have to phone someone to ask for directions to the venue or to say that you're going to be late. Professional dealers sell goods before they've even bought them – be it at fairs, auctions or centres. How do they do that? By phoning their client first.

Why You Need a Phone

◆ Communication – you'll need to be able to keep in touch with your family and friends while stuck in the middle of a field or during a long day (or days) at a fair.

◆ Business – ring your clients to say that you have what they're looking for and to tell them at which fair they can find you – sell the goods before you've even bought them or put them out on your stall.

◆ Car troubles – most dealers have tales of breaking down in the middle of nowhere with a car or van full of stock. Play it safe and carry a mobile so you can get home –

or have your car repaired by the road – as quickly and safely as possible.

♦ Ring the organiser to say that you're lost or going to be late – they'll appreciate it, help you to find the venue and keep your stall for you. If you arrive after the fair opens, you could find that your pitch has been given away to someone else.

♦ It's easier to give potential buyers a mobile phone number than your home number. There are various reasons for this but one of the most important is that you don't want them to know whereabouts you live for security reasons, you also want to control when you get phone calls – people outside the business won't appreciate the hours you keep and could ring you at 11pm when you have to get up at 3am the next morning. Mobiles can be switched on and off as required.

Coverage is as important as cost. The situation can change but, in my experience, BT Cellnet, Vodaphone and One-to-One often have poor reception and can be very problematic in some of the most popular venues – my BT Cellnet and Vodaphone phones would not connect at Newark, the largest of the fairs, and were hard to impossible to use at other showgrounds. Friends have had a similar experience with One-to-One whilst Orange seems to work everywhere – including Alexandra Palace, a fair notorious for its bad reception. There's no point having a phone, no matter how cheap or attractive, if you can't use it. Phone cards also have problems. It can be the cheapest way of using a mobile but they do tend to run out when you need them most – unless you're really well organised. Shop around before committing yourself.

> ### *Useful tip*
> Mobile phones are essential for dealers but make sure that they work where you need them to – Orange (at the time of writing) is the best supplier but shop around for the best deal. You don't have to have a monthly contract but be wary of getting a phone which needs topping up with phone cards unless you're well organised – you could be stuck with a phone which doesn't work when you most need it to.
> Don't forget to charge the battery before you go out.

You might decide to have more than one mobile phone – one for business use and the other for personal use. This means that you decide when to receive business calls (eg when you're not busy doing something else such as working in another job, driving, at an auction or dining out) and allows you to use your other phone the rest of the time for personal use, when you don't mind being interrupted. It's also handy to keep your business expenses separate which makes it easier for your accounts.

Walkie-talkies

Some dealers use their phones to ring their partners at fairs, especially if one is manning the stall and the other wandering around the fair, buying stock. If the phone has no reception, the battery or phone card has run out, this can make life really difficult. Some dealers have got round this problem by investing in walkie-talkies. These cost around £75– 100 for the pair and are available from many electrical retailers (see your local telephone directory for details) and at some of the larger fairs. They need regular battery changes but calls are free.

> *Keyword*
> **To man the stall – to run a stall.**

Walkie-talkies are a very convenient method of communication but they come at a price – that of privacy. You won't be the only person using walkie-talkies at the larger fairs and you'll quickly realise that you won't be the only person speaking on your frequency. This can have two detrimental effects – you'll think that you're being called when you're not, which can lead to terse conversations between you and your friend/partner who will immediately answer any call and be convinced that it is for them – just as you will be that it is for you. More importantly, anyone on the same frequency can listen in to your conversation.

This can be fascinating if you are the person listening in but it can also warn others that you've found a must-buy piece of stock and where you've found it. Play safe and speak in code. It's not as complex as it sounds. You can ring in and ask for a coffee and say where you are (eg I'm in the big hall). Then ask if they want to see what you have found or should you just buy it? (Do you want anything? Ooh, that reminds me, have you put the pig out yet. You know, the CW [Carlton Ware] one?) – or just return to your stall and send them out. It's up to you but walkie-talkies can save you time and let you buy that must-have piece. I use mine when I'm sharing a stall with a wandering friend and want to know the price of their unmarked stock or just need a toilet break. They're very useful.

Business Cards

It's useful to have a business card whether you deal or just like buying antiques. Giving people a contact number means that they can contact you if they find something which you'd like to buy. As a seller, you provide a would-be buyer an opportunity to buy from you at a later date.

The Dos and Don'ts of Business Cards

◆ Do include your name, name of business (if applicable) and a short description of your business. This can be very basic ('antiques and collectables dealer') or more specific to remind people what sort of goods you sell ('costume jewellery dealer' or 'Royal Doulton, Beswick and Carlton Ware stockist. If we don't stock it, we can find it').

◆ Do provide a contact telephone number – as discussed previously, it's best to give a number which you can control and which reveals as little about where you live as possible. Ninety-nine per cent of the people involved in the antiques business are honest but protect yourself from those few who aren't. On a practical level, this stops you being disturbed when you're at work (if you have another job) or other inconvenient moments.

◆ Do give an e-mail address if you have it – with the increasing use of the Internet, especially amongst antiques dealers, e-mail is a fast and effective method of communication. Like mobile phones, it's a good idea to use a separate account for personal and business use and choose your e-mail address carefully – you'll want to be taken seriously. If you specialise in something such as a make of china, try to incorporate that into your address, eg *SylvacExpert@aol.com*.

◆ Don't use your home address – you'll be inviting trouble. Some stallholders leave their business cards on their tables at fairs. It's surprising how trustworthy some of them are, especially at the multiple-day fairs. You don't know everyone who goes to these fairs so why tell a complete stranger where you live – especially because they know what stock you have and how long you'll be away from home. Keep it safe and don't disclose your address unless you really have to (eg if someone's sending you goods by post). If you decide to expand into mail order, speak to your local post office about opening a post office box – it's relatively cheap and it's a safe address to use.

◆ Don't use your home number unless you really want to. Keep personal and business lives separate and use your home to relax.

◆ Don't produce jokey cards – you want to be taken seriously to increase sales.

◆ Photographs of your stock can prove relatively expensive when reproduced on a business card, but they are also eye-catching and likely to increase sales – an ideal marketing tool.

Business cards can be produced very quickly and easily. There are machines at train and some tube stations as well as service stations and many post offices. Decide what you want to say before you insert your money, decide on the design and just follow the simple instructions. The smaller cards cost £3 for 50 (at the time of writing) and are the best size because they fit into card cases and wallets. The larger cards are neither as practical nor as cost efficient.

> Fiona Shoop
> Antiques Dealer
> Art Deco specialist
> Mob Number, E-Mail

> *Fiona Shoop – Antiques Dealer since 1982*
>
> *Studio pottery and Costume jewellery*
> *expert and general dealer*
>
> *Mail order available – PO Box somewhere*
> *or other*
> *Mob number, E-mail address*

As you can see with these examples, cards do not need to be complex to be effective, you just need to give your basic information:

- Who are you?
- What do you do?
- Are you a general or a specialist dealer – or both?
- Do you offer extra services such as mail order or restoration?
- Do you have a business address (never a home one)?
- What's your mobile number?
- What's your e-mail address – very useful in this international trade?

Later on, you might decide that you want better quality cards, possibly with a photo of your favourite piece of stock reproduced on them. Speak to other dealers and see what they have. If you see an example that you really like, ask where they got it and contact their supplier. Costs vary but shop around and don't stick to plain white unless you want to – silver-grey is very stylish and your card will stand out from everyone else's. Be discriminating and don't just give your card to everyone or leave a pile on your table for anyone to pick up. They can be relatively expensive but they can pay for themselves in the long run.

If someone is after something particular, write something on the back of your card (unless it's laminated) to remind them who you are, what you've got, how much it is and where they can see you next, eg Charlotte Rhead, rare Arabesque bowl, £375 (trade price). May 9th, Alexandra Palace, stall N22.

If, for whatever reason, you don't have a card, simply use a page of your notebook to give out the same details along with a contact number. It won't look as good but it will do the same job and at a fraction of the price. That said, it's unlikely that people will keep a scrap of paper whereas most dealers and serious buyers keep business cards in a box or file for future use.

PART TWO
Where to Buy Goods

CHAPTER ONE

Let's Start at the Beginning – How Much Should I Pay for Things?

The answer to that is easy – you pay as little as possible. Now for the more complicated part, how much is that? It doesn't matter if you're buying for yourself or buying to sell, you want to pay less than the 'market' value (if there is such a thing) and you want to know that there is sufficient profit for you to sell on (if you wish), not just to a buyer but to a trade buyer. The difference between the two can be around 20% or even more. Basically, you don't want to buy at the top or near top price but allow, essentially, for at least two other people further along the chain – your buyer and their buyer. Or more if you want.

Whether you want to be a dealer or not, I want you to think like one. I don't care if you're buying a present, for your own collection or for stock, the principle is the same – you want, if not a bargain, at least something fairly priced.

And that is the problem. How do you, someone starting out or wishing to increase their knowledge, know what a fair price is? The most obvious way to learn is the wrong way.

Be Careful About Using Price Guides

Before you start forking out money for costly books with price guides (or just price guides), stop. Let me explain something about publishing. By the time a price guide appears in a bookshop or at a fair near you, it is already out of date. Why? A writer will sit down and suggest writing a book in a letter to a publisher. The publisher will (eventually) accept. The poor writer then has to run around doing as much research as possible – including checking out the subject matter's prices (eg Wade china, one of the more popular subjects of price guides on the market) – before they can sit back down and start writing their book. This process can take months or even years. The prices should be updated at this time but are not always. The publisher gets hold of the book and will often demand a rewrite. The author takes a month or so doing the changes. The prices remain the same in the book during this process (with very few exceptions). The book is published – several months later. It can take 18 months between writing and publication. Assuming that the price guide was the last part of the book to be written, it is still 18 months out of date.

But it gets worse. Not all of the authors who have written these price guides deal in their subject matter. They are relying not on their own experience, but on others to assess market value. I hate to be cynical but this can lead to unreliable data with dealers thinking in terms of their own self-interest, not the poor readers who, rather naïvely, place a lot of trust in these price guides.

Case Study

There was a scandal amongst a certain group of dealers (not in this country, I hasten to add) when one of them wrote a book which was published to coincide with the sale of their collection. The market said something was worth £35, the book put it at £85 (for example). People believed the book and got ripped off.

There is another example closer to home where either the author made a mistake or there was a typo (printed mistake). According to the book, an ornament was worth £750. Sales rocketed as dealers got greedy and bought hundreds of these ornaments for around £25–30 and that was a mistake because the piece *was* worth £25–30, not £750 as published. It proved to be a very costly mistake for the dealers who had believed a book, and not the market value, and found themselves lumbered with ornaments which then reflooded the market and stuck (didn't sell) because, by that time, everyone knew their 'true' value.

And that is another problem – there is no such thing as a true value. You can't go into your local supermarket and pick up a vintage Steiff bear at a recommended retail price (RRP) – because there isn't one and yet these books try to force the market or gullible buyers into accepting one.

There is also a danger that you are relying on books written by someone who might deal in the subject matter but not in this country. Canada and America have a very different market from Britain. Their prices are not comparable and yet writers have been known to use their own country's prices to determine the market in another country.

By all means buy the books for their information and pictures but not prices. If they do contain a price guide, ignore it – or you could end up making a costly error or missing out on a bargain.

When I was still at school, I helped an author to write a book on china. She bought something from me and it appeared in her book's price guide as worth the exact amount she paid me for it – that's not how to determine market value. You need a greater knowledge or an estimated price. Something is not worth £30 but £25–35.

> **Keyword**
> Book price – the value of goods determined in a book (eg costume jewellery butterfly $150–180)
> as opposed to real, 'market' price. In this case, $50–75.

The more you deal, the more you'll distrust and even dislike book prices. Would-be buyers will ask you the book price of your clearly labelled stock to find out – from you – if you're overcharging. They'll stand in front of your stall with the book open to determine the same thing. Even if the book was written several months or even years previously by someone who either does not deal in the subject matter or does not deal in this country. It's like asking a tailor the price of fish.

So, take book prices with a huge pinch of salt (if you read them at all). Where does that leave you? How else are you meant to know what things are worth?

How to Discover the 'Market' Value of Stock

There are three other methods which are far more reliable than book prices:

- Look and listen – visit fairs and see what everyone else is charging for the same or similar pieces.

- Go to mainstream auctions (i.e. not specialist ones where prices can often exceed market value with so many specialist buyers after the same pieces and also not small, local auctions which rarely realise realistic prices – great for buying but not necessarily for selling).

- Ask a friendly dealer. It isn't fair to ask a dealer if they're overcharging. Even if they are, they're not going to admit it and it will also offend an honest dealer who will be less inclined to give you a better price if you ask. Instead, go to a dealer specialising in that type of stock (or with some similar goods) and, when they're not too busy, ask them what you should be paying.

In this business, you have to learn quickly. Whenever you go out, make a mental note of what you see and for how much it sells. Never write down prices in front of a dealer as it makes you look unprofessional – something you don't want potential buyers to think about you and that's the whole point of dealing – everyone you meet, everyone who talks to you is a potential buyer. Don't be afraid of asking for help but do it nicely. Dealers get annoyed if people ask them for too much information or too many prices, especially if you're not buying anything or you're asking about things which are grossly dissimilar to what they have on their stall. You'll be seen as a nuisance, not as a potential buyer or seller. Be nice, ask them what sort of day they've had and then explain your predicament. Let them know that you're just starting up and can't afford to be caught out – but don't go over the top.

Dealers love talking about antiques. They love sharing stories about their special buys and they also do another very useful thing – they'll let you know which dealers are not to be trusted. Tell them what you want to buy and how much it is. Most of them will let you know if it's a good price or if there's no profit left. If you ask them, most will tell you if they know that the seller in question has a reputation for selling restored goods as perfect and a very few will tell you not to buy the piece and then buy it themselves but that is very, very rare. If it happens to you, never buy from them. It's unfortunate and of course it's not fair but it does happen. The way round it is to say that you saw something at a certain price and don't tell them where – if they start asking, smile sweetly, make your excuses and leave – most dealers wouldn't dream of asking you for specific details unless they have their own agenda.

No matter what you're buying, there is no definitive value for anything. It is as high or as low as its buyer is prepared to pay.

There are actually reasons for buying an overpriced piece – you might want to complete a set or just have particularly attractive pieces on your stall. It might take time to sell but there are buyers for everything and, in the meantime, you have something that attracts people to your stall who might very well leave after buying something else.

A useful technique is to buy old catalogues (no more than two years old) from good auction houses. Ignore any which are just printed on bits of paper, but go for the glossy catalogues and ask for a list of the sale prices. That way, you get to assess the rise and fall of the market and get a vague idea what things are 'worth'.

Obviously, it is difficult to determine how much rarer pieces are worth. If you really want it, buy it, but if it 'feels' too much or you don't want to pay beyond a certain price then be sensible and leave it – market value really is only as high as you – or someone else – is prepared to pay.

If you decide that you don't want to pay a particular price for something, be polite and let the dealer know that it's beyond what you wanted to pay – not too expensive because that's rude (even when it's true) and could harm future transactions – just too much for you. Another thing which you should never say is that you'll 'think about it' – unless you really mean to. Some dealers will believe you and you'll discover for yourself how annoying false hope can be. Be honest but polite – because that's how you want people to treat you.

How Do I Know What to Charge Other People?

You also have to think about your own pricing structure when you start dealing. Something might be worth £100 but if you try to sell it for £100 (or even more), you'll probably have a long wait. It could also put people off from buying other things if they assume that one top-heavy piece reflects the rest of your prices. A dealer who has paid significantly less will charge around £60–75 – this allows for around two to three other buyers to make a decent profit which makes your piece more sellable. *By not being greedy, you'll have a faster turnover of stock which allows for a higher profit.* You can either hold on for months (or even longer) for the full market value (even allowing for market changes) or you could take your profit by pricing it to sell, let someone else make some money and use your faster profit to make another profit on something else and on something after that – meanwhile, the full or overpriced stock is still sitting on the shelf while you're making more and more money by not being greedy.

If you want to be a successful dealer, don't be a greedy one and watch those profits add up.

CHAPTER TWO

Buying Tips

To be a successful dealer, you must first appear to be so. There is a secret language within the trade which separates the dealers from the public and which could cost you money unless you learn it. The good news is that it's easy – when you know how.

Learn How to Read Labels

The next time you see an antique in a shop or on someone's stall, read the label. Some things are obvious – the description (**19c** or **c19** means that it was made between 1800-1899) and the price. Or is it obvious? A typical label will read £100 **T10** or even just have a '10' by the price but what does that mean? It means that the dealer is prepared to take £10 off the price – the 'T' or 't' means trade. By asking for the trade price and not just the 'best' or the 'very best' price, you will look more professional and the dealer will give you a discount, usually in line with the 'trade' marked on the ticket, often lower than the 'best' price.

The idea of discounts is a relatively recent occurrence. It used to be given strictly to fellow dealers but now many dealers will give a discount (of varying degrees) to anyone who asks for the best price – but often giving a bigger discount to anyone asking for the *trade* price. Always check to see what trade is offered on the label – it could be a better price than you were thinking of offering. *As a rule, it's better to ask for a trade price than to offer a specific figure – you could end up paying more than the dealer was expecting.*

Many dealers refuse to give discounts on items below £5 (or even £10) because they are not making enough money on them to offer a better price. This is generally signified by the letters '**NT**' or '**nt**' on the label. It means 'no trade'. Don't forget to use it on your own labels when you're selling goods but be careful about using them on higher priced goods as this could lose you sales (eg £70 NT is not acceptable). It's normally easier to mark something '£6 T1' if you want £5, than '£5 NT' because too many people will refuse to buy something for the full price when they expect a discount. And never go back on an 'NT' – if you've done it once, they'll expect it again and you'll seriously reduce your profit margin. Always remember that you're in the trade to make money, not temporary friends.

Not all dealers are honest but those that are mark their goods accordingly. 'A/F' means 'all faults' or 'as found'. It means, quite simply, that the piece is damaged or has been restored. It's always best to check goods before buying but the use of 'A/F' is a respected institution in the trade and used by most respectable dealers. That said, many dealers also recognise that not all people realise what the letters mean and will also mention the damage before selling the goods to avoid problems.

If you sell at an antiques fair, you are '**stalling out**'. The term has become so commonplace that few dealers would expect to have to explain it but it can confuse novices. If in doubt, ask.

How to Get the Best Out of Dealers

At least 10% of all goods sold at fairs are never exhibited. Why? Because dealers put them aside for favoured customers or fellow dealers. Some of these goods have been pre-sold either from previous fairs or over the telephone. How do you get this to work for you? As a buyer, let dealers know what you want to buy from them. If you've bought something of particular interest, ask if they have any more like it elsewhere (eg at home or in an antiques centre). If they have, ask for details and, if it's what you want, arrange to buy it from them at a convenient fair. If they don't have something in stock but are likely to get it at a later date, give them your phone number and ask them to call you. Not all dealers will ring, even if they do find the stock. It's not that they're rude but some of them forget, others don't have the time or know that they can sell it elsewhere and some will just not want to do business that way because they've been let down before. Make sure that you're friendly but professional and this will encourage some of the dealers to put goods aside for you, the rest might just take a bit longer until they get used to seeing you on the antiques circuit.

Always collect business cards when you buy something from a dealer or like their stock. That way, you have their contact details and can ring them later to ask whether they have relevant goods in stock. Use these simple communication skills to beat the competition and buy stock before anyone else has the chance to see it but do be careful. If you change your mind, let the dealer know as soon as possible or they might not deal with you again.

Most importantly, *always* smile and be friendly or just polite. Dealers get annoyed by a lack of manners and could refuse to give you the best price accordingly. Also, if a dealer says that they can't reduce their price any further, respect that. Demanding a discount after it's already been refused can backfire. Manners can save you a lot of money in the long run. They're also a cheap way of making a friend out of a dealer and that could help you to be one of those lucky people who never has to run around at a fair because they know that the best stock is already put aside for them – and all for the price of a smile.

How to Get the Best Out of Your Customers

To contradict the previous paragraphs, don't put goods aside without a deposit when dealing with the general public. At least 75% will never turn up to collect the goods you've reserved for them and that's a wasted opportunity. With dealers, it's bit different, but some of them will not buy what you reserve. Use your judgement which will come with experience. Treat your regulars properly and they'll do the same to you, but when selling at fairs always do what I do and set would-be buyers a time limit. Set goods aside for half an hour, possibly an hour later on in the day when the rush has finished, but set them a limit and, if they don't return, put the goods back on your stall and sell it to someone else.

The most basic principle in dealing is to treat others as you would have them treat you – be friendly, not just polite, be helpful but don't let your or anyone else's time be wasted – and, above all, smile – you'll get a better discount and a bigger customer base that way.

So remember, whether you're buying or selling, your most powerful tool is a smile and a friendly word. That (and a little know-how) is how you can get the best out of the antiques business and become a successful antiques dealer.

Antiques Fairs

It is unlikely that you'll have decided to become a dealer without at least visiting one antiques fair. The previous chapter showed you how to get the best discount from a fellow dealer – you might not even have known that you can get discounts at all. Never buy anything without asking, 'What's the trade price?'. I know that I've already said that but they are some of the most important words in the business. To make a profit, you must ask for one.

Fair Entry

I'm going to let you into a little secret which is really going to annoy fair organisers. You can get in at the same time as the stallholders at fairs where you're not meant to and you can also enter with the stallholders at fairs where you *are* allowed – but at a fraction of the entry price! This is not allowed – but everyone does it. The small print on tickets will tell dealers, quite firmly, that they are not allowed to sell their tickets – but everybody does. Just go to any large fair and look for a dealer hanging about outside it looking a bit shifty. Some dealers will approach you and ask if you're buying a ticket – ask what they're charging and be prepared to pay it. No one haggles when buying tickets. That said, know what the entrance fee is first – you could end up spending more than it's worth! Simply ring the organiser a couple of days before the fair and ask about entry times and costs. Ask if you're allowed to enter at the same time as stallholders but don't mention wanting to buy illicit entry passes or you could get into trouble.

One of the main reasons why stallholders sell their spare tickets is not to upset the organiser or cut into their profits but to cut down on their own expenses. Spare tickets can make £5–15 depending on the fair (I would love to say which ones but I might get blacklisted!). For the stallholder, that means having £5–15 less expenses to cover. They simply deduct it from their rent, you save money or actually get into the venue early and everyone is happy. Everyone except for the organiser who is within their rights to ban both you and the stallholder from their fairs. I've never heard of anyone actually being banned, and the organisers know that some of the dealers sell their spare tickets, but it's only fair to warn you – and let you know how to save money.

> *Useful tip*
> Always take a torch to fairs which have outside pitches – especially during those dark winter and early spring months. Stallholders stall out when it's too dark to see what they're selling and you could either miss out entirely or buy damaged stock without realising it. Pocket-sized torches are also useful to carry at fairs (and centres) in case there's a power cut.

When going to fairs, make a note of how long it takes you to get there and how many miles it is from your home. This could prove very useful if you decide to be a stallholder in the future. Ring the organiser a couple of days before the fair to get details of where the venue is and, most importantly of all, that the fair has not been cancelled. Fairs do get cancelled at short notice and good organisers will carry a message to this effect on their answerphones if no one is in the office.

> *Useful tip*
> Never travel to a fair without ringing the organiser first (even the day before travelling) to ensure that the fair is still on and has not been cancelled or the venue changed. It does happen and a quick call could save you both time and petrol money.

How to Get the Best Out of Fairs

I'm going to make some very basic points about buying at fairs which most dealers take for granted but often forget to do themselves.

♦ Always be open-minded. Open your mind to other possibilities. You might go to a fair intending to buy Magic Roundabout collectables, but don't forget to look at other goods which complement your existing – or intended – stock. By increasing your own mindset, you're opening yourself up to more options and, eventually, more sales. Never be limited.

◆ Take your time. Most buyers, trade or public, rush around as soon as the doors open or make a beeline for their regular pitches or stock that looks attractive. It's tempting to do the same but don't fall into that trap. By going up and down the rows systematically, you'll spot more stock than the 'headless chicken' type of dealer. Go up one side of an aisle and come down the other – avoid crossing over as you could miss out a stall or get caught up in the general rush forward. Some buyers walk straight down the middle of an aisle looking left, right or just straight ahead. They'll see around 50% of what's on offer – if that. Don't be afraid to stand in front of a stall to see everything. The dealer will probably assume that you're interested in buying something and offer to help, but just smile (frequent but essential advice) and let them know that you're just looking. Compliment their stock if it deserves it – even if you don't want to buy anything, the dealer will be happy and, if you do want to buy something, they'll be even more helpful – which can take the form of an extra discount. If they can afford it.

◆ When you see something that you want to buy, check it over carefully. This is especially relevant for breakables. Never take a dealer's word that something is perfect. Goods get damaged *en route* and not everyone has the same definition of perfect! Check the label for that telltale set of initials, 'A/F' (showing that an item is damaged) and don't be afraid to ask where the damage is. Some dealers are extra scrupulous and what they refer to as A/F is another dealer's perfect (i.e. minuscule, almost impossible-to-find chip).

◆ Ask for the trade price before buying anything over £5 or £10 (depending on individual dealers) but don't ask for any discount if the label is marked 'NT' (No Trade), as you'll end up looking ignorant. For higher priced goods, never offer a better price (eg 'Will you take £20?') because you could end up paying more than the dealer expected. And never take it for granted that you will be given a discount, even if trade is marked on the labels – it's considered both rude and unprofessional just to assume – ask first and don't just hand over the already discounted amount (eg £20 for £22 T2 pieces) – they could refuse to give you a discount for being so rude.

◆ If you're buying a lot of things or just one heavy piece from a dealer, ask if they'd mind holding onto it for you – but only after you've paid them in full. Most dealers are fine about this and the more professional ones will give you a slip of paper with their stall number on it to remind you where they are – if they don't, ask. You might think that you'll remember but it is easy to forget – especially if the dealer is selling a lot of stock or tucked away behind a set of shelves.

- Bring your own bags – not all dealers remember to bring any and some of them supply light-weight or holey bags which are not suitable for breakables or heavier items.

- You might want to take your own wrapping to a fair as well – you might feel embarrassed to rewrap goods in front of a dealer or to offer them your bubble-wrap or other packaging, but they're used to it and won't mind.

- Ask for a receipt. The dealers don't have to give their addresses but their stall number and fair details (eg Peterborough Showground, Nat West Building H15) will suffice. Always keep records when you can – it reminds you how much you've spent and is good business sense, even if you don't intend to become a dealer. You *will* need to keep receipts for all transactions if you are going to become a dealer (see Section Six, Chapter 1) for tax purposes.

- Keep a notebook to note down transactions and an opinion of the fair – you might want to stall there later or there might be something which puts you off ever doing it (eg bad facilities or signposting). Make notes so you don't forget. Take plenty of pens as well – they're sure to go missing.

- Go round a fair at least twice, especially if you're there early – make sure that you don't miss anything.

- If you meet a particularly helpful dealer or one with interesting stock, ask for their card so that you can get in touch at a later date. Ask them what other fairs they do – in any other business, this would be referred to as networking. In antiques, it's common sense.

- If you see something that you like at a good price, buy it there and then – fairs are competitive and someone else could snap it up while you're still thinking. Some buyers expect to find exactly the same goods on every other stall and waste time shopping around for the best buy – this can work out for less unusual goods but, more often, you lose out on something that you really want. Act fast to prevent missing out on must-have items.

To get the best out of a fair you must take time. There is a huge temptation to scurry about, especially if you spot something desirable across a crowded aisle, but don't do it – you could miss something even better.

Take the time to be friendly, but not too much. If you meet a good dealer, or one who has tempting stock, explain that you've only just arrived and, when you've finished or almost finished, return to their stall and speak to them then. Dealers do not have time to talk to anyone at the start of a fair when they're setting up and you could get in their way, which will not endear you to them. Likewise, at the end of a day, let them pack up in peace. They're tired, which can make them grumpy. All they want is to pack up their stock and go home – they don't want to talk. Speak to them when they're not serving anyone but be prepared to move on when they get a customer and never stand blocking their stall. Stand to the side of it (not in front of someone else's stall) and be friendly but not overly so – it's a small point but dealers don't like people who want to know their life history at first meeting or just want to get a lot of information out of them without any return. *Above all, remember the one basic rule of antiques – dealers are there to sell.*

> **Keyword**
>
> The 3Ps or PPP. I can guarantee that you'll have been guilty of the 3Ps. It stands for pick up, put down and piss off. It's probably a very offensive code to those not in the trade but it's something which really annoys dealers. Someone comes along, picks things up from their stall and leaves. That doesn't sound too bad but I'm not talking about one object. To be a member of the 3Ps, you must pick up at least three objects for no valid reason. People love touching things and the 3Ps are an extreme example of this – it's also one of the many secret terms known only to dealers – and now to you.

Should I Haggle?

In the last chapter, you read about how to ask for a better price. There are some very simple tips for getting a better price – one of which is knowing when to stop. There is a new game in dealing called the 'better price' and it is tedious for all concerned. Honest buyers and sellers should not get involved in it but you might not necessarily know that you've gone too far.

First step is to look at the price on the label or ask how much it is if it's not labelled. There is a popular misconception amongst buyers, especially those new to the trade, that an unpriced piece is a dangerous one. They believe that a dealer is waiting to evaluate the would-be buyer and their purse/wallet potential before deciding on a price. The idea being that the better dressed you are, the better your jewellery, the more money you'll be charged. That just is not true. There are two basic reasons for something not being labelled – the label has come off or the dealer is disorganised. That's a bit unfair. We all have unpriced goods on our stall at some time or other, we run out of labels or just don't get around to it. Dealers are busy people, they don't just come to life at a fair but often work all week – either as a dealer or in a different job. It can be difficult to price all goods before attending a fair, you might even buy something at a fair and sell it at the same venue but not have time to reprice it – or maybe even be writing the label while it's on display. I always seem to have one or two unpriced goods on my own stall, generally due to labels coming off, often helped by would-be buyers removing them to try to find scratches (which some dealers hide behind labels – I never do, but people always check).

Many people are afraid to ask the price of something. There's a silly theory that if you need to ask the price, you can't afford it. Just ask and don't make another common mistake – that of being rude about unpriced goods. It won't stand you in good stead if you want to buy the piece and get a discount.

Be realistic, if the price is much more than you can afford or want to spend, thank the dealer and walk away. Don't complain about the price or be rude in any way. It might sound obvious, but it is surprising how many people think that they can offend dealers. Realistically, the antiques world is a small one and you might be able to buy from that dealer another time so treat them with courtesy.

Trade Price

If you think that you'd be willing to pay either the set price or less than that then ask for the trade price. I've mentioned this before but it is one of the most important aspects of dealing and could save you a fortune. There are strict rules to 'haggling' in the trade. If something is priced £32 and you ask for the trade price (not the 'best' price, remember), then you would expect to be told £30 or £28, sometimes even less but not often. If you are willing to pay, then pay up. If you're not willing to pay the trade price, thank the dealer and move on. Don't slam the goods down and storm off – it might sound strange but this can be a common occurrence at fairs and makes the would-be buyer look extremely stupid and unprofessional. Don't keep demanding a better price – no means no and you'll only alienate the dealer if you try to badger them. I never play games, I put a little extra on my price and take that little off to give buyers the best possible price. If I could give someone a better price, then I would do so immediately and not waste everyone's time by playing games and that's because I'm professional.

There are various reasons why dealers will not lower their prices. They're not being petty but they, like you will, have a business to run and expenses to cover. Sometimes, they're just not making enough money to take any more off. Some dealers need to take a certain amount of money and cannot afford to give an even bigger discount, others know that they're offering a fair price and have a business to run. And, yes, there are dealers who are stubborn or rude but they are in business and it is their business not just to sell but to make money doing so. Some will be greedy, whilst others have a greater need for money (eg bills to pay, food to buy – not holidays but basic living requirements). Always take 'no' as just that and pay up or leave.

There is a new game where certain dealers will lower their prices so that you get an even bigger discount either than you expected or were first offered. You're more likely to buy the piece if this happens, thinking that you've beaten the dealer into giving you a really good bargain. But it's a trick – you're not winning the game as you might think but they're overcharging in the first place to make the goods appear more tempting when they give you a discount. They end up with the exact figure – or more – that they wanted in the first place and you think that you've won. WRONG. This is a dangerous game as you could start believing that all dealers operate this way and miss out on good buys when the honest dealers refuse to play this new trick.

> Good dealers will stick a bit extra on their prices to allow for discounts. If I want £28, I charge £32, no more, no less. Some buyers believe that my final '£28' is actually the starting price and offer me £25 – that's £7 off the original £32. I lose a lot of customers who believe that they shouldn't have to pay the same trade price as everyone else and use that £28 as a starting point for haggling – I don't care, I also get a lot of buyers who pay the full £32 not realising that they could pay £4 less for the same goods.

The reason I don't put loads of money on is that I don't want to con the people who don't ask for discounts. I don't want someone to pay over the odds or higher than they should because of a few people who want to waste my time by bargaining. You wouldn't dream of going into Marks and Spencers or one of the multinational supermarkets and demanding more off their sale prices or even normal prices and *they* could probably afford to give you a better price – most dealers can't so treat them with respect and accept that their best prices really *are* their best ones. The people who deal in antiques are just like you – they're just trying to earn their living or a bit extra. They don't have time for games and, if they do, they're in the wrong profession.

If a dealer says no when you ask for a better price, accept it with grace. They're not playing hardball, they're not playing at all but just trying to earn an honest living. It is the dealers who have introduced the game who should lose the sales because they're confusing a very simple business.

Dealers hate being insulted – either by a would-be buyer offering a ludicrously low price (often half the price and still expecting the dealer to make a profit) or the way that they try to get a better price. One of the worst things you could ever say to a dealer is, 'I'll give you...' The only way to ask for a better price is to ask for the trade price – anything else is unprofessional and could cost you your discount. Dealers have been known to refuse to serve or even acknowledge the worst offenders, especially those who say that they'll give them half the marked price – or even less.

Accepting the Trade Price

The basic rule is to know what you're prepared to pay. If the piece you want is still too much for you after the trade price has been given, ask yourself how much you really want it. If it's still too high, thank the dealer and walk away. Don't insult them by offering them anything below their trade price – especially if they've already told you that they can't afford to take less. If a dealer explains that they're not playing a game and their best or trade price really is as low as it gets, whether you're buying one piece or ten, then accept it. It can make both buying and selling very unpleasant otherwise.

You might want to ask what the trade price is for several pieces. Some dealers are able to offer an extra concession – often a small one – for the extra sale but others can't. Again, they're not being difficult but they have still paid the same basic price whether you're buying one, two or a dozen goods. If I've paid £10 for something and want £12, your wanting to buy a couple or a couple of dozen extra goods is not going to change the fact that I've paid £10 for one of the goods in the first place. Remember that. Some dealers will tell you how much they've paid for goods. This is a common technique used to show a demanding buyer that they simply cannot afford to reduce items any further. Accept this and either buy something or move on. Never tell a dealer that you don't care what they've paid and continue to offer less – you'll look ignorant. *Learn when to stop and spend your time looking for something else instead.* Unless you really want the stock but are just playing a game, in which case you're in the wrong business. You are *not* there to 'get the better' of dealers but to buy stock at the best price – that's the best price for all parties, not just you. Buy or don't buy, just remember to be friendly because you could need the dealer later on – you could even stall next to them at your very first fair!

> ### Useful tip
> **Most dealers will generally discount their goods by around 10%, with no price reductions for goods under £5 or £10. This is not always the case, many dealers will round their goods down to the nearest final 5 or 0 with no regard for percentages, just clean numbers. Expect realistic discounts and ask nicely – or you could end up paying the full price.**

How to pay

If you want a dealer to give you a discount and you are not intending to pay cash then be up-front and tell them. Some dealers accept credit cards, but they are charged by the card companies for taking them so you should expect to be given a lesser discount or no reduction at all if paying by costly cards. Not all dealers will accept cheques and many resent giving discounts only to be confronted by a chequebook when the price has been agreed.

Credit Cards

Credit cards can be a precarious method of payment. For a start, not many dealers actually take cards. There are some fairs where the organisers will accept some credit cards (normally only Mastercard and Visa) on behalf of the stallholders, but not all stallholders like having to wait for their money and pay the charges so can refuse to use this facility, even if it means losing a sale. You should expect to pay extra when paying by cards. Strictly speaking, this is against the rules imposed by some of the credit cards companies (normally where an electronic swipe machine is concerned) but a dealer could argue that they will not charge you if you pay the full price – expect to lose any form of discount or to receive a lesser one if paying by card. If it is accepted at all.

We live in an age of plastic but, to a dealer, plastic is not convenient. They have to pay a certain percentage of their transaction (or a set fee for Switch and some other debit cards) and often have to wait up to a month for their money. Many dealers who do take cards will not accept them for smaller transactions because of this inconvenience.

The best way to pay for all concerned is by cash. However, you might not feel safe carrying large amounts of cash with you. The larger fairs have facilities where you can withdraw money or change currency, but don't rely on them unless you get caught out as they are time consuming and their charges can be unexpectedly high.

Dealers are used to taking a deposit for goods, with the buyer returning within an agreed period with cash. Sadly, they are also used to putting aside goods for people who 'just have to nip to the bank' and are never seen again so don't be surprised if the dealer does ask you for a deposit, especially for more expensive items. In their opinion, if you refuse to pay a deposit, you're wasting their time and would probably not have returned anyway. If you cannot return to the fair, arrange to meet the dealer at another event or convenient location with cash – and expect to pay a deposit.

Some dealers are very generous and will let you pay for the goods over the course of days, weeks or, on rare occasions, months. They will hold onto the stock until you have paid in full. Do not expect this service as it depends on the dealer and their needs. They might be able to do it once but don't take it for granted. Always get a receipt for each payment you make to avoid trouble later. Don't forget to ask for their address so that you know where to send the next payment and know where your money's going.

Cheques

Not all dealers will accept cheques. They are not being awkward but there are too many cases of bounced cheques in the trade, with the more frequent perpetrators having their names printed in the trade press or on notices clearly displayed on the dealers' stalls. Dealers hate to be ripped off and take care to warn other dealers if this happens. If you know that you do not have sufficient funds in your account, either don't buy anything or explain to the dealer that you don't have the money at the moment but ask them to hold on to the goods for you if you will have the money soon and pay a deposit – or ask them to take the goods to another fair if they still have the goods in stock. Not all dealers will agree to this, but all of them would rather you be honest and they lost the sale than have to lose money and stock because of a rubber cheque. They could refuse to deal with you ever again and tell their fellow dealers to do the same.

That said, there are occasions when cheques will unexpectedly bounce. If this happens, contact the dealer as soon as you can (if possible) to explain, apologise and arrange to pay them. If you can't contact them, send them a letter care of the organiser (you'll have their name on your bank slip or receipt), apologise and arrange to make a payment or wait until you see them again and apologise. By apologising, you've reassured the dealer that you're not dishonest but just had an unfortunate financial hiccup. That said, don't be surprised if they'll only accept cash payments in future.

Please note that many dealers will only accept payments up to your card limit or will take several cheques to cover the transaction – all up to the card limit to avoid problems.

Travellers' Cheques

Travellers' cheques are accepted by some but not all dealers. Carry some ID with you to prove ownership – a passport is the preferred option because it has a photograph of you in it but some dealers will also accept a driving licence.

Cash

Ideally, take cash to fairs – it's the dealers' flexible friend and it could earn you an extra discount, especially towards the end of the month when many dealers are worried about paying their mortgages and are aware that cheques might not clear in time. But don't stress the fact that you have cash as it could annoy some dealers who feel that you are suggesting a backhander – not all dealers declare cash transactions to the relevant authorities.

Useful tip

When you carry large amounts of cash, never keep it all in one place or produce a wad of cash when paying for goods. There are two reasons for this – by keeping it in one place it's easier to steal, and by flashing your cash around, not only are you showing potential thieves what you have to offer but you could annoy a dealer – especially if you've had or demanded a large discount.

Getting Your New Stock Home Safely

Badly handled goods can get damaged on your journey home, ruining all of your hard work. If you intend to buy fragile items, it might be worth your while taking extra wrapping with you. Some dealers find this amusing but they shouldn't. You're just being practical and ensuring that what you're buying from them gets home in one piece. It's much better than having a smashing time and that is exactly what can happen if you don't handle your purchases – your stock – carefully.

Always take a strong bag with you to a fair – more than one if you have the room. This can be canvas (which gets wet so is not advisable for use when it rains or snows), a strong, plastic coated bag or even a supermarket bag. The latter are designed to carry a lot of food and are surprisingly strong, but throw away any which have even the slightest rip – these could spread. Stallholders can either forget to take bags or run out quickly. Some of their bags are not always strong or large enough so always remember to take your own.

You might notice some buyers walking around with brightly coloured checked bags. These are sold very cheaply at the larger fairs and can look very practical, but they can be troublesome. They are slightly too big to carry with ease which can mean that they get bumped by other buyers at crowded fairs which, in turn, can damage the goods. They're not all as strong as they seem, but they are large which can encourage the unwary to overload them which can cause the handles to snap – often at very difficult moments with a painful crash. However, whilst their zips are not always as strong as they can be, they are perfect for using in your car to keep your goods safe – that or a box which, like the bag, will also stop smaller goods from falling out of normal supermarket bags and slithering around your car – a costly but common occurrence.

Some dealers, especially those who have come from overseas and need a convenient method to transport their buys back to the Continent by train, use an old-fashioned looking shopping trolley. These save having to carry goods but their capacity can be limiting and they can get in the way at crowded fairs, banging into other people. They are not popular with others but they are a very handy way to transport goods. Some of them come with an extra, useful accessory – a seat. Useful for long days and tired feet, queuing outside or sitting out in the sun (or sheltering from the rain) and having a drink.

Useful tip

Folding seats such as shooting sticks are very useful for the larger fairs where seats are at a premium and not always where you need to sit down. They're also handy for those long, pre-entry queues. They can be bought from department stores (luggage departments or the picnic area), specialist luggage shops, garden centres and shows, outdoor shops or sometimes at larger fairs. Buy one which folds up so it doesn't get in the way when you're looking around.

Getting Furniture Home

That's assuming that you're after smaller items. If you want to buy furniture, find out in advance by ringing the organiser whether they have arrangements for buyers to drive in and collect larger goods. Carry a suitable trolley in your vehicle if necessary and ask the stallholder to help you load your buys if you need help.

If you want to buy furniture but don't have suitable transport or have run out of room, speak to the stallholder about arranging delivery. They normally charge a fee for delivery but this is often nominal and far cheaper than either hiring a vehicle or arranging for the goods to be delivered by a removal firm. When buying furniture, use old blankets or bubble wrap to wrap the goods carefully before transportation – it avoids costly bumps and scratches.

Getting Around the Fair

Some dealers ride around the large, outdoor fairs on bicycles, motorbikes and scooters. These might be a convenient way of getting around the thousands of stalls but watch out for people who won't expect any moving vehicle – accidents are bound to happen. There is also a danger of overbalancing if you buy larger items. Stick to walking – it's simpler and safer.

CHAPTER FOUR

Antiques Centres

Antiques centres are like living fairs but they also have a sense of security missing at fairs – you know where you can find the dealer if something goes wrong or if you want more stock. You can also be lulled into a *false* sense of security by believing that you will see the same stock day after day. Sometimes that's true, especially if the unit-holder doesn't change their stock around every few weeks, but don't get too complacent, you could miss out on that must-buy piece of stock.

> ### Keyword
> **Unit-holder or cabinet-holder – someone who rents space or a cabinet in an antiques centre.**

There are many true stories of would-be buyers going off for a coffee before returning to find their sought-after goods have already been sold. If you see it and the price is right, buy it. The centre or unit-holder will look after it for you while you're having your coffee.

> ### Useful tip
> **There is a simple rule for antiques centres which is true for all aspects of buying – if you want it, buy it. As the old saying goes, he who hesitates loses out.**

Magazines such as *The Dealer* (*The Antique Dealer Newspaper* to give it its full name – which the trade rarely do) and *The Antique Trade Calendar* contain details of centres, but another good way to find out about them is to ask around. If you see a stallholder whose stock you like, ask if they're in an antiques centre. Speak to dealers at your local fair and ask them if they can recommend any centres. Many of them will display leaflets advertising centres if they're in one – it's a free and useful way for them to tell buyers where they have more stock.

The main difference between fairs and most centres is the lack of dealers present. At fairs, most of the people behind the stalls are selling their own stock and can generally speak knowledgeably about their stock (but not always, especially general dealers who cannot possibly know everything because they are covering such a wide area). In centres, it is different. Not all unit-holders will be there to sell their stock and those with cabinets often only turn up to change their stock around or collect their money.

The people who are there to sell are one of three types:

- dealers who are also unit-holders and have to work a set amount of time every day, week or month (for more details, read Section Three, Chapter 5 on selling at antiques centres)

- dealers who are paid to work there

- or paid staff who have no knowledge about antiques but are good at selling.

Whatever type they are, they might not possess the relevant knowledge. In theory, unit-holders should write detailed information, telling you the dates and maker's name, but this is not always the case. You might not want to buy something without knowing more about it – about the potter, the type of wood or whatever. If this is the case, ask the person behind the till to ring the unit-holder and ask them what you want to know.

Dealers are used to this but are not always in. If you hesitate, you could lose out but you might not want to be rushed into buying the wrong thing and this is the negative aspect of centres. But there are more advantages than disadvantages in visiting centres.

- There is no feeling of being rushed and harried which can happen at fairs, especially the busier ones.

- There is no need to arrive at crack of dawn or rush your Sunday lunch.

- You don't have to worry about arriving too late and finding that the stallholders are packing up.

- You can take your own time and look without feeling that you are being watched by an over-eager – or pushy – stallholder.

Buying at an Antiques Centre

Centres give a standard 10% discount – but only if you ask for it. Some dealers are prepared to offer more or sometimes less than that and this is marked on their label. It is worth asking if you can have a bigger discount, especially if you are buying more than one item. This works better than at fairs because the dealer's cost is spread over the month instead of having to cover all of their expenses at one fair. Many dealers will price their stock expressly for the centre. In real terms, however this means that they are unable to go below the set discount because they have already calculated all of their costs (including the extra costs charged by the centre) and priced their goods to sell. This is particularly true of dealers who are very busy and know that they cannot always be reached by the centre for price queries. A centre has no flexibility itself and will be unable to discount goods (except for the set 10%) without the dealer's permission so there is no point being demanding – it's not their stock.

Some centres are better than others. Some centres will promise to ring you when relevant stock comes in and some will actually ring you. It really depends on how busy or how professional they are. The bigger centres have more stock and more staff but can be too busy to have time to note all of the new stock. The smaller centres might make the time knowing that it brings in business. There is no set pattern but always ask a centre to get in touch if you want special stock – leave them your phone number.

As with all forms of buying, take your time. Some cabinets or units are crammed with stock as the dealer tries to capitalise on their space – don't be afraid of looking as hard as possible, tilting your head to look at makers' names or prices which are at an angle or underneath the object in a glass cabinet. Pick goods up but be careful – you will be expected to pay for breakages and the majority of the centres now employ CCTV (closed circuit television) so they can see *exactly* what everyone is doing.

If you see something that you like and the unit-holder is not there to help, take a note of the unit or cabinet number and go to the front desk for help or find one of the staff and ask to look at the item. Cabinets are generally locked so they will have to find the right key. Be prepared to wait for service at weekends when centres are particularly busy.

Useful tip

If you haven't been to the centre before, ring in advance to ask about parking. Not all centres have car parks and you might need to park elsewhere, whilst others have very small parking facilities and it's advisable to arrive before the centre even opens in the morning to ensure a space.

Go round a centre at least twice as you could have missed something the first time around and don't be afraid to talk to the dealers, especially if they are putting out stock. That's the best way to get what you want before anyone else has even seen it. Dealers like centres as it gives them a showcase for their stock. If you find a unit of particular interest, give your phone number to the centre and ask them to forward it to the dealer – you might be able to buy more stock for less that way as dealers love to sell their goods up-front and, if you arrange to buy things outside the centre, they don't have to worry about commission charges (see Section Three Chapter 5 for more details). Centre management and owners don't like it when this is done but they accept that it is business, especially if you continue to visit their centre and buy other things.

> **Useful tip**
>
> If you find a centre which you like, become a regular. That way, the staff will recognise you and will inform you of relevant new stock as soon as you enter. You'll also be invited to their special events if they have any.
>
> The best day to visit a centre is a Monday when dealers bring new stock into the centre after doing a fair or buying at fairs. Some centres are closed on Mondays so ring first.

Some centres hold special events. They might not sound very appealing but they are a very good way of meeting the stallholders and fellow dealers who turn out for the occasion. They are popular with the unit and cabinet-holders who do not often meet, especially the cabinet-holders who rarely visit the centre. They tend to be very gossipy events. Gossip might not sound appealing but it is when it's all about the trade. You'll find out who the best and worst dealers are, and hear about bad organisers and which fairs are worth doing. It's also an excellent time to discover new centres as many dealers are in more than one centre and are happy to talk about other centres worth visiting whether they buy or sell there.

Networking is an important part of any business but the antiques trade is very informal and special nights at centres provide an ideal opportunity to discover what is going on within the trade. Professionals as well as newcomers find them useful. Don't be afraid to ask questions if you'd like to find out anything else – that's what they're there for.

Some centres have mailing lists – ask about joining it when you find a good centre. That way, you won't miss out on any special events and promotions.

How to Pay

Most antiques centres nowadays accept credit and debit cards but they do charge for them. You will either be charged a set percentage on top of your purchases (often 5%) or they will not allow any discounts. The centre's dealers are charged every time you use credit cards and this is taken into account by the refusal of discounts. *Ask about credit cards before payment to avoid problems.*

Cheques are accepted at most centres but some will accept them to the card limit only. Cash, as with all aspects of dealing, is the most popular option. If you're not carrying any and they won't accept a cheque over your card limit or plastic, ask them to hold on to the goods (a deposit will probably be required) while you find a cash machine.

Some centres will hold on to goods (reserve them) for a set period, if you don't have cash at the time or wish to pay in instalments. If there is something which you'd like to buy but can't afford at that time, speak to the unit-holder or the centre's staff and see if an arrangement can be reached. Don't expect to collect the stock until full payment is received.

Arranging Delivery

Keyword
Shipping – to arrange for delivery, especially used in connection with overseas transactions but also used (wrongly) for national delivery.
Shippers: the firms who arrange shipping for buyers.

Centres are used to delivering goods. If you are buying larger objects or are buying goods at an inconvenient time (eg when on holiday), ask about delivery charges. They are surprisingly competitive. Some unit-holders will arrange to deliver furniture for no fee at all (especially locally) or for a small payment – ask before you buy anything.

Some centres have regular shippers who arrive at regular intervals and buy goods on behalf of their clients or arrange to pick up goods which their clients have bought. It's worth finding out when they're due. Not only will they buy huge amounts of stock, potentially leaving the centre depleted for other buyers, but the dealers will bring in stock especially for their visit – get in there first and buy what you want before they arrive. Ring before you're intending to travel and ask if they've got any shippers due. This works especially well if you're a regular and the centre knows what type of stock you buy, but most centres are proud to attract shippers and will be happy to announce when they're expected.

> **Useful tip**
>
> Don't take a centre for granted, dealers move on and stock turns over – what you've been intending to buy for several weeks might not be there next time you go. If you want it, buy it.

There is a popular theory amongst non-dealers that centres are just retail outlets and that the trade never bother visiting them, let alone finding anything worth buying. This theory extends to prices which are also believed to be far higher than market value and aimed at taking advantage of those outside the trade. This is completely wrong. Some dealers only sell through centres and most price their goods to sell. Of course there are going to be overpriced goods at some centres – just as there are at fairs and auctions. But most centres offer very good buys and not just from new stock.

I once went into a centre in the popular antiques city of Bath and saw a very dusty dog. I bought it for £20. It was a rare, unmarked, standing Disney Wadeheath puppy (one of Pluto's puppies) and worth £350, but it had been sitting there for weeks literally gathering dust and ignored by hundreds of buyers.

Some goods are snapped up whilst others remain on the shelf – buy them while you can.

When a Centre is Not Just a Centre

You might want to visit a centre as part of a day out. That's fine if you're by yourself or with someone who likes antiques, but what do you do if they don't? That's easy, you go to a centre which is not just a centre. A prime example of this is The Antiques Centre in York. Set in a busy tourist city full of overpriced tearooms and restaurants, it has its own good value tearoom/restaurant. It's the perfect place to leave an antiques-loathing or just tired partner and/or children while you look around. The food is exquisite and extremely good value (at the time of writing a huge, beautifully cooked main dish starts at £4.95, including vegetables or a salad with a sumptuous sauce) with a surprisingly varied menu. It's a restful place with lovely clean toilets – a change, sadly, from many centres.

Star centres

The Antiques Centre and Cavendish in York (01904 635888)

Hemswell Antiques Centre (three in one) Lincs (01427 668389)

Bartlett Street Antiques Centre in Bath (01225 466689)

It probably isn't fair to single out only three centres from the dozens I have visited, reviewed for *The Dealer* or sold through but these are just some of the centres which are more than just centres. As well as having very good stock, they have clean toilets and good food. Not all centres have a restaurant or even coffee-making machines, either preferring to use their space for antiques or just not being big enough for extra facilities. Some have no toilets for visitors – ask before travelling if this will be a problem, they can usually tell you where the nearest facilities are (such as a pub or supermarket). Not all buyers view these extra facilities as important but, to others, they're vital.

Interestingly, of my three personal favourites (at the time of writing) only Hemswell has parking, which is superb. The other two are in tourist city centres and rely on car parks and street parking (difficult at the best of times) but are well thought out with first rate staff and all the other extras so necessary in such a competitive market.

The Internet

One of the latest, most innovative extras used by centres is the global highway – the Internet. From the comfort of your desk or armchair, you can 'visit' a centre in advance and see if it appeals before you travel. What you'll find in this business is that what's right for you might not be right for someone else and vice versa. By checking it out on the Internet, you can save time or discover that perfect centre. Details vary with some, such as Hemswell (*www.hemswell-antiques.com*) having an extensive, frequently updated catalogue showing some of their stock. Other centres' websites only contain very basic information such as opening times and contact details whilst some include maps, essential for centres like Hemswell which are not that easy to find. The Internet is a very useful tool for finding phone numbers and discovering new centres, no matter how simple or complex the actual sites.

If the Internet is not for you, don't worry – they all have phones and front doors as well.

Disabled Access

If you are disabled or travelling with someone who is, ask about disabled access before travelling. While all centres will be as helpful as possible, many centres are in old buildings which just don't accommodate such needs but the centre staff will do everything within their power to help. Some centres, such as Brackley Antiques Cellar, Northants (01280 841841) have disabled parking and lifts whilst others have deliberately created extra large aisles to accommodate wheelchairs and prams with comfort.

If your, your friend's or partner's disability affects your ability to walk, some centres might be too awkward to be practical. These include Acorn Antiques (01279 722012) and Riverside (01279 600985) which are both in Sawbridgeworth, Herts. Unlike Herts and Essex Antiques Centre (01279 722044) which is on the same complex and has a ground-floor selling area, the other two centres have steep stairs to their first floor entrance rendering them virtually impractical for those with disabilities. Always ask before travelling and ask if there is convenient nearby parking as well.

CHAPTER FIVE

Antiques Shops

Antiques shops tend to be owned and run by one dealer but can have a number of staff as well. The person behind the till or desk can either feel very welcoming or quite intimidating. You have to remember that you are the customer and, as such, are more than welcome. Like all shops, treat the stock and the staff with respect and take time to look around.

People are often nervous about buying from antiques shops because they can be quite crammed or look very expensive. Just make sure that you're not carrying any bags which could knock something over and if you're worried about your coat, ask if they can look after it for you. A fair proportion of the damage done at fairs, shops and centres is by people's coats and handbags – a lot of people don't realise just how far they stick out and many coats and jackets are the perfect length for knocking goods off tables. Just be careful.

You will probably be asked if you would like some help. This is not the sales staff being pushy but a polite way of letting you know that they're around if you would like some service. Simply thank them and say that you're just looking or ask them if they have what you're trying to find. The dealer or their staff are there to help you so take advantage of it. Don't waste their time, if you like something but are not going to buy it, then tell them. Most dealers will be happy to offer you more information, even if they know that they won't get a sale from it. By being helpful and friendly, they'll encourage you to buy from them in future. You'll probably have encountered a rude dealer before and this may have put you off buying something from them – good service should have the opposite effect.

It can be very boring working in a shop so don't be surprised if the dealer is very friendly – some will even offer you a drink. If you have time, accept the drink and they'll fill you in on the local trade and tell you about other shops, centres and fairs in the area.

Some shops offer very competitive prices, some are even cheap whilst others seem more expensive. (This will be covered in more detail in Section Three, Chapter 6.) Always remember that shops have higher overheads than virtually all other forms of dealing and the dealer has to pass their expenses on via their stock. Some places have higher rent and rates than others, which will probably be reflected in their prices, but most dealers try to be as competitive as possible to increase sales and cover their overheads.

Hidden Treasures and Useful Information

Some shops are like Aladdin's Caves, full of hidden treasures. Take the time to look carefully and be prepared to move goods if necessary – ask for help if you'd prefer. It's surprising what you can find. Many of them have a homely feel which can make furniture particularly tempting. Ask about delivery before buying anything – some shops will provide free local delivery whilst others will charge a nominal fee. Explain in advance if they will have to negotiate stairs or other awkward barriers as this could cause problems on arrival. It's easier to be honest so that they can arrive prepared – some shops have been known to refuse delivery if they encounter unexpected problems, with the buyers incurring extra costs and ill-will.

Shops are not only useful for buying stock but also useful sources of information with some offering extra services such as restoration. *Unlike fairs, you know where the dealers are the next day which can give buying an extra sense of security.* Always ask for the trade price and ask them to look out for particular items if you're trying to find goods. Shops attract regular buyers by offering better service.

> ### Useful tip
> **Asthmatics are advised to be careful when entering some antique furniture shops as the scent of polish can be overwhelming and trigger attacks.**

Look in your local phone directory for details of your local antiques shops, pick up leaflets in local centres and fairs or buy one of the publications mentioned at the end of this book.

CHAPTER SIX

Auctions

Buying at auction is not only a very good method of buying cheap (or rare) goods but can also be very enjoyable. For first-timers or novices, it can be a nerve-wracking experience with many admitting that they were too embarrassed to bid in case they did the wrong thing, but it can also offer bargains on an incomparable scale – you can buy vases worth £750 for only £48, an Edwardian washstand worth £50 + for £2, and mixed job lots for £20 worth ten-times that. Auctions are a fantastic source of bargains and good stock – but only if you know what to do.

> *Keyword*
> **A viewing – the time given prior to an auction (varies from several days to several hours) to allow would-be buyers to look at the stock, see what they want and check it for damage.**

How to Buy at Auctions

> *Keyword*
> **A lot – an item or group of items entered into auction and sold in one go – or lot.**

There is no secret to easy bidding but some dealers make it harder than it should be. Follow these simple rules to ensure that you get what you want and don't inadvertently buy what you don't.

- First of all, register to bid. This is a simple process but varies from auction to auction so ring before arriving. Some auction houses require a form of ID with an address (eg driver's licence or utility bill) before they'll let you bid for the first time but, once your details are on file, you won't have to carry such information with you on subsequent visits. Most auction houses will just ask you to write down your name, address and phone number. A mobile phone number is acceptable.

- Register to bid as soon as you arrive to avoid queuing later.

- You might be required to leave a cash deposit (£20–30) before being allowed to bid. This is not common but check before arriving.

- You will probably be given a bidding paddle (often a cardboard rectangle with a number on it) in return for your registration – keep it safe as you can't bid without it but remember to give it back at the end of the sale.

- Arrive in plenty of time to view the lots at the viewing. Some people arrive for the first viewing which can be several days in advance but others leave it until the day of the auction to check for subsequent damage. Goods can be damaged (or even stolen) prior to the auction so check that everything is there and perfect before bidding – *Buyer Beware*.

- Buy a catalogue. Copies are kept on display around the viewing or auction room but buy your own copy for private reading and note making. Prices vary from £1 at weekly or fortnightly general auctions to £10+ for better auctions. Glossy catalogues have a resale value but generally not as high as their original price, so buy to use or keep as a record, not as an investment except for very special auctions such as the Duchess of Windsor's jewellery.

- Walk around carefully and see what interests you *before* you read your catalogue. Many buyers, especially inexperienced ones, just read the catalogue and miss out on other goods which are not properly catalogued or do not look interesting in print. Look around first, noting useful lots, and then read the catalogue before walking around again, checking lots which you missed but are of interest according to their description in the catalogue.

- Never make notes in front of your intended buy as you could alert other buyers to it. Instead, return to your chair or a quiet corner and make a note of any damaged goods to prevent you from bidding for them by mistake, as well as interesting lots.

◆ Handle *every single* lot which you intend to buy – you'll end up paying too much for useless, damaged stock otherwise and have no redress. It is up to the buyer to spot damage as not all auction houses will tell you.

◆ Read the rules before bidding – auctioneers charge commission rates which will add 10% + to your buys. Take this into account before bidding as it could leave you with little or no profit – or you could end up spending more than you can afford.

◆ Stand at the back of the hall if you can or sit as close to the back as possible. This allows you to watch all of the other bidders – including those bidding against you.

◆ Reserve your seat or space as soon as you've registered by putting a coat or bag (but not handbag) on it – some people use their bidding paddles but these can go missing prior to the auction and you'll be unable to bid.

◆ If you are a non-smoker and cannot tolerate smoky atmospheres, ask if the auction has a non-smoking area before deciding where to sit or stand – many of the better auctions operate non-smoking policies or have separate areas for non-smokers to sit, but some can get very smoky and asthmatics and others with breathing difficulties should go prepared.

◆ Know when to bid. Never be the first bidder, either wait for someone else to start or for the auctioneer to drop the starting price – they can go as low as £2 from a starting bid of £30!

◆ If you can, wait before joining in a bidding fight or you could force the price up unnecessarily. Wait until one or more of the parties have dropped out before bidding. Your aim is to bid against one person only – if that – to keep prices down.

◆ Bidding is easy, raise your hand, paddle or catalogue in a clear gesture and meet the auctioneer's eye. Auctioneers like clear bidding. Some dealers will give subtle head nods to ensure that other interested parties do not see them bidding but it should only be done when you are more confident and the auctioneer knows you – the auctioneer could miss your bid otherwise.

♦ If the auctioneer takes your bid as higher than your actual bid (you might have been bidding £20 against someone but the auctioneer took their £20 and your £22) and it's higher than you want to bid, say 'no' quite clearly – explain that you were bidding £20 if necessary. Auctioneers are used to it, so don't be embarrassed but keep quiet if you were prepared to bid £22 or higher.

♦ Bids are raised by set amounts – some auctions use 2s (eg 2, 4, 6 etc), others in 5s and the more expensive lots go up in larger stages, possibly starting in 10s or 20s, going up to 50s and then 100s or more. It's useful to know how the auctioneer works before bidding so listen to the first few lots if you are not intending to bid that early on in the auction. Once you get a sense of their rhythm, speed and the pattern of their bids, you'll feel a lot more confident.

♦ If you don't want to pay the full bid (eg from £45 to £50), offer something in between (such as £48) by simply shouting out '48'. This is not a good idea if it is a popular lot but if things have slowed down or there are no other bidders, it's worth trying.

♦ When you are the highest bidder on a lot, the auctioneer will want to know your number (on the bidding paddle) or, if they don't use them, your name. If they can't see your bidding paddle, you might be required to shout out your number or (if they don't use numbers) your name for at least your first two buys. Speak clearly and don't be embarrassed. Repeat yourself if they haven't heard – auctions can be noisy places. They'll get used to you after the first few lots and regulars are often given the same number or asked for their paddle number by the auctioneer before the auction begins.

♦ Auctioneers get to know their buyers very quickly and they could look at you in case you want to bid before bringing down the gavel (hammer) on relevant bids. Smile and shake your head unless you intend to bid and then do so quickly.

♦ Don't get distracted by talking between lots or you could miss your lot, and always go to the toilet before the auction starts so that you don't have to rush out and miss your intended lot.

♦ You might be tempted to turn up later in the auction if your lots aren't at the beginning – do this at your peril unless you know the auctioneer very well and know how long he takes to get to each lot – you could end up arriving too late.

♦ Queue up when you've finished bidding (not necessarily at the end of the auction) and pay before collecting your goods. Either a porter will take your receipt for you and gather all of your lots together or you will collect them yourself and then be asked for your receipt before you are allowed to pack them and leave. This ensures not only that no one takes lots by 'mistake' but that no one forgets any lots, especially in the case of job lots with several pieces in the lot.

♦ Be prepared to take your own packaging and boxes with you as not all auction houses provide any.

> **Keyword**
> **Job lot – a box of goods sold in one go. They can contain hidden treasures such as rare chess pieces or fabulous jewellery – because not all auctioneers know what they're doing!**

How to pay

Payment methods differ from auction house to auction house so ask before travelling. Some will only accept cash until they know you better, others will take cash and cheques and some take plastic, including Switch – but not all credit and debit cards will be acceptable at all auctions. You could incur charges if you do not pay for the goods at the end of the auction and, if you renege on payments, you could be banned from the auction house and other auctions in the locale. The antiques world is a small one and reputations travel – especially bad ones.

Those who accept cheques will work in different ways – some will take a cheque for the full value, even if it is over your card limit, others will take a number of non-consecutive cheques, dated differently up to the cheque limit, whilst others will only accept a banker's draft or a single cheque to the card limit with the rest in cash. It's safer to arrive prepared. You might also have to wait for the cheque to clear before removing your goods.

General *vs* specialist auctions

There are many different types of auctions but, in this section, we're looking at traditional auctions. Internet auctions will be discussed in Section Four. They have their own section because of the tremendous impact that they have had on the trade but that does not mean that traditional auctions should be ignored – far from it. They are a very easy source of buying and you could decide to be an antiques dealer one day, go to an auction the next and buy enough stock to set you up in business the day after that – in theory. In practice, a little preparation brings its own rewards.

There are two basic types of traditional (as in non-Internet) auction –

◆ the general
◆ and the specialist.

Different auction houses call their general auctions by different names – sometimes the grander the auction house, the more elaborate the name but they are all the same – you can buy anything from furniture through china and glass to jewellery. There are bargains to be had at all auctions, especially general auctions, and there is one very good reason for this – nobody knows everything that there is to know about antiques. Nobody at all.

> **Useful tip**
> Profit from auctioneers' lack of knowledge but don't draw attention to it or you could give yourself unnecessary competition.

General Auctions

The better auction houses will have a limit as to what they sell at general auctions so expect to see only antiques and collectables. Other auction houses are not so fussy and you can pick up cut-price electrical goods from vacuum cleaners (including the latest models) to computers and office equipment. Gardeners can have a field day at some of the country auctions and buy stone bird baths for as little as £5 – expect to pay £90 + for similar goods at garden centres – with brand new £500 UPVC doors selling for £20 or even less. You can furnish your house, including furniture, windows and carpets, for a fraction of the normal price at some auction houses, or you could see a load of rubbish and not buy a thing – it all depends on the day.

Just because goods are sold at general sales does not mean that they're not worth buying – far from it. Many dealers buy their entire stock from auctions and make a hefty profit from a couple of hours' work. It is a very easy way to buy stock at good prices.

Specialist Sales

Sales such as Art Deco, posters, pop memorabilia, sporting memorabilia – you name it, there's a specialist auction with specialist prices. So why should you bother to attend? Because there are still bargains to be had, even though there are not as many as at a general auction. If you want to be a dealer, there is no better school than a specialist auction room.

Not only are you surrounded by top-quality goods (and a few other bits) but you are also seeing some of the best dealers in their field and some of the most knowledgeable collectors. Take your time, arrive early and open your ears, not just your eyes. *What you will hear will be some of the best information ever spoken about your specialist field. You will hear deals being conducted, meetings arranged and you'll get to hear who has what and where. This is the place to be if you want to learn and you must learn if you want to be a dealer.*

Talk to people when they're not busy, ask them to recommend fairs and centres but never ask them what they're there to buy – they'll walk off. Dealers are at auctions to buy – as are collectors – nosiness is viewed with suspicion but an honest appreciation is welcome. Let them know that you're just starting out or that you love what you see and wish you could get more of it – you might just be offered a deal of your own.

Specialist auctions are where the 'big boys' come out to play. The prices reached can be astounding. They can also be disappointing. Some dealers use them as guides for market values but the prices realised are often exceptional because you have so many interested parties bidding for the rarer pieces. That is why they succeed, because rarity is common, but only for a few hours and everybody wants a piece of the action. There will be collectors who will be willing to pay hundreds, thousands – even hundreds of thousands – over the estimated price because they need, not just want, that piece for their collection. And then there are the lesser pieces – these are the ones you should be considering. Never buy a piece of Clarice Cliff (or whatever) because it is Clarice Cliff but buy it because you can sell it.

Some of the more common pieces are sold at specialist auctions. There are various reasons for this, maybe somebody is selling their entire collection, including the lesser pieces, or maybe someone had a relevant item for sale around the time the auction was accepting lots. It doesn't matter, but what does matter is that you have a chance to buy some good stock. *Set your limits.* This is true of any auction but none more so than a specialist sale when bidders can go mad and be willing to pay anything to get something. Set your limit and don't exceed it – if you pay over the odds, you'll get stuck with stock and that's dead money.

Keyword

Dead money – money which is tied up in hard-to-sell stock instead of making a profit for you.

Specialist auctions are very useful to visit or for their catalogues but not always for buying – unless you're buying for your own collection.

Estimates

An estimate is the price an auctioneer expects goods to reach at auction. In theory. Some are hopeful figures aimed at encouraging higher bidding (especially for commission bids from novice buyers) or are aimed so low that buyers will be tempted to bid, believing themselves to be getting a good buy. And then there are the good auctions with realistic auctioneers with realistic estimates.

Take estimates with a huge pinch of salt and follow your own instincts and/or knowledge instead. Ask the auctioneer what the reserve price is if you are interested in particular lots – that's a far more reliable guide than an estimate, especially if the auctioneer doesn't have sufficient knowledge in that area.

Keyword

Reserve price – the lowest price for which the seller has agreed to sell their lot.

Goods can vastly exceed estimates, especially at specialist auctions when two or more buyers are competing for the same lot. They can also sell for far less than the estimate – there's no way of telling.

Commission Bids

A commission bid is a way of bidding when you're not able to attend the auction. You 'commission' the auction house to bid on your behalf. This is an easy way of dealing. All you have to do is fill in a form (a signature is needed to prove consent) at the viewing, agreeing to pay up to a certain figure. The auctioneer or one of their staff will then bid for you during the auction up to the price you agreed. This works very well for most auctions but some auctioneers will actually start at your highest bid, virtually guaranteeing you losing the lot. If this happens and you find out about it, refuse to place another commission bid with them. Some auctions can be listened to live over the telephone or via the Internet and this is an easy way of discovering what happened to your commission bid. Some people ask friends to bid for them but this can lead to a conflict of interest if your friend is interested in the same lot and knows how high you're prepared to bid. *Commission bids really are the best option if you can't attend the auction yourself and are not free for phone bids.*

Some auctioneers will ring you during or after the sale if you have been successful, while others will either write to you with an invoice or expect you to ring them – ask the auction house how they operate. It's also worth checking how soon you have to collect lots before being penalised – they will make special arrangements if you're on holiday or unable to collect for a valid reason such as hospitalisation, especially if you're a regular buyer.

Keyword

The wrong leg. This is an archaic auction term used when placing commission bids at auction. It is possible to lose out, not to a higher bidder but by being on the 'wrong leg'. Even if you have left a bid for £100 and the goods sell at £100, if the person bidding on your behalf is the lower bidder (i.e. bids up to £95), they are on the wrong leg and you have lost out to the person who tops that bid. There are two ways to avoid this common occurrence – either place surplus bids (eg 'plus one' or, more safely, 'plus two') – thus allowing the person to bid once or twice above your 'maximum' bid – or attend in person.

Telephone Bids

This is popular with people who want more control than commission bids. This is especially useful if you are desperate to buy the item and don't want to limit yourself by pre-determining your highest bid for a commission sale – it gives you more flexibility. This service is used by most auctioneers and makes auctions even more exciting for those attending. It also allows you to bid when stuck in traffic (pull to the side of the road first) or from the comfort of your home, office or even supermarket – if you must. It is also very useful for those who find getting out difficult, such as those with young children or the disabled. Not all auction rooms have disabled access so this is a very popular facility – ask the auctioneer if the goods are damaged before arranging a phone bid. They're normally honest if asked outright and they will check it on your behalf, especially if you can't actually get to the viewing or the auction in person.

Speak to the auctioneer to find out how they operate phone bids. What normally happens is that you arrange for them to ring you when the lot in question is about to come up. They will ring you a couple of lots earlier to make sure that you are there and everything is in place and, when the bidding starts, they will keep you informed about the other bidders. They'll tell you if you're competing with a buyer in the room, a commission bidder or another phone bidder. You'll have the option of bidding every time the bid is raised. They're used to hesitation so take it slowly (but not too slowly) and don't panic. Tell them that you're thinking (if you are) and they'll signal to the auctioneer to wait for you to decide if you're going to bid again. Speak clearly and let them know when you don't want to bid any higher. It's that easy.

Egos at Work

There is a common danger when buying at auctions, I think of it as a macho battle – because it normally concerns men. It's overbidding not to acquire a lot but to prevent another person (normally also a man) from getting it – and beating them. Be careful not to get caught up in such juvenile behaviour and set yourself a clear limit before bidding. Women are also to blame but normally because they want something, not to beat someone else, but to acquire it. Go into an auction with a clear understanding of your budget, including commission and, if applicable, any VAT on lots.

Lots with added VAT (the buyer is VAT registered or some other, similar reason) are clearly marked in the catalogue – usually with a dagger or similar symbol.

Buying Unsold Goods After the Auction is Over

If you want to buy an unsold lot after an auction, speak to the auctioneer as soon as the auction finishes. You will be told the reserve price and can either pay it or not. If there is no reserve price, you might be able to buy the goods for as little as £2, depending on the auctioneer's discretion (a lovely term meaning that it's up to the auctioneer how much – or how little – they'll charge you).

Some dealers run a business out of buying unsold lots once the auction has finished but it can be risky. If you want a lot, bid for it. If you missed out on a lot, speak to the auctioneer after the sale to determine whether it sold or whether it failed to meet its reserve price – you might get a second chance when the auction has finished. But don't count on it.

Know Your Auctioneer

A good auctioneer is a friendly one. They can be men in suits (or, less often, women) but they can also be found in jeans. There is no set style for an auctioneer unless they work for one of the top auctions houses (such as Bonham's, Christies and Sotheby's – Phillips was taken over by Bonham's and, at the time of writing, is no longer in business under its own name) for which they will be expected to wear suits. It doesn't matter what they wear, all auctioneers, be they owners, directors or staff, have one common goal – to sell.

Use this to your advantage. *Get to know your auctioneer and let them know what you want to buy. They will go out of their way either to get the goods or to let you know when they're about to be sold.* Give them your phone number and remember to inform them of any number changes.

A good auctioneer will greet you by name after two or three auctions and will tell you of any particularly good lots which might be of interest. Many – but not all – of them will also advise you against any over-priced lots or bad buys.

Auctions are one of the most enjoyable aspects of dealing as long as you stick to your budget and take the time to look at goods before bidding. *Never* bid on lots which you have not checked and always ensure that you have enough money to buy the lots for which you're bidding – don't forget to add the commission (10–25% +) to the final total.

Tricks of the Trade

There are certain aspects of auctions which are not fun and which could cost you money.

◆ Check where the auctioneer has attached a label – some sticky labels are used to hide scratches or other damage. If you're worried, ask one of the auction staff to remove the label for you. Be careful about doing it yourself as they could assume that you're up to something illicit, such as label swapping to confuse other dealers.

◆ Don't believe catalogue descriptions. This is more pertinent at smaller auction houses where the truth can be stretched – sometimes just out of ignorance. Some of the lesser auction houses describe furniture as 'Edwardian' or 'Victorian' regardless of their actual age, but their small print advises you not to rely on catalogue descriptions – just as well because the furniture in question is often modern. Be careful.

◆ Dealers have been known to hide some lots. If you can't find something mentioned in the catalogue, ask the auctioneer and make a point of looking in chests, cupboards and wardrobes – you'll often find the desired lot secreted in them!

◆ Some auctioneers take advantage of wardrobe and cupboard space and store their lots in them – it's honest but can lead to would-be buyers missing out on lots because they haven't seen them.

◆ Some dealers hide good pieces in job lots deeper in the box to make it harder for other buyers to spot must-have lots. Have a good rummage and take out everything if you wish but be careful as this could alert another dealer to a good find.

♦ If you write anything in your catalogue, make sure that nobody reads over your shoulder. It does happen so use symbols – but stick to ones which you'll remember (such as Roman numerals or mathematical signs – if you remember any).

♦ Be careful when buying furniture. Lick your finger and rub it gently over any questionable areas – you could rub off scratch-disguising polish!

♦ Remember to remove drawers when thinking about buying objects such as bureaux, any desks or chests of drawers – they could fall apart at that stage and you'll have saved yourself money. Treat them gently so that you won't be made to pay – the auction house will know how badly damaged they were, even if they haven't mentioned it in the catalogue.

♦ Look at crazing (cracks in the glaze) very carefully when buying china, especially so-called 'Staffordshire'. There are thousands of reproductions being sold as originals and the best ways to recognise them is to look at the crazing which is normally too symmetrical (seems to have a pattern and is not just random which genuine crazing is), too clean (the authentic crazing attracts dirt and dust) and the base is very clean, with extra pieces of white china where the base has not been evened off properly. Unless you know what you're doing, avoid these lots or only buy them from reputable dealers or specialist auctions.

Know Your Rights

Most auctioneers will have rules printed in their catalogues which let you know how long you have to return goods which are not in working order as described (generally only applicable to electrical goods and clocks). Your rights extend further than that in one, key area. *If you are sold goods other than described – especially fakes or reproductions – then you have the right to get your money back.* If the auction house refuses, report them to the police and your local Trading Standards (see your local phone directory for details).

Some auction houses will knowingly sell goods as something which they are not, sometimes claiming that unmarked goods are actually unsigned pieces by collectable makes such as Wade or knowingly sell fakes such as 'Carlton Ware' Guinness pieces as genuine. If you buy a lot like this and discover that it is not as described, then demand your money back. They are obliged to pay up.

Do remember that honest mistakes can be made but the auctioneer's reaction will suggest their guilt or otherwise. If they get aggressive, leave but write a formal complaint and demand your money back. Speak to your local Citizen's Advice Bureau (see your local phone directory) about getting your money back.

If you do get caught out at any auction house and things are not resolved to your satisfaction, report them to the police and Trading Standards immediately with as much detail as possible. Auction houses have been fined and even shut down for such behaviour. If you wish, tell other dealers, to prevent them from being tricked as well.

This is not meant to scare you but is just a word of warning to put you on your guard and stop you from being yet another victim of dishonest dealing.

An auction is only as good as its bidders. If you have no competition and there are either no or very realistic reserves, you'll have some very good buys and that's the way to successful dealing. When you find a good auction, keep quiet about it – the more people who know about it, the more competition – tell people about fairs and centres but not auctions – that's what the canny professionals do.

CHAPTER SEVEN

Markets

This is the hidden side of dealing. People who buy and sell at markets are a hardy breed, willing to work in all weathers and it pays – not all the time but enough. There are markets throughout the country, there's probably one near you but do you know about it? Many general markets turn into antiques markets one day a week. Strictly speaking, they often sell more than antiques with secondhand books and clothes a popular feature, attracting students and other buyers, not just those interested in antiques. They're normally advertised in your local newspaper and phone directory but there are new markets all the time. As with all events, ring before travelling to ensure that they have not been cancelled – especially in the cold winter months.

> **Useful tips**
> Famous London markets includes Bermondsey on a Friday, Portobello Road on a Saturday and Camden Passage (Islington) on a Wednesday and Saturday. Oxford market on a Thursday is a gem which few dealers realise exists.

Markets are exciting and unpredictable, full of regulars and newcomers. The regulars know that they need fresh stock to appeal to their regular buyers and price their goods to sell, counting on a high turnover to buy new stock on a fortnightly, if not a weekly basis. Other markets are monthly and all outdoor markets can be at the mercy of the weather, so dress accordingly.

There are not many first-time dealers at markets as they can be very hard work and aren't protected from the weather. The dealers who go are working dealers which means that they price their stock accordingly – they're there to sell. Markets are strange affairs, the dealers seem to have more time than their fairs' counterparts, no matter how busy it gets and buyers stop by for friendly chats – something which is not so common or popular at fairs.

Market dealers tend to be very friendly and can form a close-knit community as they work side-by-side week in, week out, no matter what the weather. Dealers at fairs don't work next to each other as often or in such conditions, which doesn't lead to such a community feel. Market dealers are generally local (but not always) and often socialise outside the market, leading to a very friendly and happy atmosphere – something which, in turn, is very welcoming to buyers.

The regular markets outside London don't seem to attract as many trade buyers as they should which means that there are very good buys to be had with little or no competition. Some of the dealers specialise in house clearances, which means that they empty people's houses or excess for them, often when they're moving or when someone dies. *They price the goods to sell quickly and might not have sorted things thoroughly, enabling you to pick up bargains.* Ignore the condition of the smalls and furniture (within reason), some of the goods might be filthy but dirt is easy to clean (see Section Three, Chapter 9 for more details) and polished or shiny goods are much easier to sell – for a healthy profit.

Markets open early so pop by on your way to work and get to know the regulars – they'll reserve stock for you once they recognise you and know what sort of goods you buy.

CHAPTER EIGHT

Car Boot Sales

Some people believe that the days of amazing finds at car boot sales have gone. They're wrong. If you look hard enough (and arrive early enough), there's a magical find at every car boot sale. It might not offer you thousands of pounds worth of profit but you can still get a bargain for £5 – or much, much less.

There's a simple trick to car boot sales. You need plenty of change. You can't haggle and then expect change from a £20 note, that's flaunting it and will not endear you to the seller who might not be quite so generous next time. Save your change and take it to the boot fairs. You'll need plenty of silver (5p-50p) and lots of £1 coins. A few £5 notes will also come in handy but what can you really get for your money? These are just a few of my own buys in recent years:

Item	Paid	Sold
Art Deco mirror	£5	£60
Arts and Crafts chair in need of restoration	£5	£75
Art Nouveau napkin ring	20p	£35
Villeroy and Boch trinket box	£1	£15
Incomplete Art Deco china tea service stored in a wooden chest.	£8	Sold tea service for £55, chest for £20 Total £75
1950s studio pottery coffee set	£1.50	£35
1950s, stylised clock and mirror	£5 the pair	Sold the clock for £18, the mirror for £35. Total £53
Hunting picture	£5	£75
Pewter teapot, jug and sugar	£3 the lot	£25 the set
1960s dress	20p	£35
Florenza costume jewellery brooch	20p	£35

These are relatively modest buys but the profit margins can exceed all other forms of buying, including charity shops which offer far less bargains than they used to with many of them pricing their china and glass at a higher rate than most dealers!

It is still possible to spend a few pennies and realise thousands of pounds but it can require specialist knowledge. That said, take the time to trawl through your local car boot sale or, if you can travel, I'd recommend one by Ashley Heath near Ringwood (07977 715121) every Sunday during the summer but get there early and be prepared to queue to leave.

Take your own food as the catering at car boot sales is not always good and toilets can be filthy. Go before you arrive.

Better Prices

You are expected to haggle at boot fairs but too aggressive bargain hunting can lead to the loss of a bargain. Be polite but quick – if you hesitate, someone else will get there first. Ask for the best price or offer about 25–30% less than they're charging – some people will steam in at 50% (or more) but that could offend the dealer who could refuse to serve you. Be realistic and don't be too greedy – let them make a profit as well. But only if you're going to make a much larger one.

Don't forget to look at hardback books. You could snap up first editions worth £400 + (especially crime ones) for as little as 10p. Take plenty of bags with you and leave your goods in your car when they get too heavy. You need to keep your hands free for rummaging through boxes and it's not always easy to keep an eye on your bags at the same time.

Types of Sellers

Professional boot sellers buy goods to sell, and their prices are not always realistic or profitable, but it's still worth looking to see what they've got – not everyone knows everything and they could be wildly underpricing certain items. Some of them are antiques dealers who use boot fairs to clear excess or tired stock – even damaged pieces – whilst others are house clearancers who use the boot fairs to sell the cheaper or mundane pieces of stock, including damaged pieces, so examine everything before buying but be fast as someone could take it off your hands – literally. The professionals are easy to spot – they have proper tables, clearly labelled stock, some of it new and aren't as excited or disorganised as the real boot sellers, the people who are clearing their homes.

These are the people you want to find. They don't know what their goods are worth and just want to clear space at home or raise a bit of money. They might not be expecting you to haggle so go in softly. One first-timer refused to serve the professional buyers who hovered around her table and some even took her boxes out of her car but she did serve me – because I hung back and smiled. I got some very good bargains and have a feeling that she'll never sell at a car boot again. Be gentle and don't get too excited – they could realise that you've found a bargain and refuse to sell it or even up the price. Don't be surprised if goods aren't priced – just ask.

There can be a snobbery amongst antiques dealers, some of whom regard boot fairs as the lowest of the low, but those in the know realise that there are bargains and good buys to be had and that's what it's all about. It's an enjoyable way to spend a morning but get there early for the best buys and easy parking. I loved filming Meridian's version of *Boot Sale Challenge* as it introduced me to new boot sales – where I picked up bargains – as well as working as their TV expert.

How to Get the Best Out of Car Boot Sales in Summary

◆ Arrive early for best finds and easy parking.

◆ Be careful where you park – make sure that you're not going to get stuck in a muddy field or trapped in by selfish parkers.

◆ Take plenty of change – the seller might not have any and you could lose out.

◆ Take your own bags and packing (but keep the packaging in the car – looking too professional can raise the prices).

◆ Rummage around boxes and under tables for those special finds.

◆ Don't hesitate – you could lose a good buy.

◆ Be polite – it will get you an extra discount.

◆ Don't pay the full price unless it's very cheap or the sellers are first-timers who have priced their goods cheaply anyway.

◆ Don't forget to look at books – hardback first editions are very cheap and sell well at fairs.

◆ Look at clothes as well – 1950–70s clothes (and earlier) are good sellers and can be picked up at boot fairs for 10p!

◆ Check out furniture. Some people are moving house and chuck out some really good pieces such as vintage 1950s plastic chairs for £5 or less – sell them on for £75–150+ depending on style.

◆ Look at old curtains, some of them make great cloths for covering your stall at antiques fairs whilst others are collectables in themselves – 1950–70s are best. They're easy to spot by the bright, stylish designs.

◆ Remember to look at accessories such as compacts, hats and real or costume jewellery – there's a very good market for them, especially the signed pieces.

◆ Enjoy yourself – car booting is not hard work unless you make it so.

CHAPTER NINE

Damaged Pieces

Dealers are divided over damaged pieces. Some, especially newcomers, won't buy them at all whilst others know that they're easy money. You might be wondering why anyone would want to buy a damaged piece. Some people use the cheaper pieces (often under £5) to practise restoration. The better pieces allow people who cannot afford perfect items to have an example of the piece in their collection or on their stall.

There are some very good restorers around who snap up good but damaged stock and return them to the market intact (sadly, not always sold on as restored). Small chips on glass are relatively simple to restore using glass files. A lot of people intending to 'repair' glass will buy cheap, damaged goods to practise this technique and are often able to buy the better pieces for a pittance because of small, easy-to-erase chips.

Money is a factor when buying damaged goods. Some dealers will not take damage into account when pricing and find it difficult to sell the items, whereas others go for a small profit, high turnover and have a very successful business selling (amongst others) damaged goods.

There are dealers who choose not to have any damaged goods on their stalls, believing that it reflects badly on the rest of their stock. It can happen, especially if a would-be buyer picks up several pieces in a row, only to find them all damaged, but it can be unrealistic for a dealer to refuse to countenance damaged goods.

Keyword

A/F or a/f: as found or all faults. Often seen on labels, this means that the item is damaged in some way. It can mean major or even very minor damage. Not all dealers will tell you if their goods are damaged and even honest dealers can get caught out when their goods are damaged *en route* – always check before buying.

If you find that an item is damaged but the dealer has acknowledged this damage on the label *and also* made a point of telling you about the damage before you've bought it, they have probably taken this into account when pricing their stock. Some of them will even make a point of telling you how much the goods would be if perfect. A dealer who has done everything in their power to inform you of any damage is a good dealer so don't offend them as you might want to buy from them in the future.

If, on the other hand, you want a piece and discover that it is damaged *before* you have bought it, point this out to the dealer. There is a possibility that they didn't know about the damage and will be very embarrassed about it. Some will offer you a drastically reduced price on the spot, whilst others will withdraw the goods from sale completely. However, if the dealer does not seem to care and refuses to reduce the price, unless it is still very cheap with the damage taken into account, walk away – why should you be landed with damaged, overpriced goods?

Summary of the Argument

Ultimately, it's up to you whether you buy imperfect goods. Many collectors will buy them because they want an example of a rare piece in case they never see it again. Those who wait for a perfect example might never find it and could regret passing on an imperfect example. There is a very basic rule – if it's too damaged (eg great big chunks out of china, heads missing from figures, several legs missing from a table), it's best to leave it – some things are too far gone to be restored or to attract any buyers. The following summary is based on the assumption that the items are not too badly damaged and covers selling, as well as buying – something which you have to consider if you want to be an antiques dealer.

There are grey areas where pieces are not damaged *per se* but are missing vital components – such as the lids of teapots. The good news is that these can be good buys – *if the price is right*. Some dealers stock spare lids and, whilst it is not easy, it is possible to match teapots with lids. Decanter tops are more difficult to find but not all of the tops sold with glass/crystal decanters are the authentic ones and not even the dealers can tell the difference – unless they're specialists or collectors.

Incomplete sets such as tea services can be sold on as they are or can be matched by patiently trawling around antiques venues or speaking to specialist 'matching' services (if applicable).

Pros	Cons
You get to buy an example of a good piece at a cut price	The goods are not perfect
You can always sell this piece on when (or if) you acquire a perfect example	You won't get top value for it
Restorers or people with restorers will buy the piece from you – or collectors who want an example but can't afford or find a perfect piece	Would-be buyers might be put off from buying other goods if they find several damaged goods on your stall
It might just have a small chip	Cracks can spread
You can get the piece restored and keep it or sell it on for a better profit	Restoration costs, takes time and is not always effective – some people won't even buy restored items

If a spout, leg or head of an object is missing, unless you know exactly what shape or how long it should be, it's best to leave it – guesswork, even by an accomplished restorer, can backfire and you could get stuck with an unsellable piece and an expensive restoration bill.

Restoration

A well restored piece can be a very good buy. If the dealer knows that it is restored and prices it as such (and tells you about it), they can be bargain finds and allow you to have an example of a piece which could be beyond your pocket otherwise.

A badly restored piece is not worth buying – even the best restorer could have problems correcting someone else's mistakes.

The best restoration is not always easy to spot and even long-term professionals get caught out.

How to Spot Restoration

You might have spotted someone raising china to their mouth and seem to nibble it. This is a very strange sight which can shock novices into believing that someone is about to bite the head off their figure. They're not. Our teeth are very sensitive and what the buyer is doing is checking that the piece has not been restored by relying on touch, not sight. A restored piece feels rough to the touch (as sensitive teeth quickly discover) and slightly warmer than the original china. Restoration is about filling in missing pieces and non-authentic materials are used. In terms of china, this feels different and the paintwork doesn't quite add up, especially for heavily glazed pieces.

Unless you know what you're doing, don't use your teeth but your fingertips and your eyes – look for irregularities. This can be hard if the lighting is bad so check for roughness with your sensitive fingertips. With experience, you'll be able to feel the exact point where the china stops and the restoration begins.

It's up to you if you buy restored goods – some people do, others don't but only buy it if the piece is below market value – restoration might 'mend' the piece but it's still not perfect and this should be reflected in its value.

There is no guide to how much cheaper it should be but it *should* be cheaper and always tell the dealer if a piece is restored and not marked as such – that way, no one else will get caught. Assuming that the dealer is honest enough to tell other, would-be buyers.

Furniture restoration can be equally easy to spot. Like china, the colours don't quite match, additions can be felt with fingers or seen with eyes – screws won't be authentic and the restored section won't 'feel' the same as the authentic part of the furniture. This might seem like a very vague description but, like many aspects of the antiques trade, experience is the only way to learn. Once you know the warning signs by sight, you won't be caught out again – but you have to see it first.

Finding a restorer

For details of good restorers, speak to other dealers or a good auction house (see your local phone directory for details). Restorers do go to major fairs, offering their services, but ask for at least two references and a chance to see their work before agreeing to anything and ensure that you have an address as well as a phone number – you need to know where your stock/possessions are going and exactly when they will be back. If a piece has still not been touched a fortnight (or week if you need it faster) after the agreed delivery date, demand your piece back and find a more reliable restorer. That said, good restorers are in demand and their quality work takes time so your patience is as much a requirement as their skill.

PART THREE
Where to Sell

CHAPTER ONE

Can I Sell Anywhere I Want?

You *can* sell anywhere in the country (or even abroad) but you might have to **register** to do so first. At the time of writing, the Home Office is analysing the possibility of having a national register for second-hand dealers. This will cover antiques dealers, junk dealers and car boot sellers. The whole aim is to stop the trade in stolen goods. Opinions vary but the common belief is that it's a waste of time and paperwork but an excellent way to catch any dealer who is claiming any benefits for which they are not entitled (eg invalidity) or those not registered for tax. Many of the public believe that it is a very good idea as they think that many dealers are knowingly selling stolen property – this, of course, is not true but is a popular misconception of the trade. I believe that a national register, if properly administered and decided on by those who understand the trade, is no hardship but we need a *national* one. At the moment, there are 11 regional ones with different rules requiring different records to be kept for each different area. For the dealer, the paperwork is getting out of hand with many refusing to sell in the affected counties.

I've written several articles on the Kent County Council Act, the most recent of these Acts, and I can see that it has frightened many long-term dealers but it shouldn't. Yes, the paperwork is a hassle but it's easy to do and registration is easy. I'm not sure that we actually need a legal mandate to keep us honest, many of us have managed for years without it and it can all be seen as bureaucratic nonsense with the money better spent elsewhere but, as far as it goes, it's easy to register and the record-keeping is simple enough.

How Am I Meant to Know if I Should Register or Not?

When you want to sell in a county or area, be it in a shop, centre or at a fair, just ask if you need to register. You can ring the council – speak to Trading Standards – or ask the fair organiser. It's that simple. But it's not so easy trying to find out from other sources, except for local knowledge. If you're not sure, ask around and be advised that more councils are expected to ask their dealers to register before selling (or even buying regularly) in their county.

For example, if you want to sell in Kent and live there, you need to register; if you want to sell in Kent but don't live there, you need to register; if you want to buy in Kent on a regular basis, you need to register but you don't need to do so if you intend to buy there once in a while. And the registration process is so simple – it only takes a couple of minutes and doesn't ask any intrusive questions at all.

I'm not going to list all of the terms, such as what records you need to keep, because all of this is subject to change and is tiresome for those not affected by the various Acts.

One of your main requirements will be to display a certificate each time you sell in the county or keep one permanently on display if you have a shop.

At the time of writing, those with registration requirements include, in order of enactment:

- ◆ South Yorkshire
- ◆ County of Merseyside
- ◆ Greater Manchester
- ◆ Humberside
- ◆ Lancashire
- ◆ Hereford City
- ◆ Worcester City
- ◆ North Yorkshire
- ◆ Newcastle
- ◆ Kent
- ◆ Scotland – not the most recent but the biggest.

If you want to trade in any of these areas, speak to their local Trading Standards for further information and application forms. Once you are registered, you are free to start dealing.

CHAPTER TWO

How to Sell

You might not realise it, but there is a technique to selling and it's surprisingly easy to learn. The next time you buy something from a dealer or a shop, think about the service you received. Did it make you want to buy more than you were thinking about or did you get so annoyed that you didn't buy anything at all, even though you wanted something? Think about why you reacted this way.

Smiling is one of the easiest ways to attract customers. You don't have to be insincere to smile, just think about the people that you're serving – or their money. Some customers are rude and you have two choices – either send them away by telling them how rude they've been (or treat them accordingly) or be friendly. Not only could you win them around but, even if you don't, you'll have their money and that's what it's all about. No matter what type of dealer you are, even if this is just your hobby, you have expenses to cover and money to make and you'll get it faster by being nice. Even if you feel lousy, grumpy and just wish that you were at home in bed.

It can get boring when there are no customers around, so take a book with you but remember to keep looking up for potential customers. If you don't notice them, they will walk away and you'll lose a sale. There are few things more off-putting than being ignored. If you get caught out, apologise for reading (you don't really have to but it starts things off on the right footing) and smile. Whatever you do, don't read a newspaper – it looks bad and can give the wrong impression. Remember that you're there to sell, not read, so keep one eye on your book and the other on your stock.

One of the hardest aspects of selling, if you're not used to it, is how insignificant
you become. Your only role in such circumstances is to serve when you are wanted and not
when you aren't.

You are seen to have no personality and can be at the mercy of some insulting comments. Take a deep breath and remember that this is not about you but them. They are the people who can send you on your dream holiday or pay your mortgage. They might have had a bad day and normally be charming – they could, if handled properly, become your regular customers. Or you could send them away with a flea in their ear, feel superior for a few minutes and then accept that *you* lost the sale – not them. Selling is all about egos – theirs and the suppression of yours. But not always; some sales are easy, some are lovely and others are very, very hard work.

One of the most important methods of selling goods – besides that all important smile (sincere ones only, please) – is to know your customers. Not as individuals at first but as types. To know them is to understand them.

Types of Customers – and Time-Wasters

- **Dealers** – often knowledgeable, always out for a bargain – don't be pushed into dropping your trade price. Don't let their profit be at your expense.

- **Fellow stallholders** – this can be very awkward. They try to con you into believing that they deserve a better rate than the trade price because they're stalling at the same venue. Don't fall for it – they, just like you, are in business and *you* need to make a profit too. If you don't agree with me, think how you'd feel if they beat you right down and then put what they've just bought from you at a bargain price on the stall *right next to you* at twice the price. It happens, so don't do it – price your goods fairly and stick to your trade price, no matter what.

- **Knowledgeable** – know what they want and can rarely be swayed. Good buyers – you either have it or you don't. Often serious collectors or specialist dealers.

- **Collectors** – not always willing to pay for what they want. Sell by giving them knowledge about the piece in question but not too much – some just want information.

- **Regulars** – improve on your service, not your prices for this welcome type of customer. Tell them that you have something which might interest them as soon as you see them. Ask about their family/life and remember what they said so that you can refer to it the next time you see them. These small, personal touches won't cost you a penny but will make your regular buyer want to buy from you even more. It's a useful way of making friends, whatever your business.

♦ **Lovely** – they want it, they buy it. Sometimes even for the full asking price.

♦ **Like what they see but don't know what it is** – these need careful handling to convince them to pay the price, be it £2.50 or £2,500. Some buy, some don't and that's often down to your service.

♦ **Want something for the home** – they need careful handling but can be awkward. If you don't feel that you're getting anywhere, politely let them know that you're going to leave them to think about it and sit down – they'll either walk away or buy it without feeling crowded.

♦ **After a present** – similar to the above type but ask a few more questions – what type of person are they buying for, how old are they, do they like cats (or whatever it is you're trying to sell)? Give them a couple of choices if they haven't already picked something out, but not too many as they're easily confused. If they have too many options they'll probably walk away, but if they're hesitating over spending £30, find them something similar for a bit less – £20–25. You'll probably clinch the sale that way.

♦ **The novice** – lovely buyers who need careful handling to reassure them that they're doing the right thing. Just remember how you felt when you were first starting out.

♦ **The ignorant** – will be rude about what they don't understand but might buy if you overwhelm them with knowledge – but nicely.

♦ **The bargain hunter** – a tedious type, they want to pay less than you did and won't always take a polite 'no' for an answer. They can be talked around by confirming how cheap your price really is. If there is a similar piece at the same venue for much more, tell them about it. It's one way of getting rid of them and they could come back once they've seen that your price really is a good one. Don't let them bully you – they'll only do it again. Stick to your price and, if you've had enough, let them know that they're insulting you and sit back down behind your stall. If they carry on like that, they won't be buying it anyway. Never reduce your trade price – especially for aggressive non-dealers!

◆ **The thief** – buy one, take one – if you're lucky. Don't be too worried about theft but be advised that it happens so watch out. Pay particular attention if you feel that you're being diverted down one end of your unit or table – the thief (or thieves) could be active at the other end. If you're worried, ask another stallholder for help and be careful.

◆ **The lonely** – they do buy so handle them carefully but don't be too friendly or you'll never get rid of them. Some just want to talk, others will pretend to be interested in something whenever you make it clear that you have other things to do. Don't waste too much of your time on them.

◆ **The amorous** – a tedious type but, handled carefully, they can buy but generally only after a long time. If you're not interested, tell them. It can save you a couple of hours of embarrassment. Please note that this type normally starts by pretending to be interested in your stock – not you.

◆ **Pricers** – they don't want to buy but love knowing the value of things. Maybe they've got one at home or have seen one elsewhere. Spend as little time with them as possible and don't give them too much information. They're not buyers.

◆ **Pickers up** – they might buy so be polite but they probably just like talking and playing with your stock. Leave them to it.

◆ **Readers** – if you're selling books or pamphlets, someone is bound to read at least one from cover to cover with no intention of buying anything. Either ask them if they want any help or ask them to leave – they can damage your stock and are not buyers. If you don't want to ask them to leave, keep offering them help – they'll get the hint and move on. You are not a library and they could stop a real buyer from buying the book or seeing the rest of your stock.

◆ **Mothers' meeting** (with apologies) – at every fair or centre, there is a group of friends who meet up to chat. Nothing wrong with that, you might think. There is if they do it in front of your stall and block it off from real buyers. Don't be rude but just ask them to move while you fiddle with something (anything) on your stall – you'll get in their way so they'll move on with no offence caused.

Buyers are a mixed bunch, some are easy, others hard. Some are rude every single time you meet but they buy. It's a cliché, but take the rough with the smooth. Not all sales will be easy but it's the hard ones which you'll remember. One of the most important things to remember when you're trying to sell is that you're a buyer too – treat people as you would wish to be treated, give them space but be there to help when they need it, sense their moods and react to them.

If someone is standing in front of your stock for more than a quick glance, stand up – this makes it clear that you have noticed them and are willing to help. Smile. Some people will ask for help at this stage, others ignore you – either by accident or deliberately. People want to look without being hounded. If you feel that they need help (i.e. continue to look at your stock or handle a piece and don't just put it back down immediately), say, 'would you like some help?' or 'I'm here if you'd like some help.' Even, 'if you'd like some help, please ask.' Said with a smile, these are pleasant, non-aggressive ways of offering to sell something. They remind the would-be buyer who you are and why you're there. They also make it clear that you respect their space.

This might sound like mumbo-jumbo to you but it works. When you are buying anything, especially something which you do not necessarily *have* to have, you want to feel comfortable doing so. You might feel guilty about spending so much money – even if it is for stock. You might just want someone to come along and tell you that you *deserve* a treat. That's called sales technique.

Don't push but don't ignore.

Some customers are impossible to satisfy. You might offer help and they'll snap that they don't need it, wait for you to sit down (always useful to do if your offer of help has been refused – however politely, it stops the would-be buyer from feeling crowded) and then demand help. Ignore their rudeness, they're almost hoping that you'll react so they have a valid excuse not to spend their money. Smile, stand and serve.

Sharing Knowledge

There is a fine line between sharing knowledge and lecturing, between imparting knowledge and being used for it. It's advisable to give enough to show your expertise but not enough to bore or act as an unpaid valuer. Your customer might buy or they might not but you want them to feel confident in your knowledge.

If you know the dates, tell them, 'Kitty Evershed was a studio potter from the 1920s–30s. She won a lot of awards.' Note that you have told the customer quite a lot in that statement. You're using the maker's name, confirming that she was a studio potter, i.e. that her goods were not mass-produced. You've let them know in which era she worked and you've confirmed their own beliefs that the potter was a good one because she won awards. Note also that all of the information is not only accurate but also succinct. You don't bore but inform. Another important thing to note is that you have not mentioned the price. You are selling the figure, not its price. At that point, they can walk away if that's all they wanted to know – and you haven't even had to tell them everything you know – or they can ask for the price. 'It's £330.'

Giving the Price

Always give the marked or actual price first. If you start by saying, 'the best is £300,' they'll immediately offer you £275. Why? Because they assume that you're playing games and that £300 is the starting, not the finishing price. When they ask you if £300 (or whatever) is the best that you can do, smile regretfully and say yes. Maybe give them a bit more information, 'Yes, sorry, but it's a good price. They're very hard to find.' You're confirming that your best (or trade) price really is your best price, apologising that you can't offer an even better price and enforcing that the piece in question is not easy to find and, therefore, a good buy.

If you are selling a more common item, repeat all of the above comments (or similar) and finish by confirming that it's a good price. Say how much other dealers charge (if applicable). 'It's got to be £45. It's a good price. Other dealers charge £60 – or even more.' Stress the fact that they're getting a bargain. If they ask (as someone is bound to do) why you're not asking the full price, just smile and say that you're not greedy, that you paid less or that you never charge the full market price as you sell to the trade. The latter will appeal to members of the public who are determined to beat you down or get a bargain – at your expense.

Selling to Regulars

Some of your buyers will be lovely. You'll end up selling goods to them for years so treat them well. Try to remember their names. This is not always as easy as it sounds, even if you are good with names. You will see thousands of people in your life as a dealer – they will meet about a dozen or so regular sellers. There are times when you won't even be able to place them, especially if you see them at a different venue to their normal ones. This can be very embarrassing but it's easy to cover up your confusion. Be pleased to see them – which you will be, regulars are really sweet and often very profitable – and ask how they are. Let them know that you hadn't expected to see them there. They'll say enough to answer those bland comments to remind you who they are.

A harder trick is to remember what you sold them last time. You should sell dozens of goods every fair (depending on what you sell, you'll sell less if your stock is better quality than if most of it is £50 or below) and you can't really be expected to remember who bought what, except for exceptional pieces. They *will* expect you to remember and will be hurt if you can't. Don't let on, just ask if they're still happy with it or that you're pleased they bought it. It might seem a little bit dishonest but it isn't – you're making someone happy and they'll go away knowing that you're a good person and that there are nice people in the trade.

Your regulars will always have a tale to tell about bad dealers. By knowing you and by your treating them properly they'll still attend fairs and that should make you proud of yourself as a dealer.

Case Study

As a dealer, you'll get to hear about unpleasant experiences which your buyers have had. They'll often be angry about it and often rightly so. I met a buyer who had asked for the price of a brooch. The dealer refused to answer, telling her instead that she couldn't afford it. Quite rightly, she left, vowing never to buy from that dealer again and I don't blame her. When I spoke to her, she was very hurt and my reaction (anger on her behalf) confirmed that she was right to be angry and that the dealer had no right to talk to her that way, whether she could afford the brooch or not.

It's dealers like these who make our job harder. It's completely unnecessary. Good selling is simple — don't be pushy or rude but treat customers how you would like to be treated. Even the rude ones.

Just because someone has bought something from you does not mean that your job is done. Show them matching or similar goods but don't be pushy, just ask, 'Did you see this?' and say that it matches or would go with what they've just bought (if it does). They'll know what you're doing and some will say that they've bought what they wanted. Respond that that's fine and thank them for buying from you. Others will be grateful and, maybe with a little, *gentle* persuading from you, will buy it as well. Thank *them* very nicely.

Ending the Sale

Always end each sale with a personal comment (wish them luck if they were talking about a job interview or are doing a fair the next week which is why they bought your goods, tell them that you hope they enjoy what they bought from you or that the person for whom they bought it likes it – anything like that). It's free but puts the buyer in a good mood, so much so that they might become regulars or buy something else from you before they leave. Even if they don't, they'll remember you next time and be positive about seeing you again – this puts them in the right frame of mind to buy from you – if you have the right stock for them.

No matter how good you are at selling, if you don't have what someone wants, you can't make them buy.

They might be buying with the intention of getting something specific and end up with something else, but if none of your stock appeals – or they can't afford it – you can't sell it.

Making Selling Easier

Never take it personally if you don't sell something. They're after antiques or collectables, not you. Selling can be a challenge so treat it as such. You want people to buy from you and it is your job to sell. Make this as easy as possible by following some simple rules:

◆ Price your goods to sell – most sales are lost by unrealistic or top of the range prices.

◆ Arrange your stock attractively – think about layout, group similar objects or makes (brands) together to make it easier for buyers, maybe colour co-ordinate sections, use stands to give different levels. Put your most attractive or eye-catching pieces at the highest point on your stands (being careful that they are not too big, little or heavy for such a site).

◆ Arrange flat objects at the front of a stand with taller objects closer to the back so no stock is unintentionally 'hidden' from view.

◆ Keep clashing colours away from each other – red, orange and pink can be an eyesore and detract from individual pieces' attractiveness.

◆ Hide your food and wrapping behind the stall.

◆ Use floor-length cloths to hide boxes and wrapping.

◆ Use lighting (if applicable) to highlight choice items or shine through glass.

◆ Clean or polish goods (see Chapter 9 for advice on safe cleaning).

◆ Dress casually smart – depending what you sell, dressing too smartly can be off-putting whilst dressing too casually can cheapen your stock to some would-be buyers.

◆ Wash your hands after unpacking your stock – they get dirty from the newspaper wrapping which can be transferred to any goods which you handle afterwards and might deter buyers.

◆ Arrange your goods attractively – colour co-ordinate jewellery or keep similar stones together, arrange furniture to look as homely and uncramped as possible, even use fresh flowers to add that extra special feeling. Homely sells – people aren't always imaginative so make it easier for them by letting them see how it would look in their own homes.

◆ Be friendly but not overly so (it can drive customers away) and don't be rude or arrogant, however tempting. That said, if someone *is* obnoxious where your stock or prices are concerned, look at them nicely and say, 'Oh, but if you knew what it is, you'd realise that's it's a good buy.' Well, you're not actually accusing them of ignorance but you are reminding them that you're the dealer and have the necessary expertise to know how much your own stock is worth – even if you're just starting out.

◆ And smile – I keep saying it but smiles win sales, especially for undecided or reticent customers.

CHAPTER THREE

The Importance of Careful Wrapping

This might seem like an odd, even slightly patronising chapter but it's not meant to be. What this book aims to do is to stop you making the common mistakes made by all dealers from first-timer to professional – including me. The obvious comment to this chapter – especially for those dealing in smalls – is to wrap everything, but do you really know how?

Keyword
Smalls – smaller items of stock such as china and jewellery. Excludes any furniture.

If you don't already know about it, invest in some 'bubble wrap' – this is the plastic sheeting which comes with protective bubbles – so popular with children for popping. If you do have children or can't resist it yourself, cut off a small square and pop away but then throw it away – the bubbles form a protective layer around your stock and the plastic sheet is useless without them. Bubble wrap is available from garden centres as greenhouse insulation and from packaging firms, while small, often overpriced packets can be bought from some stationers (see your local phone directory for details) or buy a roll at larger fairs. You might even be able to get it free from supermarkets or double glazing firms.

There are no set rules for the use of bubble wrap – some dealers use it for everything, others selectively and some don't use it at all. What I would suggest is that you:

◆ Use bubble wrap selectively but thoroughly. Wrap it round an object at least twice for maximum protection, especially when sending goods by post.

◆ Cut off strips and wrap them gently around extra delicate protuberances such as heads (especially with easy-to-snap hats or delicate hairstyles), limbs and fragile flowers. Wrap bubble wrap around the whole object at least twice and be careful about how you do it – too tightly can snap an object, too loosely won't offer any protection.

◆ Always use it on more expensive objects (eg £100+).

◆ Keep it after use and carry a spare bag of bubble wrap to fairs or centres whether buying or selling – you never have enough when you need it.

◆ Avoid stepping on it or playing with it as this makes it unusable.

Some of your customers might request a piece of bubble wrap for even solid-looking items (i.e. no delicate, easy-to-snap bits such as arms or heads). It's up to you but remember that bubble wrap is not cheap and has to be added to your budget. Also remember that you only have so much with you (unless you waste space in your car and under your stall or in your centre by packing extra rolls of bubble wrap). This means that a delicate piece would have to be wrapped without a protective layer of the bubbles. If you wish to save the packaging, politely refuse by explaining that the piece in question didn't come with any and make a great show of using extra tissue paper or newspaper to wrap the goods.

The Joys of Newspaper

Purists dislike newspaper but it is the saviour of many dealers. It is free, easy to find and thicker than costly tissue paper and does not have to be worked into your budget. It doesn't tear as easily and recycling it is helping the environment. On the negative side, it makes your hands dirty. Some buyers don't like it (eg for certain makes such as Pendelfin, best known for its resin rabbits, believing that it marks the goods) but most accept that it is a cost-effective way of protecting their goods. Always take extra newspaper to fairs (one or two papers will suffice) as it never seems to last as long when leaving as arriving. That way, you don't have to skimp when packing goods for buyers – or rewrapping your own goods which you have just bought.

Paper Bags and Jewellery Bags

It is not always acceptable to wrap jewellery in newspaper (even fresh broadsheets) and your more awkward and demanding customers might complain. Either ignore them or make a small investment in paper bags. These are available from larger stationers, packaging shops and sometimes at larger fairs. They come in several sizes with the larger bags being more costly and generally thicker.

More costly still are jewellery bags. These come in different designs and different sizes and are sold at fairs, packaging shops, some stationers and various jewellery suppliers. Generally made of plastic with resealable tops, they are often sold in packs of 100. On the plus side, they keep your jewellery safe from scratching and keep earrings together but their main disadvantage is that they do take time to pack at the end of a fair when each bag has to be opened, the goods inserted and then sealed. Canny dealers get round this by using the bags when selling goods and wrap the rest of their stock (if not very expensive) in newspaper but more costly goods, especially precious stones, should be treated with care. One chip or scratch can render them unsellable so take care and treat them accordingly.

Useful tip

When wrapping teapots and other lidded goods such as decanters, always wrap the lids separately. Some dealers choose to Sellotape their lids to their goods to prevent damage by careless customers, but this is not advisable when packing as the lids could come loose and chip. Sellotape if you must (can stop lids from falling off and smashing when unwary customers lift them from your shelves/stall) but be prepared for interested parties to want to remove the Sellotape to check that the lid and teapot (or whatever) rim is not damaged – be wary of dealers who will not allow you to remove the Sellotape as they could be hiding damage. Don't forget to put extra packaging around the teapot's spout to avoid damage.

CHAPTER FOUR

Antiques Fairs

Antiques fairs are possibly the most important aspect of dealing. They give you a feel for the trade and an idea about both your prices and your stock. Are you selling the right things, are your prices too high or too low? Or have you got it just right?

> **Keyword**
> **Stalling out – to sell goods at an antiques fair.**

Before you stall out at a fair, you have to decide which fair is right for you. If your stock is general, you might not be able to do specialist fairs; if it encompasses all eras, avoid dateline fairs. That's the simple part but choosing your first fair isn't always that easy. There are two very common mistakes made by first-time dealers which could prevent them from ever dealing again. First, think about why you're stalling out in the first place.

Whether it's love, money or need, whether you're a full-time, part-time or hobby dealer you are in business to make money. For that reason, I would advise against starting at a really small fair.

This probably doesn't make sense but think of it this way – the smaller the fair, the lower the attendance. I could be wrong and you could ignore this and be very lucky. You could be lucky and have the perfect stock or the perfect customer but, like thousands of dealers, you could also discover that no buyers at all can be very costly – and very dull. Of course small fairs have their market – they wouldn't exist otherwise – but it is a mistake to start out too small. It's best to leave it until you feel more confident and have your regular customers. Most dealers who do small fairs (as in about 30 stalls) are hobby dealers who don't really need the money but enjoy getting out about once a month or once every other month. They are normally claiming a pension or have some other income and this can be reflected in their higher prices which deter trade buyers who often avoid the smaller fairs. This is because they are generally not worth travelling to see, unlike larger fairs which offer more choice and better prices.

Unless you live in an area with few fairs or there are several fairs in the same locale, small fairs are rarely well attended, giving you a smaller chance of finding buyers.

Paradoxically, I would also suggest that first-timers avoid the huge fairs which are teeming with buyers.

In the same way that you would not enter the Grand National when you've just started riding, so I would advise against entering the antiques trade at its busiest. Quite simply, you're asking for someone to take advantage of you at worst or, at best, you could lose out on some sales.

The larger the fair, the greater the number of buyers, the busier it is. There is a knack to selling antiques. Some of it is very easy – people see something they want, hold it out, you wrap it and take their money, but what are you missing when you're doing that? What about the person who is just looking at your stock – are they too shy to ask for help or maybe they just need some help to make up their mind. Then there's the person with big pockets who wants your stock but might not want to pay for it. You need eyes in the back of your head to be a dealer and that comes with time, but not when you do your first fair. You need to unwrap your stock at your own pace, not have impatient dealers unwrap it for you (it happens) and you also need to work quietly without being flustered which can be hard for newcomers at the massive multiple-day fairs. It's not only that but everything will be new for you, from checking that the table is secure to putting up your shelves, taking time to clamp them in place and putting up your paste table – and that's only after you've parked the car in the best position for you, unloaded it and have mastered trolleying your stock into a crowded hall. But don't let that put you off larger fairs. Once you have the knack of dealing it becomes a doddle, but if you go too big, too soon, you might never stall again.

The right fair for a first-time dealer is an easy one. You need to be at a mid-level to small fair of about 75–100 dealers. It's large enough to attract both buyers and trade without being too overwhelming. Only ever do a one-day fair when you start out. They can be very tiring and it will give you time to evaluate how you've done. Two days or more is excessive at the beginning of your career or hobby as an antiques dealer.

How Do I Find Out About Fairs?

Most dealers buy the three-monthly white book, *The Antiques Trade Calendar* for £1.50 at most fairs and antiques centres or by subscription for £9 (inc. p&p).[1] This guide lists most of the fairs held throughout Britain and includes the phone numbers of the organisers with many fairs handily listing their size (eg 500 stalls). It is an essential guide for any dealer from the novice to the experienced. There are other guides available but the three-monthly guide is the dealers' bible.

The fairs are listed by county but it's surprising how many people don't really know what other counties are close by so, before you go any further, sit down with an atlas and see what's near you. Some dealers will stick to fairs within a 30-mile radius, others travel further either through choice or limited nearby options. For one-day fairs, it's worth looking at distances of up to around 90 minutes, which opens up possibilities whilst any longer can be too tiring to be practical. This is assuming that you have transport. If you only have access to a taxi or public transport, stick to something closer to home until you decide whether it's the right trade for you, but you really ought to think about driving or getting a car if you want to have more options. Many of the larger fairs are held at showgrounds which necessitates the use of a car for non-locals.

> **Useful tip**
>
> Outside stallholders are at the mercy of the weather (include stock-destroying wind) but can sell more than cramped, inside stallholders for less rent. Consider selling outside during the hot summer months but be aware that you might have to pay to stall out even if it's too wet to do so. Or you could just get a lovely tan – invest in some sun cream when doing outside fairs. It's easy to get burnt but enjoyable to work outside when the weather permits. Long-term, think about buying a small marquee or large tent to protect your stock from the weather.

Once you've worked out which areas you want to cover, look at the listings. As a rule, I would recommend starting at a Sunday fair which, traditionally, is one of the best days for fairs. Obviously, if you have religious objections or, for whatever reason, cannot work at weekends, look at other days. Many dealers don't like trading on a Saturday which they regard as shopping day for the public. This can lead to limited attendance or an overflow

---

1 G.P. London, 32 Fredericks Place, North Finchley, London N12 8QE (020 8446 3604).

of 'browsers' who have no intention of buying but will waste your time talking about anything except buying your stock. Be polite as they could turn into buyers, but save your time and, with a nice smile, go off and serve someone else or excuse yourself and go to the toilet or sit down with paperwork. A Saturday fair is generally not the right first-time fair for you so stick to Sunday if you can.

Ideally, visit your chosen fair before stalling out and speak to some of the stallholders when they're not busy serving someone else. Most dealers are happy to help as long as you're not interrupting them with a sale or some other form of business. Remember, they are there to sell. Explain that you're thinking of stalling there and ask them how they've done – you don't have to say that it's your first fair, it's up to you. Some might patronise but others will be full of helpful advice.

What to Ask a Stallholder

The following pointers are a guide to what you need to ask about any fair that you're thinking of doing regardless of location, size or type (i.e. specialist or general):

◆ Is it a good fair? Obvious but many people don't think of asking before they go and find out to their cost when it's too late.
◆ Has it been busy?
◆ Have you had a good day?
◆ Do most things sell here?
◆ What's the organiser like? A very useful question, especially if the organiser has a reputation for being aggressive, overly familiar with women or, more positively, is really helpful.
◆ Are you doing it again? Another useful way of discovering if the fair is worth doing.
◆ Can you recommend any other fairs?

It's always useful to ask advice from a dealer who has similar stock to that which you're intending to sell. Some people think that this is a strange concept as, effectively, you're asking the competition for advice but dealers are not competitive in this way. The dealer will not see you as a future rival but as a possible buyer and will be happy to share their knowledge of fairs with you. If they've been in the business for a long time, they'll know which fairs are right for your stock and will be happy to tell you so. It might be worth writing it down or asking them to write a list for you. You will have a lot to remember so don't just rely on your memory and they'll be delighted to see that you're taking their advice so seriously.

Always check out the facilities before stalling out if you can. To put it crudely, some toilets are so filthy that they can put you off stalling at that fair but, if everything's suitable, your next step is to speak to the organiser. Either ring them up or, if you're already at the event, ask them some questions.

What to Ask the Organiser

- How much is the stall?
- How many stalls are there (unless you already know)?
- Is there parking?
- Is there even unloading or will I have to take my stock up stairs?
- Is there room for a paste table?
- What time does the fair open for stallholders?
- Is there anything I'm not allowed to sell?
- Do they supply the chairs or will I have to bring my own?
- Is the venue easy to find (if never been before) and can they supply either directions or a map if not?
- Is there signposting (a useful tool for finding a fair and essential for bringing in buyers)?

> **Useful tip**
> Avoid fairs which clash with important sporting fixtures such as The Grand National or the FA Cup. You might not be interested but thousands of buyers are and the fair could be empty all day. Mothering Sunday is also a very bad day for fairs with everyone leaving in plenty of time for lunch (if they come at all) and arriving back just as you're ready to pack up.

If you feel happy and are free to do the next fair, book it then and it's all sorted out. You might have to pay a deposit or the entire stall rent up front. All organisers will accept cash or cheques, with others taking credit or debit cards, and not many of them give receipts but, if you're worried, ring up the day before a fair to ensure that it's still on. The organiser will take your personal details, including a phone number, and 99% of them will ring if there are any problems. They will also have your details on file and can send you details about their other fairs. If you're not happy, smile nicely and say that you'll have to check your diary/with your partner (or anything, really) before booking. They're used to it so don't worry about upsetting them – smiling goes a long way in this business and a good organiser can become a good friend.

One of the most important questions that you'll ask them is the stall rent. There is no set price for stalls which is a pity. Some organisers charge more than others, some less so but, in some ways, you do get what you pay for – although many dealers will disagree with me about this.

What you want is to pay a fair price for a well-advertised, well-organised and pleasant fair. On average, stalls cost around £30–35 for a one-day fair but some organisers charge £12, others £65 + . These are for average fairs, the big, impressive fairs cost a lot more but, like most dealers, you'll be starting off at normal fairs and paying around £30. On top of that, you need to consider petrol costs. Obviously, the closer to home, the lower the cost.

Keyword
Trade fair – a fair held in the middle of the week when non-dealers (i.e. non-trade) are working –
in theory. In reality, anyone can stall out or buy at a trade fair and they're often more competitive
than weekend fairs.

There is a hierarchy at fairs and you'll notice that most organisers charge extra for a 'wall stall'. Why? Some fairs are so cramped that you can only have extra tables at wall stands so it's worth paying the extra (around £10, usually). If you are selling pictures, wall stands are good for exhibiting your stock. Another advantage is that you have no one behind you and one of the most annoying aspects of dealing is a bad neighbour so wall stands can be great for preventing someone else from encroaching on your space. You might also have more space (eg for a paste table at events where centre tables can't have spare tables). The only negative, apart from the extra cost, for a first-timer is that you'll have less dealers around you which is a shame as it's an ideal opportunity to find out about other fairs, news or anything to do with the antiques trade. But that's assuming that it's busy. You might be nervous at your first fair and not want to leave your stall (if stalling alone, always ask your neighbour to watch your stock when you go to the toilet) so won't have the opportunity to ask around but, if it's quiet, dealers often congregate in front of their stalls for a talk.

Most dealers are friendly; if you find one who isn't, just talk to someone else. You're not stuck in an office so it doesn't really matter if you don't like the person stalling next to you, just be friendly, smile blankly and get on with paperwork – or reading a book. There will always be quiet times at fairs, no matter how good they are, so take something to read or you could get bored.

Shopping List

There are a few things which you will definitely need to buy before your first fair while others will be useful for later on. Remember to start off small and save your money. You could hate stalling – some people do – or you could decide, after only one fair, that antiques is your life and want to expand immediately. The following is a shopping list, with the essentials listed separately from long-term needs:

- *The Antiques Trade Calendar*
- cloth
- plastic boxes for stock – or use free cardboard ones from the supermarket
- notebook and pen to record sales
- labels to price goods
- bubble wrap or newspaper for wrapping
- bags
- calculator
- flask
- food
- map
- petrol
- a float (as in change – you'll need plenty of £1 coins and £5 notes; ask your bank if they would change £20 into £1 coins and at least another £20 into £5 notes).

Long-Term Needs

- shelves – two sets
- clamps for shelves
- paste table (with a spare cloth)

- ◆ trolley
- ◆ receipt book.

Let's take some of these items separately. Some of them are self explanatory, such as bags – most of us save money and recycle supermarket bags which we use when selling stock. It's amazing how many dealers, even long-term full-timers, forget to take any bags with them. The same goes for wrapping – take a bag of old papers with you to wrap up goods when you sell them (or small bags if you're selling jewellery) and your own goods at the end of the day. You might have enough when you arrive but, for some reason, there tends to be less at the end of the day than at the beginning so take a couple of old newspapers with you when you stall out.

Cloths

Too many novice dealers either forget to buy a cloth or take the wrong type. You need a cloth to cover your stall. Not only does it look professional, but it also softens the impact when would-be buyers put your stock down. This might sound funny but a fair or two will show you just how careless other people are of your stock.

What type of cloth is best? Always go for a plain one. Patterns can distract from the stock and smaller goods (eg small pieces of china) can get 'lost' in the patterns. Dark colours are best – not aesthetic but practical; it's surprising how quickly those cloths get dirty. For this reason, stick to easy-to-clean materials which won't shrink or crinkle fatally on washing. Velvet looks beautiful and some dealers use old curtains (bought cheaply at car boot fairs) to cover their stalls but they are dry-clean only which can be very expensive in the long run. Most dealers go to their local market and get a cut of dark, plain cloth 7 to 8 feet long (tables are normally quoted in the old measurements, not metres) with blue, green and black being the most popular. Reds tend to clash with stock and browns are too dull. Black is especially popular as it offsets all types of stock, lending it a richer colour and appearance. Avoid plastic cloths which look tacky and can get sticky and retain fingerprints too easily. This makes them look dirty and can reflect badly on your stock.

Useful tip
Buy a longer length of cloth than you'll need – 7–8' instead of 6'. This allows for an attractive overlap and, more practically, shrinkage when washing. Don't worry about width as most cloths have a standard width which is suitable for your needs.

There are two types of dealers – those who iron and those who don't. I don't think that it really matters but I fall into the second category. Some dealers, especially those with more expensive stock (eg £250 minimum per item), think that a smart cloth suggests better quality goods. It's up to you – next time you go to a fair, look at the cloths and see what other dealers are doing. In the end, if you have enough stock, the cloth should just blend in and not be an issue – life's too short.

Boxes

There is much debate amongst certain dealers as to what type of box is the best – plastic or cardboard. For your first fair, I'd suggest starting off cheaply and speaking to the manager of the fruit and vegetable section of your local supermarket. These days, banana and apple boxes are squashed as soon as the stock is unpacked but, if you ask the manager to reserve you some (let him know how many you'll need), then you have free boxes to protect and carry your stock. Never say that you're an antiques dealer but, if they ask, say that you're cleaning up at home or something like that.

Some dealers use bags for their fragile stock but boxes are much safer – they protect your well-wrapped goods from getting squashed or accidentally knocked and they're easy to store. Banana boxes are the best as you can fit about four on a standard upright trolley, which saves time and energy wheeling goods into the fair. You can also pile them up under the table, unlike apple boxes which are more problematic, being that much taller, but are useful for larger items such as taller vases.

The disadvantage of banana boxes is that they absorb water and fairs can get wet, especially if you're hanging around outside before the doors open. They also need repairing every so often but they're free, light and a good size for storage and loading a car. Only ever use boxes with lids – whether they're cardboard or plastic – that way, nothing ever falls out if you tilt the boxes at the wrong angle or do not put them down properly. They're also easier to stack without any annoying slippages and breakages.

Plastic boxes are more solid than cardboard ones, it doesn't matter if it's raining and some people think that they look smarter. *But* they cost money (around £5+ per box with lids often costing extra) and most dealers take around six to ten boxes per fair with more boxes containing spare stock at home – that's quite a hefty initial investment. They can also be relatively heavy even before goods are put in them but some dealers prefer them and they are often bigger than the other boxes, allowing for larger or more stock to be carried at one time – which can present a problem when storing them under the table at a fair. Ultimately, it's up to you but save money where you can when starting out. Plastic boxes are not essential for your first ever fair.

Notebook, Pens, Labels, Calculator and Receipt Book

Whether you're a full-time, part-time or hobby dealer, you will need to keep records (see Section Six, Chapter 1 for further details) and it's best done in a notebook which is kept solely for use at fairs with a stockbook used to record purchases. You are very lucky that you're starting out now so you can avoid the mistake made by most experienced (but lazy) dealers. Start as you mean to go on and give your goods a stock number. Make it sequential so that you can find it easily in a stockbook. Some dealers try to be clever by having a different code for different types of goods (eg AR for silver and RD for Royal Doulton). This is fine if you keep a separate stockbook for each different type but it is very time-consuming if you don't. Imagine having ten different types of codes, each with around 20 goods – more when you become more experienced. Now imagine trying to find the relevant number when you're in a hurry. Keep it simple and stick to sequential numbers but always use a letter in front of them (eg the initial of your surname – S in my case) to prevent them from looking like prices – buyers can get easily confused. Labels have already been discussed in detail but remember the basics – always put the date and maker's name (if known) on the label, along with the price, trade discount (eg T5) and your stock code. Keep it tidy and clear to avoid problems. Would-be buyers will walk off if they can't read a label.

Dealers always seem to lose pens at fairs so take several with you. Keep one in your pocket or purse and at least one behind the stall to make your life easier. Even take a spare one for your neighbour who will probably forget – it's a way of starting a conversation and, if you're lucky, a friendship.

An increase in the need for receipts with various Registration Acts (as mentioned in Chapter 1 of this section), and the need for overseas buyers to have a record of sales for Customs purposes, has meant that you will be asked to provide a receipt at some time or other. Go to your local stationers or a big office supply shop (such as Office World – see your local phone directory for details) and buy a simple receipt book which will allow you to record the item purchased, where it was purchased (eg Wood Green Animal Shelter antiques fair, stall number W34), from whom (your name or business name), method of payment and the amount. Buy one which copies automatically without the need for messy extra carbon paper and keep it in a bag which you take to all fairs – buy a cotton or other, hard-wearing type of bag which you'll get used to carrying automatically to all your fairs.

You'll also need a calculator to add up multiple buys, your takings and, most exciting of all, your profit.

Flask and Food

There is a basic rule to most food and drink at fairs – it's expensive, dull and, worryingly, often out of date. Always supply your own food and take a flask of hot water with you – or make the coffee in it before you go. Tea lovers should take their own teabags and milk can either be brought in a bottle or carton. That said, some dealers bring tiny, individual cartons which they get from the supermarket or, dare I say it, help themselves to extra milk pots at service stations or fast food restaurants – which seems to be where most dealers get their sugar. I am not suggesting that anyone steal anything, merely mentioning where many dealers seem to acquire their milk and sugar. Don't forget to take a spoon with you for stirring it – it's another common item forgotten by dealers. The flask is especially useful when you arrive early and are sitting in the car before the doors open, especially on a cold morning.

Cold drinks at fairs can be astronomical so buy your own before you go. In the summer, water is best because fizzy drinks can have unwelcome side-effects and juice can get a bit sickly. Water can also be used to clean your hands which attract dirt and dust, especially in the summer at the two-day fairs.

Sandwiches are easy to eat and practical at fairs. You can rarely eat your lunch in one sitting so don't take anything complicated or fiddly. Think of your neighbours and avoid pungent smelling food. Many dealers will make their own sandwiches or cook chicken legs, whilst others raid their local supermarkets – it all depends on time, budget and taste. Biscuits, carrot sticks and baby tomatoes are also popular at fairs but crisps are best avoided – as are any other foods which leave sticky fingermarks on your stock or could make you thirsty.

Whilst buying food at fairs can be expensive, the toasty (hot, toasted sandwich) has become an institution at the trade (mid-week) and multi-day fairs and, whilst relatively expensive (just under £3 at the time of writing), they are a pleasant treat with some fairs going even further and providing not just chips and greasy-looking bacon sandwiches but homemade doughnuts (sticky and fattening but irresistible) and even Thai food – not as authentic as it could be but normally very good value and tasty.

As a rule, stick to easy to eat, clean food which is easy to clear up afterwards, won't leave you with sticky fingers, smelly breath, dirty clothes or a filthy mouth.

Trolleys

Long-term, no matter how often you intend to do fairs, you will need a trolley. These come in different shapes and sizes from flatbeds to uprights and opinions vary as to the best. Flatbeds can often carry your entire stock, including extra tables and shelves, plus your food and fair bag (containing notebook, bags etc) in one go. On the downside, they can be hard to steer and things have been known to fall off. An upright holds less but is lighter and easier to manage. It's also advisable to invest in some 'spiders' (they look like colourful bungee ropes) which, like the trolleys, can be found either in DIY stores or at the larger fairs. These bind your stock to the trolley and are easy to apply. You can either get single ones or the multiples which are more effective and have six ends, all with the hooks which make spiders so useful. They do stretch but be careful of overstretching, they have a habit of 'pinging' if incorrectly applied which can be painful.

Be careful about wheeling your trolley over steps and always take it backwards if there is a small step at the entrance to the fair – it's safer that way and prevents the trolley from getting stuck, causing both a traffic jam with queuing dealers and embarrassment. If in doubt, carry your stock, but most dealers use a trolley where they can. Whilst it is acceptable to use a fellow dealer's trolley with permission at one fair, it is generally frowned on to do this too often – you can end up looking not only cheap but unprofessional which could lose you sales.

Spare Tables

Most first-time dealers lose out by not having a spare table. It doesn't have to be a paste table – which is what most dealers use – it can be anything from a card table to a picnic table but it needs to be strong, have its own cloth and be small enough to fit in your car. Long-term, a folding paste table (available from most DIY shops) is an essential tool of dealing.

Why do you need a table when the fair organiser supplies their own table? Quite simply, if you bring your own table (check with the organiser that spare tables are permitted), then you will double the size of your stall at no extra cost and that could double your profits. By doubling the space, you're doubling how much stock you have on offer. Paste tables cost around £30 and are not only excellent ways of capitalising on your profits but can be used in the home when you're not at fairs. Perfect for picnics, car boot sales and party food, not to mention wallpapering.

Shelves

Like the spare tables, shelves can double the amount of stock on display. Not only that, they also look good and are safety features. Children love handling antiques but they can't reach the shelves, so put your best and most expensive goods on the top shelves – it will also give them status.

The best shelves are the folding, three-level ones which most dealers use at fairs. These are easy to fit in most cars when folded and don't need time-wasting and fiddly screwing back together at fairs.[1] There are alternatives and the normal, folding sets might not even be suitable for your stock – jewellery dealers rarely use them except to exhibit necklaces on display stands, whilst furniture dealers don't use them at all. However, if you are intending to sell 'smalls', or accessories such as hats and handbags, they are a must. Always carry a screwdriver with you because the supports often need a bit of tweaking.

Always check that your shelves are secure by pressing down on each level before clamping them and using them.

Clamps are very useful when using shelves. Not everyone who goes to a fair realises how precarious shelves can be and it is not uncommon to see elderly ladies making their way from stand to stand at a fair by holding onto the shelves! If they're not clamped, the whole lot could come crashing down and you could lose it all.

At various times, department stores and large supermarkets sell shelves under the guise of bookshelves. Some of them are very attractive; Asda produces especially well-made ones with similar, but far more expensive versions, found in branches of John Lewis. However, they are designed as bookcases and can be too heavy to lift. Remember that you have to lift them from your house or garage into your car, from there into the venue and then, hardest of all, onto your table. If they're too heavy for you, leave them.

You might find it useful to nail some picture nails or picture hooks into the shelves where the shelves meet the main frame. These are great for displaying wall clocks, necklaces and goods designed for hanging such as wallpockets (vases which are flat-backed and designed to be displayed on the walls – especially popular during the 1930-50s). This can save you room and show the would-be buyer how attractively they will hang – which sells them much more easily than laying them flat on your stall.

---

[1] Folding fairs shelves are available from B. Pitcher at £28 each + P&P (Tel: 0121 378 1529) and Bobby's Books (01474 823388) – good quality but more costly.

Table size differs from fair to fair with some organisers using metal tables. Do be careful if you are unlucky enough to encounter these. They are rarely even and stock can bounce across the table, breaking it. Shelves *must* be clamped if metal tables are used to counteract the 'bounce effect'. Some tables are wide enough for you to have the shelves sideways on as opposed to the more traditional face-on. This means that you can have two sets of shelves, one at each end of the table with a third set in the middle – essentially, allowing you to display another box of stock – that can be worth £1,000+ and all for a minimal outlay.

> **Useful Tip**
> Always find out where you're going before you set out. Either get a map or ask the organiser for directions (or both). An alternative is to use the Internet. Some sites will give you detailed directions to venues (or roads) with a very useful estimate of journey length. Remember that you'll be travelling before most people are awake so the roads will be clear on the way there but slower on the way home. Useful sites to check routes are *www.theaa.com* and *www.rac.co.uk/plan_route* whilst *www.streetmap.co.uk* is very handy for checking out streets (eg you know how to get to Brentwood by using one of the other sites but then use Streetmap to find Doddinghurst Road where the fair is held in the Leisure Centre). Print out the maps/ instructions and carry them in the car along with your tickets for the fair – put them in the car the night before so that you won't forget them.

The Day of the Fair

◆ Dealers have had their cars stolen along with all their stock and this can be avoided by loading the car on the morning of a fair and unloading it as soon as you get back home in the evening instead of leaving it until the next morning. If you don't do this and your stock is stolen, it is unlikely that your insurance company will pay out – unless the car is locked in your garage at the time.

◆ Always arrive early at a fair so that you have easy parking and easy unloading. The later you arrive, the further you have to trolley your stock when unloading – unpleasant at the best of times but worse during the wet winter months.

♦ Before you leave your house, check that you have got everything you need. It sounds obvious but it's amazing how many dealers forget simple things like bags, wrapping, pens, clamps and even their cloths. You might like to write a checklist until you get used to doing fairs – it could save you a lot of unnecessary trouble.

♦ Make your flask before you go and leave it in an accessible place so you can have a coffee or other drink while you're waiting outside the venue, especially if, like most professional dealers, you arrive around an hour before doors are due to open.

♦ Fill up with petrol before you leave so that you don't have to stop on the way back – you'll probably be too tired then and will be grateful for your forethought. It's also not always easy to find a garage when you're stalling outside your locale.

♦ When you arrive, if it's dry, unload your stock near the hall (see what the other dealers are doing). Again, it will make your life easier. When everyone else is running about, getting caught up with each other, all you have to do is trolley your stock from near the door of the hall (or wherever) into the venue itself. Obviously, if you're doing an outdoor fair where you park on your pitch, this is not relevant.

♦ When the door opens, take your time and don't panic because others will. Take care and ignore everyone else scurrying round. They're not you. This is when trolleys tip and stock gets broken.

♦ Set up your stall by putting your cloth on the table once you've checked that the table is secure (look under it and check for the wobble factor by giving it a slight push before doing anything else).

♦ Erect and clamp the shelves (if applicable) and then set up your spare table (if applicable) with its cloth and start unloading *in your own time*.

♦ Don't let anyone hurry you and ask them to stop if they start trying to take things from your boxes. It does happen and it shouldn't. Just because this is your first or one of your first fairs does not mean that anyone has the right to take advantage of you. Just ask them politely to wait, maybe ask them what they're looking for and tell them if you have any. If you have some at home, but not with you, let them know and tell them to come back later when you've unloaded. Most dealers are fine, some might go off in a huff but you don't need customers like that. Just keep smiling and watch that money come in.

♦ Make a note of sales as soon as they happen so that you don't forget, and keep all of your labels so you can match them with sales at the end of the day – it's a useful tip, especially if you forget to write something down or to note down the stock number.

♦ You might be asked to keep something for someone. That's fine but always tell them that you'll only keep it for a certain period of time (half an hour to an hour, it's up to you). You might never see them again otherwise and, meanwhile, no one else can buy the goods. At larger fairs, I always offer to write down my stall number with a note of what I'm holding for them. It's a useful trick as it not only reminds the would-be buyer what it is and where but reinforces the fact that I'm doing them a favour by reserving it – it's much easier to sell goods by appearing helpful but professional. By writing things down, you're emphasising that you're there to sell, that you're running a business not just show would-be buyers pretty bits and pieces.

Useful tip
Don't stick to the same area when stalling out or you'll end up taking the same stock to the same buyers. Ask the organisers which other fairs they hold and be prepared to travel to maximise your sales potential.

Keep calm and don't let it get to you. You're there to sell. It doesn't matter how much they want to pay, you know how much you need them to pay so stick to your prices, relax and enjoy yourself. The antiques business is only stressful if you let it be. So, sit back, smile and be there to serve when you're needed – give information about pieces but not too much as it can intimidate would-be buyers who will leave very quickly without spending a penny.

Talking of which, take extra tissues with you – the toilets at antiques fairs aren't always very pleasant and always seem to run out of toilet paper. Often very early on in the day, so go prepared.

Recap

- The best day to stall out is a Sunday or a Bank Holiday Monday.

- Do your homework before booking – check out the fair, the organiser and see if it clashes with an important sporting fixture (avoid it if it does).

- Go shopping for a cloth and other basics such as a notebook and calculator.

- Get a map (or directions from the organiser) so you know where you're going.

- Clearly price all of your stock before wrapping it carefully and putting it in boxes – never cram too much into a box or you could have costly breakages.

- Write a list of what you need to remember and check it off as you load the car the morning of the fair. Don't forget your ticket if you have one.

- Load the trolley last (if you're using one) so that it's accessible, and keep your flask and food bag where you can reach them with ease.

- Fill up with petrol before you leave to avoid having to do it when you're tired on the way home.

- Park with your boot closest to the venue for easy unloading.

- Take your time.

- Don't be bullied into lowering your prices.

- Smile.

- And enjoy it – that's why you're there.

Fairs

If you have a problem with a fair or the organiser, speak to them or put your complaint in writing. If you are not happy with their response, or important matters such as signposting, parking or their attitude does not improve, do not return. *The continual support of inferior or overpriced fairs will not help to improve them.*

There are too many fairs to list in this book with more starting up all of the time and, sadly, long-standing fairs being forced to close down.

I'm only going to list three organisers, not just because I do or have done their fairs but because their fairs are good and that's what you need in this business.

- **Aztec** (01702 549623). Fairs in Cambs, Essex, Norfolk and Suffolk. Best fairs are Norfolk Showground and Brentwood. Good, friendly and helpful organisers with well-priced stalls and good fairs. Perfect for first-time, novice and professional dealers as they are well-attended and easy to do. Their stalls start at £35.

- **Bob Evans** (01664 812627). Fairs in Cambs, Hereford and Worcester, Leics, Norfolk, Northants, Shrops, Warwickshire and Wilts. Best fair is the Festival of Antiques at the Peterborough Showground which is far too big for first-timers to stall out but offers terrific value (around £40 for three days) and is possibly the best multiple-day fair in the business. Good organisers with well-priced stalls and good fairs. Their other fairs are worth doing by all dealers, including first-timers. Their stalls start at £28.

- **DMG** (01636 702326). Fairs in Kent, Notts, Somerset, Suffolk, W. Sussex, Worcs, France and USA. One of the priciest organisers on the market (most single day fairs start at £65 +) but it can be worth it and Newark is the best fair for buyers – too big for first-time or novice dealers to sell but *the* place to pick up a handful of bargains, no matter what you buy. Shepton Mallet is possibly their nicest fair (but not first-timers – slightly too big and hectic). DMG is possibly the biggest of the organisers with fairs to match – you can't call yourself a dealer unless you go to their fairs at least as a buyer.

CHAPTER FIVE

Antiques Centres

Antiques centres do not always require their dealers to be present, which offers you a chance to sell your goods when you're busy elsewhere, even when you're on holiday. Used properly, they provide a good source of income and a place to display your stock instead of keeping it boxed up in storage when you're not at a fair. Some dealers find that centres provide them with all the income they need whilst others use them as just one aspect of their business, using fairs and/or auctions as well. Many dealers will exhibit in more than one centre at a time whilst others don't use them at all.

Finding a Centre

Always shop around before you commit to a centre. Most centres will ask you to sign a three-month contract with a month's written notice required before you can move out. This can cost you a lot of money, especially if the centre does not work out, so choose your centre carefully. Ideally, speak to other unit or cabinet holders with similar goods to your own before you sign a contract.

You might find it strange that anyone would want to exhibit in the same centre as someone who has similar goods but the more dealers there are, the more buyers. For example some centres have several cigarette lighter dealers (such as the Admiral Vernon in London's Portobello Road) which means that would-be buyers know that they have a good chance of finding what they want. Similar dealers grouped together attract buyers who might not be quite so willing to travel to a centre with only one relevant dealer.

The wrong location can ruin a centre before its even opened, but if there are several centres within one small locale it doesn't matter how far they are from a motorway or city centre because buyers are prepared to travel if they have so much on offer. Sawbridgeworth is on the Hertfordshire-Essex border, near Harlow and Bishops Stortford. The town itself has nothing much to offer most people but there are five antiques centres there, within a few minutes walk from each other and handily located by the station.

Buyers travel from all over the country and even overseas to visit the five centres but they might not bother if there was only one centre there. This is a useful guide to assessing the potential usefulness of a centre.

If it is by itself with no other antiques outlets (including a good auction house or regular antiques market) nearby, then it might be too quiet to be successful.

There are of course exceptions. Hemswell in Lincolnshire is in the middle of nowhere but attracts buyers from all over the world. This is because the centre itself is huge. In fact, it is so big that it inhabits three enormous buildings and has plans to expand. A smaller centre in the same location might not have the same success.

Assessing the Centre

One way to assess a centre's success is to ask how long-term their dealers are. A centre which cannot keep its dealers for longer than a year (unless it is a new centre, of course) is worrying. Long-term dealers are a sign of the centre's success – dealers leave when they are not taking enough money to cover their expenses, let alone making a profit.

Turnover is a major factor in a centre's success and unit-holders are aware of this. Regular buyers grow complacent and don't bother looking too hard if everything appears to be the same. For first-time visitors to a centre, a dusty cabinet is a sign that stock is sticking which could stop them from buying, especially if they are not professional dealers who will know that even dusty stock can contain good buys.

When you have found a centre which you like, sign up for three months. For most centres, this is the minimum stay required. If three months seems like a long time to you, especially if you are just starting out, you have to remember that it takes time for dealers to get established in centres, even if they do manage it properly. Some dealers (and centre owners) would argue that you should allow at least six months before assessing the situation but this can leave you with a costly loss, especially if the centre is obviously not working out for you within the first three months.

You have to be practical when establishing how well you are doing in a centre. You cannot expect to do well during quiet months (the summer months for any non-touristy area) and you are not going to take the same amount month after month or week after week. Sales are unpredictable and, no matter how good your stock, you will have the odd bad week. However, if during the first two months you are nowhere near to covering your expenses, let alone making a profit, put your notice in writing so that you can pull out at the end of the three months' cycle and not waste any more money. Most centres require one month's written notice.

> **Useful tip**
>
> It is a bad sign if there are too many available units or cabinets in the centre which you're thinking of joining unless the centre has just opened or expanded – more than five in an average sized centre (100–150 dealers) is too many. If they have only just opened, ask about special offers. Some new centres will offer half-priced cabinets for the first three months to attract dealers – it's better business for them to be virtually full, even at a loss for the first few months to attract buyers and other dealers. Olney Antiques Centre (01234 710942) did this and had a waiting-list of dealers willing to pay the full price when the special offer was up, replacing any dealers who moved out after the offer finished at the end of the first three months. In fact, it proved so successful in attracting unit-holders that they had to expand in their first three months to satisfy demand – something which might not have happened without that initial centre-filling offer.

What Expenses Should I Expect to Pay?

◆ **Rent** – £35–90 + pcm for a cabinet or £150–250 + pcm for a unit for an initial three-month period. Some centres might ask less, others more. Please note, this rent is not normally negotiable unless you are moving into more than one unit or cabinet or the centre is just about to open.

◆ **Commission** – Some (but not all) centres will charge a percentage of your sales for commission on top of your rent. This varies between 3–10%; 5% is the average and any higher can be too expensive to be practical. Remember to work out the commission before pricing your stock – add an extra percentage to cover commission charges.

◆ **Petrol** – You will be expected to drive to the centre on a regular basis to change stock and, if applicable, pay your rent and collect your money. Take this into account when budgeting.

◆ **Miscellaneous** – Some centres will charge you an initial, one-off fee before you move in for various reasons. Some charge £10 for the key in case you take it away by mistake (it happens), others £10 for packaging. Work this in to your expenses when calculating if the centre is practical. It's a small amount but has to be considered.

Discounts

To be a successful centre dealer, you have to price your stock to sell. This doesn't mean too cheaply but realistically. When you sign up for a centre, you are committing yourself to at least three months' rent and that has to be covered. By hanging out for the optimum price, you might not even cover your basic expenses. Many centres will ring you up to ask if you can give a further discount on your trade price because they have an interested buyer. This can be worth agreeing to if you want to shift old, more expensive or larger items of stock. It's also worth considering if the would-be buyer is looking at three or more items of stock. That said, it is perfectly reasonable to refuse. Why? Because you're there to make money and, if you reduce your prices even more *and* pay a commission on top of that reduction, you could end up losing money. Always remember that you have to pay rent and commission plus the original cost of the stock before you can begin to make money.

> **Useful tip**
> A successful centre dealer is one who knows how to make their stock look fresh even when it isn't. Simply move it around the cabinet or unit on a regular basis.

Being Paid

Different centres work differently. Some will allow you to have your takings in cash whenever you turn up (as long as you sign for them), others will pay you once a month with a cheque. Most centres allow you to deduct your rent from your takings but some won't and that can make life very difficult, especially if you've had a bad month and money is tight. Always ask about how the centre pays before signing a contract. Try to be paid in cash if possible so that you have the cash immediately and don't have to wait for a cheque to clear – this is especially important if you are a full-time dealer and need the money to pay bills or for extra stock.

Most centres will give you receipts with copies of your labels, allowing you to see exactly what was sold and, more importantly perhaps, that the centre has stuck to your discount. If they have not and have agreed with a customer to take less money than you specified without your permission, then demand that they pay the difference and give your notice in writing there and then (ask to borrow paper if necessary) – if they've done it once, they'll do it again and you could lose out.

If a centre gives you an over-the-card-limit cheque from a customer which subsequently bounces, ask the centre to pay you out of their own money. If they don't, move out. It's not really their fault but they should not be accepting cheques without writing down card numbers or accepting them for higher than the card limit – why should you lose out? If, however, a centre bounces their own cheque when paying your monthly (or whatever) takings, then give your notice *immediately*. It's too risky to stay – they could go bankrupt, taking all of your money – and maybe even your stock – with them. It has been known to happen and a bounced cheque is the first warning sign. Move out before you lose anything else – and demand your money in cash.

Most centres will pay you on a set day of the month or send you a cheque without any trouble at all, but always add up your receipts and ensure that it corresponds to your invoice – honest mistakes do happen. Just make sure that you catch them and get your money back.

If asked, get paid in cash and have your rent deducted from your takings to save time and trouble.

Display

If you're selling smaller items such as glass and china, jewellery or precious metals (eg gold or silver), opt for a locked cabinet. It keeps your goods safe and free from breakages. It also means that you only have to turn up to change your stock and collect your money. Most cabinets have glass shelves which allow in light and enable buyers to see the base of the goods (where many pieces are signed by the makers – it's called the backstamp). It's a good idea to clean these shelves properly at least once a month to keep them looking fresh and clean – dusty shelves can be off-putting and reflect badly on the quality of your stock.

Try to arrange your goods as attractively as possible instead of cramming them in. This makes it easy for buyers to see and an attractive display draws buyers in – and makes them more inclined to spend. Invest in some display stands which can be bought at most of the larger centres, fairs, specialist shopfitting firms and via the Internet from firms such as Alan Morris Wholesale (01453 861069 or *www.alanmorris.co.uk*). If you are intending to sell plates, buy plate stands (they cost about £1) which stand plates upright – not only do they look better, but they'll save you room.

Never use wire plate stands, designed to hook plates on the wall – they can damage them long-term and many dealers will refuse to buy any plates which are displayed this way just in case.

If you're selling jewellery, get some specialist stands (details as above) to display rings safely and effectively, tilting them upright to display the stones to perfection. You'll also need necklace and bracelet or bangle stands. Not only do they make your goods look more attractive but they save room. Some dealers buy black velvet material or pads (material from the market, pads from jewellery display specialists – at fairs or see your local phone directory) to enhance the quality of their goods. Black velvet is perfect for off-setting all jewellery from the cheapest to the most expensive. Some buyers even carry a piece with them on buying trips and check the colour of pearls against the cloth to check for replacements or discolouring.

Centres are an easy way of making money but you can't just expect them to succeed unless you do something to help. Go at least once a fortnight to replace stock, with a complete changeover every other month. If you don't have enough stock for that, just do what the experts do and change your stock around *within* the cabinet or unit. That way, it looks fresh and will get regulars to look properly instead of just assuming that they've seen it all before – even if they have.

Your stock is not an exhibition but a sales display so keep it fresh to make it pay.

What Makes a Centre Good?

If you are travelling a long distance to your centre, you might need to use the toilet. Some centres have facilities for all but others only have them for staff – and not all of them will mention it. Find out before you've signed up if you can use the facilities.

A lot of the larger centres have cafés and restaurants but not all do. If they don't, you should be given a free tea or coffee on arrival as a courtesy. Don't be afraid to ask – most will do it automatically but they can forget. If you can't have normal tea or coffee, take your own so that you can have a drink when you arrive.

Parking

One of the main requirements for centre dealers is parking. There's no point going into a centre when you can't get your stock there with ease. Whether you're selling large items such as furniture or smalls, you need easy unloading. If a centre is upstairs and you can't manage them, ask whether or not they're prepared to help you with loading and unloading. If the answer is no, find another centre. Some centres have no parking as such but do have areas for unloading. Ask before you sign anything and ring before travelling so that you're expected and space can be made for you. Some centres have parking restrictions because they're in busy cities or pedestrian areas; find out before you agree to go into a centre and ensure that you arrive before the restrictions are in place for easy loading and unloading.

If the centre you want has a small car park, arrive early – even before the centre opens in the morning – to park. It makes life much easier. And try not to change your stock at the weekends when it is much busier than normal. You'll get in the way and prevent people from looking at your stock as you pack and unpack it. Parking will be more difficult and the whole experience will be unnecessarily stressful. The whole point of being in a centre is to make stress-free money, so make it easier on yourself and arrive early for parking during weekdays – if you can.

Details, Details

There will be times when you're asked for an address. Maybe a dealer who lives in one of the areas covered by registration (mentioned in Chapter 1 of this section) will need to take your details when buying goods from you. Never give anybody your home address (apart from centres and auction houses who will need them before you can start trading). If you trade in an antiques centre, it is a legitimate and, above all, safe address to use in such circumstances. If someone wants to ring you and you don't want them to have a personal number, including a mobile phone, give them your centre phone number (with cabinet or unit number for easy reference).

One of the most important things which you pay for when selling at a centre is their details – use them.

Centres are happy for you to give out their details and will often ask you to have some of their leaflets on your stall. That way, they get free advertising and benefit from your customer base. Always tell people about a centre that you're in as it will increase custom and that's good for all concerned.

Labelling

There is a tedious side to selling in centres. It's called labelling. Unfortunately, different centres have different rules and that can make life difficult if you're transferring stock between centres. Why? Because they all want you to use codes on your labels. Some want your initials (or a series of letters if someone has the same initials as you) whilst others want your unit or cabinet number. That's easy enough to do if you're in only one centre but you have to remember to include your number or they won't know whose goods they've just sold.

The difficulty begins if you're in cabinet 027 (always use three numbers where possible to avoid the code looking like a price or trade discount) in one centre and 051 in another. If you change the stock around without changing the code, another dealer could take your money – if you're in cabinet 051 in one centre but have code 027 on your label by mistake (because you haven't relabelled the goods from the other centre where you really are cabinet 027), the real owner of cabinet 027 gets your money – unless the centre's manager spots your mistake first.

The other problem concerns your handwriting. If it's anything as bad as mine, you could be giving someone else your money. I'm in cabinet 051 in one centre. My handwriting is very bad and I often run out of space on my labels, which means that I'll stick 051 anywhere it fits. So, what's the problem? Turn 051 over and it looks like 150! If you are in a reversibly numbered cabinet or unit, underline the number with the line at the bottom so 051 doesn't become 150 by mistake.

Your Obligations

Some centres will want more than just your money, they'll want your time as well. If you have a unit in some centres, you will be required to man it (i.e. sell there) yourself. This is difficult if you don't want to be a full-time dealer, want to go on holiday or do mid-week fairs. Or you might just not want to be there. If your contract demands that you're there at least once a week (normally more), then you must either honour this or choose another centre. Busy centres in market towns such as Lymington in Hampshire (01590 670934), demand that their unit (but not cabinet) holders be present at least on market day (in this case, Saturday). That's because the centre is too busy to rely on its paid staff. And that can be a problem if you'd rather be elsewhere. On the other hand, no one knows your stock as well as you do. Sweet talking and honest knowledge can pay for itself and be reflected in your takings.

You might be happy about selling your own goods in a centre – many dealers know that they have better sales that way – but how would you feel about selling other people's? Some centres will expect you to man the centre for a set amount of days every month. This can be as little as once a month but it could be more and can include Sundays – a day best kept for buying or selling at fairs, or just being at home with your family or resting after a busy week. It doesn't matter how far away you live, you will be expected to maintain your days and could be asked to leave if you are unable to keep up this commitment. It is time-consuming and you might not be happy selling other people's goods as well as your own. Alternatively, you could see it as a fantastic opportunity to learn about other areas of antiques which you might not normally consider selling. It's a chance to learn about pricing as well as acquire basic or maybe even detailed knowledge of a different range of stock. It's also very sociable. You could be working on the same day as the same people every time – great if you like them, frustrating if not. It depends on you, some people like this aspect of centre dealing and use it to brush up on their sales technique, whilst others just want to sell their own goods or not have to work in a centre at all – especially if they have a full or part-time job.

Manning a Centre

There is a negative side to manning centres which you might not think about. You might be happy to man a centre yourself but are you as happy to let other people? No matter how hard dealers try to be professional, they will always try harder to sell their own goods. If a buyer is undecided between two objects, one owned by you, the other by the person manning the centre that day, they're more likely to buy the one belonging to the manner. Realistically, it might be because the person manning the centre is able to give them more information because it is their stock, they might give a bigger, more tempting discount to clinch the sale or they could be negative about your stock to get the sale for themselves. Less cynically, the buyers might have made the decision themselves and you're just unlucky.

A centre with paid staff employs professional sellers who are non-biased (in theory, at least – decent Christmas presents can add useful bias!) and can sell virtually anything, enabling you to devote your time elsewhere. Some centres use part-time staff who are also centre dealers, often paying reduced rent. These are not always the best type of staff. Some are excellent and use their knowledge of antiques to sell your goods better than those without an antiques background. Others will put their own stock first. The good news is that these are easy to spot. Before you sign a contract with a centre, go as a buyer. See what sort of service you receive. If you're being pushed towards certain cabinets, find out if the seller has a vested interest. If they admit that it's theirs, don't move in – they could lose you sales.

To man or not to man? It's up to you. If you want to use the opportunity to sell your own – and everyone else's stock – and can afford the necessary time, then do it.

It can be an enjoyable way of learning more about the business and you get to meet some interesting people whilst seeing what else people like to buy. If, on the other hand, you want to use a centre where you don't need to sell yourself but where professional staff are employed, then avoid centres with manning policies. If you do opt for a manned centre which does not open on Sundays, make it clear that you are happy to do your accepted shifts but will not be able to do Sundays if they decide to open at some point – you can change your mind later if you wish but, that way, you save your Sundays for buying or selling elsewhere.

What Sort of Centre Do I Want?

♦ Size is not everything. Big centres attract more buyers than small ones (usually) but you have more competition – are your prices or your stock competitive enough to cope with those demands?

♦ Do you want one close to home or are you prepared to travel? Most dealers stick to a 50-60 mile radius whilst others do not even live in the same country. If you have the time and desire to travel (at least twice a month), don't let distance be a barrier but be practical, petrol costs add up. That said, it is a good idea to have a centre in a different area from where you normally stall out – your stock will be seen by different buyers that way, increasing your chances of selling.

♦ Are extra facilities important to you? Do you need food and decent toilets or do you just want a centre which sells without the added extras – but are there toilets in case you need them?

♦ Are you or your partner disabled or have a potentially debilitating condition such as asthma? Can you manage centres with stairs or do you need one with disabled access and extra wide aisles?

♦ Do you want a cabinet or a unit?

♦ Are the units or cabinets large enough for your needs?

♦ Is the lighting good enough?

♦ Do you want to man the centre or want them to do the work for you?

♦ Do you feel welcome when you enter or are they standoffish? Will potential customers feel the same and could this put them off looking around and buying your stock?

♦ Is there easy parking or unloading?

◆ Are there security measures (eg CCTV, alarm systems, locked cabinets, shutters etc)? You should be able to see these without asking but, if you're serious about moving in, ask.

◆ Do they attract many shippers or overseas buyers – not necessary but often very useful.

◆ How high is their turnover?

◆ How often do they pay out? How do they pay out?

◆ Is it busy? It might not be if you visit mid-week but it should be if you're there at a weekend. If not, how will they be able to sell your stock?

◆ Do they get a lot of regulars? Either ask (they'll probably say yes either way) or watch how they greet customers. Those greeted by name or told about new stock are either centre dealers or regulars. Either way, it's a sign of a good centre.

◆ Is the centre signposted? This is not necessary but is helpful as it will attract people who don't already know about it and help those who do to find their way.

◆ Where do they advertise? The most important places are *The Antiques Trade Calendar* and *The Antique Dealer Newspaper* (better known as *The Dealer*), as well as local papers to attract local buyers who might not necessarily be antiquey people but want presents.

◆ Can you afford the rent? That's the big one, if you don't think that you can, don't risk it. A centre should pay for itself, you shouldn't have to pay for it because you haven't sold enough stock.

CHAPTER SIX

Antiques Shops

Long-term, you might want to have your own shop. It is not advisable to rush straight out and get one, no matter how cheap it might seem, before you get some experience. There are various reasons for this but the main one is financial. Most shops require a long-term contract with expensive get-out clauses. There's no point opening a shop one week and deciding that antiques is not for you the next. If you want to get a bank loan, you'll need to prove that you have enough know-how to make a go of the business and you won't get one without relevant proven experience.

Rent or Buy – the Big Debate

If you do decide to get a shop, you'll need to consider whether it's better to rent or to buy. Some people view renting as dead money whilst others see buying a property as limiting. Buying is expensive and it also means that you can't expand or move as easily as renting. However, if you find the perfect shop to rent, you could lose it if the owner decides to sell (if the contract makes provision for this or it has come to a break-clause in the contract) or ups the rent to an unfeasible level. Most contracts allow for regular, upwards only rent reviews (often every three years) which could see your affordable, successful shop suddenly become too expensive to be practical.

> **Keyword**
> Break-clause: a contractual obligation which allows you or your landlord to terminate your shop lease. This is normally set after the first, third, fifth or tenth year of the contract.

If you buy a shop, you have a huge initial expenditure after which you might discover that the shop is too small for your long-term needs or that the location is not what you had hoped.

Rent	Buy
Easier to move on	You own the property, the landlord can't throw you out or up the rent to an unviable level
You can see if the location is right for you	You have the security of owning your own property
You can move to larger premises with minimum problems	You can build up your business securely knowing that it's yours
You don't have to pay a large sum upfront	You don't pay dead-money on rent. Once the building has paid for itself, there's no more to pay
Your landlord will repair faulty wiring etc (if the lease is not a full repairing and insuring one)	You can make what improvements you want without having to get permission (unless planning permission is needed)

There are dozens of arguments about whether you should rent or buy, two of the biggest are:

◆ If you rent initially to get a feel for the business, you might not be able to buy in that area when you decide that it's time to buy or your lease comes up for renewal or is terminated. Someone else could move in and steal your hard-won regulars.

◆ You will need a lot of money to buy a suitable property (depending on the area) but it could save you time, money and heartache in the long-run – if it works out.

Location, Location, Location

One of the most important requirements for a successful business, especially a shop, is the right location. You might dream of a lovely shop in the country, nestling on the edge of a country road. Think again – how many people will know that you're there? Can you survive on local trade only? Are windy country roads easy for unloading and parking if there isn't a car park with the premises? It is an ideal but not necessarily a practical option.

Shop around before you commit. Buy *The Antiques Trade Gazette* (ring 020 7420 6601 or buy it at larger fairs) or read their classifieds on their website www.atg-online.com and see if they have antiques shops (or centres) for sale in their classifieds section. Speak to commercial estate agents (see the local phone directory – larger libraries house most, if not all, the country's phone directories) and explain your requirements or look at the classifieds section in local newspapers where you are thinking of setting up shop. You might want to drive around and get a feel of an area – you might even spot a 'for sale' or 'to let' sign on your travels.

The best locations tend to be used by other dealers and this is a good sign. The more dealers, the more attractive the area to buyers. Towns like Holt in Norfolk, Olney in Bucks and Weedon in Northants are renowned for their antiques shops and centres and people are more likely to travel a long distance for that sort of area than one which might have only one or two antiques shops.

The more antiques shops, the better the area for a new business.

There is a danger of too many shops but realistic prices and good stock will lead to a successful business, even in the most over-populated antiques town or village.

Useful tip

Look for shops with large, ground floor windows and use these as a showpiece to attract buyers and sell stock. Replace window displays regularly in the summer months – not only will you attract more buyers this way but you'll prevent your stock from fading in the bright summer sun.

Picturesque villages, such as those in the Cotswolds, attract visitors from all over the world and people on holiday spend money – as do the trade who frequent such areas – but you should be aware that property costs (for renting, as well as buying) reflect the area's popularity. The best areas cost more but they can be worth it.

Should I Live On-Site?

You might like to save money by living on-site. This has several advantages:

- You save time and money by not having to commute.
- No more traffic jams.
- No worries about finding a parking space.
- Potential burglars can be put off if they know that the upstairs of a business is inhabited.
- You save a fortune on food because you can just nip upstairs for lunch instead of buying expensive sandwiches or lunches.
- Your family can join you in the shop without feeling neglected if you're working (also a disadvantage if you want to get away from them or it interferes with serving).
- You can see your garden from your desk (if you have a garden).

But there are also disadvantages which are almost too tempting to be prevented:

- Your home could easily become an extra store-room.
- You could end up working later and later because you know that you don't have to travel home.
- You end up working all hours, especially in tourist areas in the summer, because it's so easy to open early and shut late – you're already on-site.
- You spend all your time in the shop or thinking about it because you can't get away.

If you decide to live above your shop, you will obviously be looking at more expensive or different properties from a straightforward shop. Long-term, you might want to move out and use this space as an extra sales or storage space for your shop. Effectively, this could double its size and give you a chance to expand without moving premises.

Budgeting – Matching Dreams to Reality

Once you have decided what type of shop you want, and whether to rent or to buy, you must sit down and prepare a budget. This will enable you to know how much money you have to spend. A proper budget or business plan might sound intimidating but you need to know what you can afford before you commit yourself to anything. As with all budgets, it is the little things which are often the most important and can cause problems later. You might have decided that you want a shop but do you really know what that entails financially?

◆ **Rent, the purchase price or a mortgage** – This will be the biggest expenditure. Set yourself a realistic limit (go lower, rather than higher) once you know about property and rental prices in your chosen area. Remember, you can always expand if necessary but don't start too small, you'll quickly outgrow too small a property and it could cost you more than you can afford to move out.

◆ **Deposit** – About 5–10% when you're buying or at least three months' rent if you're renting (but not required by all landlords).

◆ **Survey** – For buyers or renters with full insuring or repairing leases. About £400 + .

◆ **Lawyer's fees** – Whether you rent or buy, you will need to employ a lawyer. £400 + .

◆ **Building's insurance** – Payable by all property owners and most rentees.

◆ **Contents' insurance** – Generally available from the same company as the building's insurer but not if you are renting – you will normally be expected to use your landlord's insurance company and might not see the insurance forms. There are specialist antiques insurers (see Section Six, Chapter 3 for details) but shop around for the best deal and get full cover – you might regret it if you don't.

◆ **Security systems** – Most insurers will not supply you with contents' insurance unless you install security devices such as alarms and sometimes shutters or even CCTV. Expect to pay £1,500 + for alarms connected to the police station – this is often a minimum requirement from insurers who will check your security before granting cover. An annual maintenance fee of around £400 is payable for this service and should be calculated into your budget.

◆ **Business rates** – These vary from council to council but can be unexpectedly high.

◆ **Rubbish** – You will be expected to pay for special, commercial bin bags (often green) which the council supplies to collect rubbish from business premises. These can cost around £1 + per bag. You might try to take your rubbish home with you (assuming that you don't live above your shop) but the council could find out and pay you a visit in your shop (even when you have customers) which is both messy and embarrassing – they have been known to empty rubbish onto shop floors. You could be charged if you are caught disposing of business rubbish at home – they can check your bin bags and look for boxes or letters with your business address. It happened to me when I first opened my shop – no one had thought to tell me about commercial rubbish collection and I didn't know to ask. Speak to the council for details before you open your shop.

- **Utilities** – Electricity, gas and water. Make sure that you don't share meters with any other premises and have separate meters installed if you do – it could save you a fortune.

- **Heating and air conditioning** – They can be vital but are costly to install and run. Buy a fan initially for those hot summer days.

- **A till** – Safer than a cash box.

- **A safe** – Keep your money safe at the end of the day or during busy days (be discreet when doing so).

- **Electronic card machines** – Available free from banking services but with a monthly bank charge. They pay for themselves and allow you to take larger sales. Ring around the various banks to negotiate better rates and ask to accept Visa, Mastercard, Switch, Delta, Solo, Electron, Diner's Cards and American Express – the latter two are very popular with overseas buyers and you could lose out on their custom if you don't have the right facilities. Hand-held swipe machines have a minimum but no monthly charge, but can take a long time to process by phone and are not practical during busy times.

- **Telephone, fax and answering machine** – All vital for the modern business but don't forget to budget for phone bills as well.

- **A computer** – Keep a record of stock, produce professional invoices and advertise your shop and stock on the Internet to attract buyers from around the world. They are expensive but can put you ahead of the competition. E-mails save time and increase sales.

◆ **Website designer** – Think about having a website for your business and make it as easy to use as possible. Update it weekly if possible. Either do this yourself if you have the know-how or pay someone to do it for you. It will pay for itself in time. You might not want to do this immediately but it is worth considering – how else will people know who and where you are?

◆ **Shop signs** – Have your shop name tastefully emblazoned on the front and side of your shop to attract passing trade. Add your business phone number and e-mail address (if applicable) so that you can be contacted easily.

◆ **Shop window signs** – Professional open and closed signs are vital for any smart business. Buy one which uses a clock and avoid any 'back in five minutes signs' – they never say what time you left and are not professional. Add a special sign with your opening hours in the window so people know when they can buy stock. This will also let people know which days you're open. Buy more than one of these signs so that you can have a different one for your longer summer hours (if applicable).

◆ **Wages** – Long-term, are you thinking of having extra staff for the busy weekends or one day a week to allow you to go buying, or will you risk losing custom by shutting the shop at least once a week for your buying trips? Don't forget tax on top of wages.

◆ **Accountant** – You'll need one.

◆ **Tax** – Keep a portion of your profit in a special account for your tax bill or you could get caught short. Late payments incur fines.

◆ **Bank charges** – You'll need a business account for your shop. Every transaction will incur bank charges so shops around for the best deal.

◆ **Advertising** – You'll need it to let people know that you're there when you first open and for any special promotions and seasonal attractions, eg Christmas and National Antiques Day (not taken seriously within the trade but used by businesses to increase custom through special events such as lectures, valuations or wine tastings). It might be worth putting aside a nominal amount (up to £100) for an opening party and invite all your best customers from fairs and dealers from the other shops or centres – get to know your future buyers.

◆ **Stock** – It could become your highest expenditure but it will pay for itself. You will need a large amount of stock to start your business properly. A half-empty shop will not attract buyers and will not succeed. Buy good quality stock and avoid cheap-end stock, bordering on junk, to fill it out. That said, get some cheap but good quality stock in to appeal to all buyers, not just those with money – those smaller sales soon add up, as well as filling out otherwise empty shelves.

◆ **Miscellaneous** – Coffee maker or just a kettle, mugs, bins, stationery, toilet rolls, tea bags etc.

These are just the expected charges. You're guaranteed to face unexpected bills so allow for an X-factor when budgeting.

Bank Loan

You might want to start your shop with your own savings or an inheritance but, if you don't have the money yourself, look into taking out a small business loan. The major banks all have special packs which will tell you what you need to consider and use to prove that you're a sound investment – this is as much for you as them so do it properly. You'll need to draw up a business plan showing that you know what you're doing, that you've done some marketing and know what your future (and existing) customers will want.

Dress to impress when you have your meeting with the bank once they've had time to study your application. Don't go overboard but dress confidently so that you *feel* that you deserve more than you're asking. A good bank manager will discuss your options with you and might even offer you more than you've requested because they know more about business than you do. Take what's on offer but don't overstretch yourself. You might be asked for security such as a house – think of it like a mortgage. If you are intending to live above your shop, whether you're renting or buying, you will probably be expected to pay back your loan on the sale of your house. Don't risk your home if you're not 100% sure that you want to be an antiques dealer with a shop. It doesn't work for everybody but some dreams are worth the risk. *Stick to banks and not various loan schemes or you could lose everything.*

Is There Anything Else I Should Think About When Looking for a Shop?

There is no such thing as one perfect shop. Everybody has different needs. If you want to sell furniture, you'll need a larger property than you would for toy soldiers or dolls' house furniture.

There are some basic requirements, some of which have been mentioned before:

- **Good location** – Passing traffic or, if in a pedestrian area, sufficient passing buyers to make it noticeable (quiet, five-shop squares don't always get enough potential buyers to be worthwhile). If in doubt, do some market research of your own. Take a clipboard and count the number of passers-by in an hour and stop some of them to ask if they'd buy antiques – it could save you a fortune.

- **Large shop window** – Keep it lit at night and it will sell stock for you when you're shut.

- **Preferably parking but at least safe unloading** – Stock can be bulky and heavy. If you and your customers can't park close-by, leave it.

- **Easy access for all customers** – Don't be tempted by shops which have no ground floor but can only be approached via stairs – that could deter customers from even entering, let alone buying heavy items if you can even get them up there.

- **Other antiques shops or centres** – An established market will help your business to succeed.

- **Character** – Nice but not essential.

- **An established business** – Not essential but it might be worth paying a bit extra to take on good-will and existing customers, but ask around first or you could be lumbered with someone else's bad reputation.

- **Good location over cheap rent** – It's worth paying more to get people through the door.

I'm Going to Rent, Should I be Concerned About Anything in the Lease?

Unless you're a lawyer yourself, you shouldn't handle lease negotiations without one. That said, don't rely on them completely – you might spot something which they haven't – or which they expect you to know about already.

One of the most annoying aspects of renting a property is that you're expected to pay for the landlord's lawyers as well as your own and they're not cheap. You will still be expected to pay for them – and your own lawyer – even if negotiations fall through and you don't take the property. Some landlords will try to take advantage of your desire for a shop by suddenly demanding an excessive deposit when negotiations are almost complete, assuming that you'll be too enthusiastic to back out by then. *Wrong.* This is not the sort of behaviour seen in a good landlord so pull out immediately – even if you do lose a few hundred pounds. Long-term, you could end up losing a lot more, including the entire deposit.

You might be expected to pay a deposit up front and this should be taken into account when budgeting – it's dead money which you might either get back at the end of your lease or have to relinquish to get out of your lease early – all leases are different. Expect to pay at least three months' rent as a deposit.

Many landlords will use 'full repairing and insuring' leases. In layman's terms, you are expected to pay for the building's insurance (generally a few hundred pounds) *and* for all necessary repairs, including any pre-existing problems. If this is the case, pay for a survey. It will cost you a few hundred pounds but could save you a fortune. Use the survey to negotiate a rent-free period if repairs need carrying out prior to moving in (i.e. existing problems are discovered). If the landlord refuses or the work needed far exceeds the rent-free period or allowances, pull out immediately to save further expense.

Case Study
I once wanted a shop which needed immediate repairs costing £25,000. The landlord agreed to a rent-free period of £10,000 for me to pay for this work – potentially leaving me £15,000 out of pocket before I'd even started trading. I pulled out immediately and opened a shop elsewhere. One where the landlord paid for his own repairs.

If there isn't already one, ask your lawyer to insert break clauses. Ideally, you need one after the first year. This will let you get out with minimum pain and expense if it's obvious that it's not working out for you or if it's been so successful that you need to expand quickly. After that, they will generally be set at three or five yearly intervals. That's the easy part. With every break clause comes the nasty part – the 'upwards only' rent review. In other words, you're giving your landlord the right to raise your rent. This, unfortunately, is normal. Even if business in the area plummets, your rent will not be reduced accordingly. Be realistic when rent raises happen. No matter how much you might love your business, it has to pay for itself. If the increase is too high to be viable or will make trading difficult, hand in your notice – there are always other properties.

A shop can be a wonderful asset but it can also be a drain and a tie. Think carefully before committing yourself. Shop life without staff can be very lonely but it can also be fantastically rewarding. If you need a lot of people around you or get bored easily but can't afford staff initially, it might be worth looking at shared premises or getting a larger unit in a centre where those extra bills are not your problem.

But you might want the independence and the freedom of working for yourself with your own hours in your own premises. It's up to you.

Easy Ways to Extra Profits

Whatever you decide, there are various ways in which you can increase your own profit potential at minimal cost:

◆ Change the window display on a regular basis – fortnightly is good. Weekly can be too frequent as would-be buyers could assume that their desired item has been sold and monthly can make stock look tired to regular passers-by.

◆ Window displays should be attractive. That might seem obvious but too many antiques shops use their windows to demonstrate the variety of their stock without making it appealing. Arrange goods to look like a cosy drawing room or colour-co-ordinate your arrangement. Seasonal displays are always good sellers but avoid anything tacky – it will detract from your stock and could deter custom.

◆ Sell quality goods on commission. Charge 5–10% for space in your shop and have the sellers sign a contract to avoid problems. Commission sales are a great way of filling out your stock at no cost. Accept the goods for a set period only – you don't want to be stuck with someone else's difficult-to-sell stock.

◆ Hold special events. It will cost you a few bottles of wine and orange juice but brings people into the shop who will then buy. Give talks on your specialist areas or even arrange special days for authors to sell their antiques books in your shop. Authors love book signings as it sells their books and they are often prepared to travel, especially if they get a book launch that way – they might even mention your shop in their next book. Spend some money advertising to attract new buyers into your shop.

One of the most important things you will ever have to do for your shop is to give it a name. Quality shops tend to name themselves after the owners or use their initials eg F.A. Shoop or Shoop's. Other shops use witty names to attract customers – 'All That Glistens Is Not Gold' or 'Aladdin's Cave' but avoid anything too cheap such as 'The Junk Shop' as this could lose you customers who could take you literally.

CHAPTER SEVEN

Auctions

Let me start by dispelling a myth which has been propagated by a certain TV series – auctions are not always the best place to sell your goods. But they can be.

When Should I Use an Auction?

- If you want to clear some of your belongings but don't want to go to the time or expense of doing an antiques fair. Maybe you don't have enough goods to make a fair worthwhile or there are no decent fairs by you and you don't want to – or can't – travel.

- You're moving house or a family member has just died and you want to dispose of a lot of goods in one go.

- You want to get rid of a load of tired stock.

- You have some quality goods which will realise a higher price if sold in auction.

- You want to sell your collection, preferably for the highest possible price in one go or a series of high profile auctions.

- You find it easier to sell at auctions than fairs.

- You will realise higher prices at specialist auctions than through conventional fairs.

- You have something rare and either don't know quite how much it's worth or want it to reach its highest possible price.

◆ Your goods will reach a higher price if sold in a different area – i.e. one where it has a wider range of buyers or more interested parties – bizarrely like taking coals to Newcastle when they won't sell elsewhere. Almost the opposite of what you might expect.

◆ You like selling at auction.

A quick glance at this list will show two conflicting ideas – auctions are a place to get *rid* of stock or belongings but are also a good place to raise optimum prices. The contrast is, as was explained in Section Two, Chapter 6, the difference between a general and a specialist auction or even just a different location. For instance, Scottish glass will stand a better chance of realising a higher price in a Scottish auction than in England where there might be fewer interested – or knowledgeable – parties.

> The large auction houses (Bonham's [which now incorporates Phillips], Christies and Sotheby's) have offices and auction houses throughout the country and they might advise you to sell your goods in one of their other, more suitable auction rooms. If this happens, ask for them to transfer the goods for you – it's free of charge but they don't all automatically tell you about this time and money saving service. Be sure that you take out insurance if it is not automatically added by them – this will ensure that you get some money back should the goods accidentally be broken *en route*.

Do Auction Houses Charge Fees?

If you want to sell goods at auction you need to be aware of three basic fees:

◆ **Lottage** – this is the fee charged just to enter your goods into auction whether they sell or not.

◆ **Commission** – the percentage charged on each sale. Some auction houses will charge VAT (17.5%) on top of the commission – that's VAT for the commission, not the selling price.

◆ **Insurance** – around 1% but not charged by all auction houses.

If you want a photograph of your lot included in the catalogues used at the better auction houses, this will cost extra but will significantly improve sales for higher quality or rare lots. If you look at *The Antiques Trade Gazette*, you'll notice that many of the auction houses use photographs in their adverts – this is a very good way of attracting buyers not only nationwide but overseas as well. If you get the chance, ask for photographs to be included in the catalogue and ask if they will appear in their advertising as well.

Commission Charges

These can be the most costly of the fees, depending on the auction house. It doesn't matter what you're selling, whether you're just clearing space or selling a significant item or collection of goods, always shop around before selling your goods through auction. If you are selling a collection or several thousand pounds' worth of goods, negotiate a better commission rate. Most auction houses have lower commission rates for higher priced goods or for a collection of goods amounting to certain levels (the higher the price, the lower the commission – most auction houses set 'bands' to determine the level) but it's still worth trying to pay less, especially if you will be using the auction house for similar high-profile or costly lots in the future.

> **Useful tip**
> For higher priced or costly collections, try to negotiate a better rate of commission – one seller reduced their commission rate by 5%, saving them thousands of pounds.

You don't necessarily get what you paid for – an auction house charging 8% commission could end up realising a higher price than one charging 20%. More expensive is not always better. It's worth asking other dealers what auction house they use but don't ask them what they're charged – you might get a lower rate than them. Regular clients bringing in thousands of pounds worth of business will get better deals than a one-off seller with something worth a few hundred pounds or even less.

It doesn't matter how much money you're bringing in, make sure that you're happy with the service offered. If not, look elsewhere.

Lottage

You will be charged a fee for entering your goods in auction which is payable even if the goods are not sold. This can be a costly expense. Some auction houses will charge a nominal £1 per lot. Others will charge from £20 to a hefty £60. However, these are sometimes offset against commission costs. At some auctions, you will be charged £20 + whether the goods sell or not but, if they do sell, this £20 is taken as the first percentage of the total lot (10% of the first £200 if the auction house charges 10%). Costs do vary between auction houses so ask them to explain their costs before committing yourself. The higher lottages are fine if you are selling expensive goods but only if you can afford to pay up to £60 for goods which do not sell.

Reserve Prices

If you are entering goods into an auction to make space or because you just don't want them, don't bother to set a reserve price or you might not sell them. However, this could mean that your goods sell for as little as £2 but at least they'll sell. If you are selling better goods, it's always worth setting a reserve price. If you have something which is worth £150–200, set a reserve of around £100. This will ensure that the goods are not sold for less. You might think that if the estimate is £150–200, you should set a reserve of £150 but this is not advisable. Not all auction houses will allow you to set a reserve so close to their estimate because it might not sell and unsold lots are not good for their reputation. By setting a realistic reserve, you guarantee that the goods will not be sold for less but neither are you harming your chances of a sale by setting too high a reserve.

If you're not sure, ask the auctioneer for advice and remember that you can always sell the goods in their next sale or elsewhere if they don't sell them first time round.

If setting a reserve price, inform the auction house that this is a set figure, not a 'discretionary' one – they could sell it for 10% (or more) less than your reserve price otherwise.

Paying Out

All auction houses will work differently, with regional auctions of the same large chains sometimes having different, often faster, paying out times compared to their London houses not to mention lower commission or lottage charges. You should be paid within a month of the sale. Some auction houses will have the auction on the Monday and pay out (sometimes in cash) on the Wednesday but that is not the norm. Expect to wait at least 21 days to be sent a cheque for your goods, less expenses.

All of this should be explained by the auction house, if not in person, then in their details which are listed in the front or back of their catalogues. You should also be given a separate document listing all of their charges (including the commission rate) and terms and conditions when you enter your lots into auction – ask for it if you are not given it automatically. Don't take it for granted that your reserve prices are the ones which you set – check before signing and returning the form (if applicable). Mistakes do happen, especially if you have submitted several lots.

Your payment will be less the charges, including the lottage for all lots, including any unsold ones. Keep the invoice which you receive, as you will need it for your accounts.

How Soon Can I Sell My Goods Through Auction?

It depends on the auction house. The bigger auctions will have cut-off dates whereas the small, weekly or fortnightly auctions will accept goods on the day of sale or before the first viewings. Never enter goods which are too late to be listed in the catalogue, as they will not realise their best price. Some buyers only work from the catalogue and will not even notice uncatalogued goods.

If there is a specialist auction due, ask them to keep your goods for that sale – you'll get better prices, even if you do have to wait for weeks or even months. It can be worth it if you do not need the money sooner.

Valuations

Before you enter any goods into auction, make sure that the auction 'expert' knows what they are talking about. The larger houses will have different departments (eg Decorative

Arts, Paintings or Jewellery). Recent cuts in auction houses and staff levels have meant that many of the departments have been amalgamated, sometimes at the cost of their expertise. If your goods are run-of-the-mill, this will not be a problem but you might want to shop around to find the right expert. Why? Someone without the relevant knowledge could catalogue your goods incorrectly which could cost you money and buyers.

If you have more knowledge than the 'expert', don't be afraid to say so politely. Even the best auctioneer will admit that they don't know everything and they will be happy for your help. Auction houses and departments are tested on their profitability – higher sales lead to bonuses and promotions or, these days, a continuation of their jobs. If you can help make more money for a department or auction house through your knowledge, they'll be delighted. Don't be arrogant but don't be afraid to share your expertise – they're your goods.

Should I Attend the Sale?

It's up to you. Some people don't have time to go to auctions whilst others don't want to watch complete strangers handling their belongings or see their collections split up and sold to different buyers. Others want to see how the auctioneer handles the sale of their goods. If an auctioneer is derisive about the possible attraction of your goods or describes them incorrectly, you have the right to withdraw your goods or correct them. You also have the right to choose a different auction house to sell your goods in the future. You might want to attend to assess the interest in your stock. This is especially useful if you have similar goods which you were thinking of selling through the same auction house. You'll be able to judge whether it's worth selling through them again.

A good auctioneer is a good friend – they want to sell your goods for the highest possible price and so do you. Once you find one that you like, stick with them – they'll do their best to help you and you could even be given a lower commission rate if you are a regular customer.

There are too many auction houses for me to list them. What I would suggest is that you buy *The Antiques Info* magazine from your newsagent (ask them to order it if necessary, ring them for subscription details, 01843 862069, or check their website on *www.antiques-info.co.uk*). This two-monthly guide lists most auctions and is an essential guide to knowing what's on and where. *The Antiques Trade Gazette* (020 7420 6601) carries auction listings on a weekly basis with many of the adverts containing useful photographs showing must-buy stock. It's the main source of news within the auction and antiques trade. If you intend to use auctions regularly, you should subscribe and keep up to date with the latest developments within the antiques and auction worlds. Your local phone directory and newspaper will also contain details of local auction houses.

Star Auctioneer

Mark Oliver, Director of Design at Bonham's New Bond St, London (formerly known as Phillips). Tel: 020 7629 6602.

Four of the best auction houses are:

- Bonham's – 020 7393 3900 or 020 7629 6602 (formerly Phillips)
- Christies 020 7581 7611
- Sotheby's 020 7293 5000
  Ring the above to find your nearest regional office or auction house
- Dreweatt Neate, Newbury, Berks. Tel: 01635 553553. One of the best regional auction houses both for buying and selling.

CHAPTER EIGHT

Transport

Most dealers find it essential to have their own car or van. It *is* possible to be a dealer without one but it is very limiting, especially for visiting the larger, out of town fairs in an age of train strikes and bad service.

If you are intending to sell furniture, you will need a van. The larger the furniture, the bigger the van. Long-term, you might want to consider a van or lorry with a motorised lift for those larger, heavier pieces. Some dealers of smalls use vans to carry large quantities of stock and also for somewhere to sleep at the multi-day fairs. Not all dealers sleep in their vehicles but hundreds do and they get used to it.

Useful tip
If you are going to sleep in your vehicle, lock the doors for your safety and wrap up warmly. The long nights, even in the summer, can get very cold. Don't forget to take a change of clothes with you – you'll need them. Many of the larger fairs are held on showgrounds or airfields which offer shower facilities but check their opening times when you arrive – some are open for one hour only. Go prepared.

Some dealers sleep out at fairs but in a more comfortable fashion – they use caravans or motorvans (caravans with an engine). If you are thinking of doing fairs long-term and want to do the multi-day fairs, these are a good investment. You'll have a good night's sleep without the expense of staying in a hotel (if you can even book one close to the venue) and don't have to get up as early the next day. Dog-lovers leave their dogs in comfort while they stall out. If you have an outside pitch, you should be able to park your vehicle on your pitch which cuts down on unloading and early mornings.

The size of your car depends on your stock but, if you have a larger car, you can carry more stock. Jewellery dealers can get extra small cars such as the Smart car but, long-term, smalls dealers need to look into buying estate cars. This is not essential but it can pay for itself in just over a year with the amount of extra stock carried.

Whatever car you have, remove the section covering the boot – it forms a ledge in a hatchback and covers the back of an estate car in roll form. Next, lower the back seats to create a flat area. This will significantly increase storage room and you might find that a hatchback offers sufficient loading space for you at the moment.

> **Useful tip**
> Check that the back seats of a car fold down (ask for help at a car showroom) before buying. For example, in some models, the inside 'tilts' where the seats are lowered which can make it difficult-to-impossible to load properly. You need a car which is completely flat inside when the seats are lowered. I can personally recommend the Volvo estate or the Vauxhall Astra Estate.

Check out wheel arches before buying a car. Some arches take up the equivalent of one box which can drastically reduce how many boxes and, therefore, how much potential profit, you can fit into your car. Professional dealers will know exactly how to load their car to its maximum – but safe – capacity. Properly loaded, the Vauxhall Astra Estate can take up to 18 boxes and six sets of shelves. This is assuming that three of the boxes are apple or smaller banana boxes. It might sound very sad but it's essential to know just how much stock you can fit in your car. The more stock it carries, the greater your potential takings.

Measure a car properly and work out how many boxes you can fit in before buying it. Shop around and ask about petrol consumption. As a dealer, you will be driving far more than you did before and you need to take this extra expense into account when considering getting a new (or second-hand) car.

It is not essential to get a different car when you become a dealer but it can be worthwhile and you should consider buying for your business when it's time to change cars.

You might be tempted to promote your business on your car or van and it can bring in business, but it will also attract negative attention and you don't want your vehicle to be broken into when it is loaded with stock – and all because you told someone that it was worth stealing. It's up to you. Some businesses find car signing a huge asset, especially if they also offer house clearance but, at the moment, your business car is also your personal car so forget signs for now. More importantly put comfort alongside need and invest in a decent stereo for those long, lonely journeys. Jump leads are also a good investment – you never know when you will need them.

Useful tip

Join a recovery service such as the AA or RAC. You might need them, especially if you're miles away from home. Also visit DIY shops or Halfords and invest in some 'grip tracks' – they're useful for getting out of those muddy fields which are used for parking or stalling out at larger fairs.

Get your car serviced on a regular basis – you can't sell antiques without it.

CHAPTER NINE

Safe Cleaning

This probably seems like a pointless chapter to you. You might think that it makes sense to clean your stock so why do you need to read on? Because you can ruin your stock by cleaning it incorrectly – that's the mistake made by most first-timers and novice dealers.

Cleaning China

Dirty china is not attractive. It can also hide cracks, chips and crazing so make sure that you clean it before trying to sell it – you could lose sales otherwise. Obviously, don't put any stock in the dishwasher – it's amazing how many people do but did you know that you shouldn't soak china either? Why not? Because it can craze it – that's those annoying cracks in the glaze which can stop people from buying your stock. Don't use hot water but luke-warm water. Make up a solution of warm water with a small amount of washing up liquid – not too much and never undiluted. Dip a soft cloth in this solution and squeeze off any excess, then gently use it to clean off the china, using a corner to dip into any awkward folds, eg the neck of figures or between their arms and their bodies – do this carefully or you could snap something off. It happens.

Dry the china immediately using another soft cloth. Do the same for glass but don't clean resin or biscuit (rough, unglazed pottery) pieces – they can be porous and easily stained by liquid. Use a soft, dry cloth to gently clean off any excess dirt on these materials.

If you have a teapot or cup which has tea or coffee stains, soak their insides with denture-cleaning products. Depending on the stain, it can take hours or even overnight to remove the ugly stains.

Other stains can be cleaned with bleach. Handle this very carefully avoiding splashes and use rubber gloves to keep your hands safe. Some dealers use bleach to disguise cracks or heavy crazing. Soak the items in the diluted bleach – test one first. This should only be done for a few minutes in luke-warm or cold water. Hot water will cause crazing. Never soak anything which has its original paper label (eg maker's name or the name of the item) as this comes off when wet which can detract from its value.

Pewter

Tear off a cabbage leaf and then tear it in half. Use the ripped stalk to clean pewter and save on special cleaning products – one cabbage cleans all.

Silver, Silver Plate and Other Metals

There are plenty of silver-cleaning products which are available at fairs and from antiques shops and centres but some are harsh and can ruin your silver or silver-plated stock. These can be costly and some dealers use cabbages (as above) or even a soft cloth which can remove some of the tarnish if wiped gently and patiently.

Traditional methods involve bicarbonate of soda which can either be used sparingly on a soft, damp cloth, wiped on the silver, rinsed and then dried or you can form a paste of bicarbonate of soda and water to rub into the silver before rinsing and drying it – with a soft, dry cloth.

The brighter the silver, the more attractive it looks. Dull, tarnished silver can look unappealing which will affect both its price and sellability. As with all metals, including gold, copper, bronze and brass, bright, shiny goods are easier to sell than dull and dirty versions. If you are going to sell a lot of these goods – copper, bronze and brass are especially popular in the countryside – then invest in some special cleaning products and add their cost to the price of your goods. Or just use sauce – brown sauce or tomato ketchup to clean copper – cheap but effective. Rinse off and dry immediately.

Pearls and Other Jewellery

Pearls should never be washed as this can destroy their surface but, if your pearls have lost their colour or lustre, try wearing them. They'll absorb your body's natural secretions to regain their lustre. If it is too late for this or they are costume jewellery, ask a jewellery or costume jewellery specialist if they can recommend someone to repearlise your jewellery – it can be costly but it's often worth it. They might also offer a restringing service.

It is advisable to get all other jewellery cleaned by a professional (speak to other dealers for recommendations) to avoid problems. Jewellery should never be cleaned with water which can damage it.

Whatever you're cleaning, do it gently and carefully or you could damage it. If in doubt, leave it alone or pay a professional. There will be certain fairs where, no matter how much you clean your stock, it will be filthy at the end of it – the Abergavenny Hall with its sandy floor at Ardingly, West Sussex (DMG 01636 702326) is a prime example but dealers expect to see dusty stock there and stallholders always clean their stock afterwards. It's part of the fair. Outside stallholders are used to buying and selling dirty stock but try to present yours in the most profitable way possible – clean stock sells faster.

PART FOUR
The Internet

CHAPTER ONE

Should I or Shouldn't I?

The most important thing for dealers to know about buying and selling over the Internet is that it's not essential. If you don't want to do it, you don't have to. All I would ask is that you read on just a little bit further because, whilst you don't have to do it, it could help your business. It could even mean an end to those early starts. *But you don't have to do it.*

To many people, turning on the computer is as natural as switching on the kettle and connecting to the Internet even easier than setting an alarm clock. It's certainly true of me – I automatically switch on the computer on the way to the kettle and check my messages before the kettle's even boiled, but it is not that way for everyone. The thing is, it can be. Computers, if you're not used to them, can seem terrifying and many people believe that they've lived for X amount of years without needing one so why should they start now. I appreciate how they – possibly you – feel but I can't help thinking that they're missing out on so much, not just in terms of buying and selling antiques but so many other things – I saved 66% by booking my holiday on-line, I save up to 50% by buying books – even antiques ones – on-line without having to get dressed properly, drive to my local shops, struggle to find parking and walk anywhere when I've got better things to do – but I didn't always find it this easy.

I taught myself to use the computer but that wasn't necessary. There are many courses, some of them free and aimed at people, just like you, who want to see a little more of the world and not let their front door be their horizon. I'm proud to say that my mum is one of them – dad, on the other hand, steadfastly refuses to learn anything about computers and continues to sell at fairs instead. It's up to him, just as it is up to you but please don't shut your mind to it forever. You don't even need a computer to buy on-line or even see what's on offer. Most libraries provide free Internet access and Internet cafés are springing up all over the place and give you access not just to new people but new stock – often at surprisingly cheap prices.

What's Bad about Buying and Selling Over the Internet?

I'm going to start by answering some of the most common questions I get asked by non or new users.

How do I know that I'll get what I've paid for?

Yes, it does happen. Some people do send their money and not receive anything in return but, of the thousands of people I've spoken to who buy and sell on-line, it has *not* happened to them. The Internet auctions, the most common places for buying and selling antiques, have a 'feedback' system which allows people to make complaints. Anyone who has actually taken the money and not sent out the goods would either be blacklisted (and prevented from setting up again by some simple means, including the necessity of using their credit card details to register) or have warning, negative statements. I've written many articles about dealing on the Internet, as well as doing it myself for several years and I honestly have not known it happen to anyone, but it has happened.

How secure is it to hand over my credit card details on-line?

That depends, I would never recommend that you send your credit card details by e-mail as that's not secure. However, it is safe to give it on secure sites – that's places like insurance company sites and retailers such as *www.amazon.co.uk* – the most famous on-line bookshop.

Keyword

Secure – this means that special barriers are in place to ensure that your personal details, such as credit card numbers, cannot be read by outside sources, i.e. it's like paying your money into a bank, not shouting out your credit card number on the street where anyone can listen in. Secure sites warn you that you're about to enter (or leave them) with a clear message on the screen. You'll also see a padlock in the corner of your screen. You can only enter these sites when you're on-line – that's when you're connected to the Internet.

If you're buying something from an on-line auction or insecure site by credit card, it's safer just to ring them up and pay over the phone. Sometimes, the old ways are the best. Most of the dealers who take credit cards give fax numbers and some recommend that you fax your credit card details through, but I wouldn't – you never know where the machine is kept and who's standing by it at the time. Some buyers have a special credit card which they only use for on-line transactions but, whatever you do, just keep an eye on your statements. I can honestly say that I'm not worried about on-line security. Any break-in and breach of security hits the news but so do any bank robberies. If you're overly worried about it, don't use a credit card, but you might not be able to register for all of the on-line auctions if you don't. Just be careful and do what's best for you.

Isn't buying and selling over the Internet really impersonal?

This is one of the most common fears expressed by many people, including long-term dealers. It depends on you and the buyer/seller but I've found it surprisingly friendly. People tell me about their dogs, their daughter's wedding, their collections – anything, really and it's lovely as I have time to talk by e-mail whereas I often find myself too busy at fairs to catch up with anyone, even regular buyers. Other people have found it a difficult experience but they are not people for whom communication is easy. I find, whether you're buying or selling, a friendly thank you does the trick. It's actually a really enjoyable and surprisingly easy experience.

What happens if what I've bought is not as described?

That's the nasty one. There are either unscrupulous or ignorant dealers out there who misdescribe their goods. This is a common fear amongst Internet virgins or novices but all you have to do is write a polite e-mail to the seller, explaining your problems with the piece in as much detail as possible (eg it has a 2.5cm or 1 inch scratch across the face when it was described as being perfect) and *politely* ask for a refund. Be polite as it could be an honest mistake. There's also another reason for being polite – just as you can leave negative feedback about someone, so they can do the same for you and they will if you're rude to them. This could stop other dealers from doing any business with you – it could even prevent you from being allowed to bid by some dealers. Send the goods back (but ask for a postage refund before you do – why should you be out of pocket?) and that's the end of it. Yes, it can be difficult when buying china (or whatever) when you can't handle the goods beforehand, especially as the photos on the sites are not always very clear, but you *can* return faulty goods. If you're worried, start small, bid for a few cheap lots just to see how you get on and then go higher when you feel more confident.

Aren't computers expensive?

No. Prices have come down hugely and many people have more than one computer in their home because they are so affordable. I'm looking for a new computer at the moment – and I'm going to buy mine over the Internet or from a computer exchange shop where you can buy working computers at a fraction of the price – you can get a working computer with a modem (that's the machine which connects you to the Internet) for £150 – and you can make that back in your first month or even week dealing over the Internet.

I can just about switch on a computer, I think that the Internet is beyond me.
It isn't. You can either go on a course or buy a simple book which will explain exactly how to connect to the Internet and how to use e-mails. They're electronic letters which arrive at the touch of a button and could be from buyers asking what else you have to sell. That's the whole point of the Internet, it's there to make you and your business as much money as possible with minimal effort. It isn't scary, you just have to make that first step.

What's Good About Dealing Over the Internet?

You might have realised by now that I'm slightly biased. I think that the Internet has revolutionised the trade and for the better – but only if you use it. If you don't, you're missing out on some of the best quality stock around because canny dealers have realised that they reach a wider audience and, that way, some of the better pieces are being put straight on the Internet instead of going to fairs. And that's great if you have access to it because you get to see stock which you might have missed otherwise. If you live in the south and something that you really want comes up for sale at a Scottish fair, you won't see it, but if it comes up for sale on the Internet no matter where the seller lives, you have a chance to buy it.

You have access to more stock, even goods from overseas, and you also have access to more buyers, including the antiques-hungry American market.
One of the best aspects of the Internet is the sheer volume of people who use it. In simple terms, you get more bidders and often higher prices but it also works in the opposite way. In America, for instance, they have certain goods which they take for granted but which we want over here (eg Disney goods, novelty cruets or Fiesta Ware – simple but stylish tableware). That means that we buy low and sell high, but if they want our better pieces (especially teapots, Carlton Ware and Art Deco), they pay high and that's how to make a profit from the Internet. For many dealers, the Internet is effectively a huge auction and library unless they have their own website (which we'll be looking at in Chapter 6) and then all they have to do is price their goods, not for their local market but a vast, international one. By using the Internet, you make more money with minimal effort and you get to have

lie-ins which, for many dealers, is one of the best aspects of the Internet revolution.

Will I still have to do fairs?

It's up to you. Some of the best dealers have given up 50-75% of their fairs, saving thousands of pounds in stall rent and petrol, but they still do some fairs. Why? Because they want to sell what they bought over the Internet. They bought low and need to sell high to the right market — that's not back on the Internet but at fairs. They bought from overseas or from different parts of the UK to sell at fairs. For those with websites, fairs are useful advertising tools for their sites — 'if you like what I have here, check out my website'. Fairs are useful to form contacts and buy stock, as well as make money. Their main negative point is the early hours — I get up at 3–5am every Sunday and often during the week. By using the Internet, you can sit in front of your computer before you're even fully awake and make money while the kettle's boiling — literally.

CHAPTER TWO

Let's Start at the Very Beginning

Before you can start dealing or even browsing (that's just looking) on the Internet, you need to sign up with a server. Different offers come out all the time and there are advantages and disadvantages with most of the main Internet providers (actually known as ISP – that's Internet Service Provider). If you're sent an attachment (usually shown by a paperclip), it's important to be able to see what it is before opening it. Attachments are like extra letters which come with the main letter – the e-mail. I get them all the time, generally from dealers showing me extra photos that I've requested of their stock or maybe maps from fair organisers as well as questions for my Antiques Clinic in *Antiques and Collectables* magazine. Attachments are great but they're also the source of the dreaded Internet viruses. It's normally very easy to see a virus before you open it and then you just delete it before you get infected – think of it as being around a person with flu. You avoid them. With AOL as a provider, you don't get to see what you're opening and it's easier to get infected that way but it's up to you. AOL is one of the biggest of the ISPs and offers good value for money and many extras.

I prefer to use other providers, such as ntl or Virgin, especially since I can read old e-mails without needing to connect to the Internet and can see attachments before opening them. You see what they're called and, if they are text – that's written – files, you can see if they're viruses. Viruses don't use space so will be listed as having 0 space or will come with iffy, often sexual sounding, attachments – just delete them unopened to avoid catching them – don't forget to empty your delete box immediately to get rid of them for good. If you are going to be a frequent Internet or e-mail user, you might want to consider paying a monthly fee (around £15pm) and being able to access the server (that means connect) as often as you want for no extra charge – it could save you over £100 a quarter. Faster broadband is around £30pm.

To sign up, you need a CD-Rom (often available from record shops or computer outlets) or use the information on your computer (go to: Start, Programs, Online Services to see what options already exist on your computer). Before you start, decide on your e-mail address. Some people use names which describe themselves or their occupation (eg *fatboy@blahblah.com* or *gdjourno@blahblah.com*). I always feel that the less you reveal about yourself the better and you don't want to look stupid or unprofessional so stick to a simple e-mail address. Many people just use their names but, if you have a common name such as John Smith or Ann Jones, expect to be told to use a number as well or to use another address completely. *JohnSmith6008@blahblah.com* is a more likely option than *johnsmith@blahblah.com* – someone else will have got there first.

Some dealers have a separate address for their business to simplify their working day and separate work and pleasure.

Once you have your address, you will need a sign-in name if you want to deal on Internet auctions. I'm signed up with a few different on-line auctions and I've deliberately used different names – I just prefer it that way and it saves problems if you have an overly friendly would-be buyer (AKA a stalker – not scary but annoying) or will be selling different things on different sites. Don't forget to keep a record of your username (that's the sign-in name) and password for each site.

But I'm going too fast. Once you have an ISP, you're free to browse and it's very easy to do. Click on the Internet icon on your screen, add your password if asked (tick the 'remember my password next time' box to save you from having to type it in again) and click connect. Once you're connected (it only takes a few seconds), go to the relevant site if you know it by typing its name in the address box and you're there.

And if you don't know which site you want? Read on.

CHAPTER THREE

Buying on the Internet

You're ready to buy but you don't know where to start. Don't worry, you'll get the hang of it – even professionals have to think about it sometimes. Your best bet is to use what's called a search engine. It's a complex name for a simple function – it's the phone directory for the Internet. There are lots of them about and you probably know a few of them already but I find that *www.google.com* is the easiest and, in my opinion, the best but you can also try *www.askjeeves.co.uk*, *www.lycos.com* or *www.yahoo.com* – amongst others. If you have the option, ask it to search English-language sites only – unless you're fluent in other languages or English is not your first language.

If we stick to Google for now, you'll see that it has a 'search' box. If I want to buy, for example, a Clarice Cliff vase of no particular pattern, I'll type in 'Clarice Cliff vase' and click on the 'Google search' (enter) button. What will appear next will be a series of sites which I can click on to connect to them. Some will be completely irrelevant but it's quite easy to see this – some will be for Clarice Cliff vases, others will be sites which have a 'Clarice someone or other' and a 'Cliff something' listed. I ignore those and click on what look like relevant sites to see what's on offer.

If I want a special design by Clarice (or whatever), I'll type in 'Clarice Cliff Rhodanthe vase'. That way, I'll find the exact pattern I want. If I want a particular shape of vase, I'll list that either with the pattern I want or without any pattern at all if the shape is more important than the decoration.

I actually give as little information as possible – within reason. Some people would feel the need to add colours, dates or extra, irrelevant things to cut down the number of sites offered. I do the opposite.

I give the essential information and sit back to see what else is offered because it could lead me to something even better.

I might be looking for the rare 'Arabesque' pattern by Charlotte Rhead but it could also lead me to other Charlotte Rhead pieces or even a fantastic Deco site. I might not want to use it then, but I'll add it to my 'favourites' (use your mouse until the cursor touches the 'favourites' sign on the screen, click on the right-hand side mouse button, click on add) or list it in an address book or notebook which I keep by my computer for later use. Always try to think ahead, not just of your current needs – you'll save time that way.

I've used Deco china as an example. It doesn't matter what you buy, just type in what you're trying to find (eg 'rare Wade', 'Bakelite napkin ring', 'Chanel jewellery'). And here we have a problem – spelling. In the UK, we write 'jewellery', in the USA, 'jewelry'. You could either just type 'Chanel' or you could do it twice, using both spellings. There's a similar problem if you're looking for a brooch – it's known as a 'pin' in the US. Once you know, it's easy. The other obvious confusion will be over cruets (salt and pepper pots, often including a mustard pot). In the UK, some people will list them as cruets whilst others will call them 'salt and pepper' or even just 'salt' or 'pepper' if there's only one of them. In the US, they're known as 'shakers'. Don't worry, you'll get used to it.

Ebay

Two of the best known Internet auctions are Ebay and QXL. Ebay is probably the best of the auctions. When buying, I use *www.ebay.com* which is the American version, giving me access to a lot more goods than *www.ebay.co.uk* without needing to press extra 'buttons'. If you look at the listings, you'll notice that some of the sellers will list themselves as 'shipping to the US only'. If I see something that I like, I e-mail the seller and ask if they'll send the goods to England – 19 out of 20 will say yes – it's worth asking.

Register

First, you must register. I'm going to use *www.ebay.co.uk* for this chapter just to make it easier to explain and give you a chance to practise on the world's most popular auction site – it really is the best. Ebay has a similar process to most of the Internet auctions – they know that not everyone is a computer whizz and so they all make it really easy. Before you even connect, go and find your credit card – you'll need it to register. Speak to your bank about getting one if you don't already have one. It's just a security thing, so that they know you're not giving them fake information (well, you could be but at least you've got a fake credit card to match). With credit card in hand, decide on your username. Don't use anything which could give too much personal information or look unprofessional – sexual names are a no-no and I'd also be wary about disclosing your gender. I learnt the hard way not to use my e-mail address – you'll get inundated with 'spam' (that's computer junk mail) if you do. Go for something simple and, like the password which you'll need to invent, *write it down*. For security reasons, never use the same username as password – you could be impersonated that way if you do. Sorry, I don't mean to worry you but there are some stupid people out there who have nothing better to do with their time.

For the purposes of this section, your username is 'startingout' and your password is 'thisisfun'. You don't have to register unless you want to buy or sell anything. You can look without having to register at all and it might be worth doing that for a couple of days just until you get used to it, but try to register as soon as you feel comfortable – it doesn't take long but you'll need to wait for a special password (which they'll send you by e-mail) before your account is activated. If you see something that you want, you could miss out if you're not registered in time so sign up as soon as feel comfortable doing so.

I Want It

You've seen the perfect piece. You have enough money in your bank account so should you go for it? First step is to find it – list what you want in the 'search' bar and tick on 'search in title and description' which will give you a better chance of finding what you're looking for. You could be told that there are no relevant pieces or you could be given a list ranging from one or two pieces to hundreds. Just work your way through them.

You've found what you wanted and the description seems fine. They say that it's perfect and there's a photo. It looks fine but is it? Good dealers will list crazing, others won't. If I'm going to pay good money for something, I'll ask a question beforehand (if there's time before the end of the sale – they'll list how long it is before the sale ends). It's easy to do this, just click on 'ask seller a question' and write your message. If I'm happy with the response, I'll bid and it's really easy:

◆ Have your username and password ready.

◆ Scroll down (that means click on the arrow at the side of the Internet page or move the thick bar downwards) to the bidding section.

◆ Enter your maximum bid – this is binding so be realistic about what you can afford.

◆ You'll have a chance to confirm or withdraw your bid on the next internet page – essential if you've pressed the wrong button. One of the commonest mistakes is to miss out a decimal point so your bid becomes '£1950' instead of '£19.50' (or whichever currency you're using). Correct it if you've made a mistake.

◆ Then confirm your bid by filling in your username (startingout) and password (thisisfun).

◆ I always click the 'remember me' button so I don't have to keep signing in. It just saves time – and my memory.

And that's it – you've bid. Ebay (or whichever site you've used) will e-mail you to confirm your bid. Bidding goes up in stages. Unlike some traditional auctions, your maximum price (e.g. £19.50) is not your starting price unless others have already bid up to that level. Just look at the screen to see your opening bid. They will also e-mail you to let you know that you've been outbid if you have, allowing you to raise your bid. If you really, really want a piece, try to be online, watching the last few minutes of the auction – if you're outbid right at the end, you might still have time to raise your bid – but you won't if you're not there to see it. There are options available to prevent this from happening (see Ebay for more details), but, until you know exactly what you're doing, do it this way. I know what I'm doing and I still prefer to do this myself, someone else can still go over your extra bids unless you're there to manage it – it's also surprisingly exciting this way. For pieces that aren't so vitally important, I let my bid stand and check my e-mails when I wake up (auctions often finish in the middle of the night because of time differences between countries). You'll probably find that the seller will contact you to arrange payment before Ebay notify you that you've been the successful bidder.

How Do I Pay?

Before you even bid, check to see how the seller accepts payment. If they haven't listed it, contact them (by clicking on 'ask seller a question') and ask. You might want to pay by credit card if they take them by ringing them and giving them your card details over the phone – not by e-mail (as mentioned before).

I usually pay by cheque to UK sellers and wait a few days for it to arrive and clear before they post the goods to me. If they live near me or one of the big fairs is coming up, I e-mail them to see if we can arrange a meeting and pay them with cash while collecting my goods at the same time. I always ask them if they have any other stock which I might want to buy. It's a useful contact if handled properly.

If there is a reason why you can't pay quickly, let them know, preferably before you bid. I once went on holiday with some auctions still ongoing but e-mailed all of the sellers beforehand to explain that I was going away but would be back on a certain date. This let them know that I was not backing out of the sale and I got extra praise in my feedback for being such a good communicator. If I'm doing a fair and might not be able to send the money or goods (if I'm selling), I'll let them know – it just takes any unnecessary stress out of what should be a simple transaction.

As soon as your goods arrive, check them carefully and notify the seller that they've arrived safely – they'll really appreciate that and note it in your feedback. Don't forget to write a good feedback for a good transaction – and they'll do the same for you. Feedbacks are a way of letting other buyers and sellers know that you're a good dealer.

If there are problems, write to the seller and explain why you're not happy. Don't do it aggressively but politely. I've only ever had two pieces which were not quite as perfect as described – one was a bit worn. Because it was not an important problem, I didn't notify the seller but I also didn't give them any feedback at all – negative feedbacks are very harming and should only be used in extreme circumstances. As it was, I still doubled my money, selling the goods as slightly worn. Had it been cracked, I would have notified the seller immediately as I did with the second piece and demanded my money back *and* charged them for the return postage. I got my money, so not a problem – but a bit annoying. Two bad buys out of a few hundred is not bad.

Goods are delivered straight to your door (or business if you prefer to use that address) and it couldn't be easier. Buying on the Internet allows you to travel from the comfort of your armchair. Unlike going to fairs, auctions and centres, you can see what's available and you don't have to travel. It really couldn't be easier. You can even do it from an Internet café without having to buy your own computer.

Useful tip

If you are buying from non-EU countries overseas, your goods might be subject to Customs duties – see Section Six, Chapter 2 for details. This potential extra cost should be taken into account when bidding.

CHAPTER FOUR

Selling Over the Internet

Many of the same rules for buying are relevant to selling where the Internet is concerned. If you are thinking of dealing in an on-line auction, you need to register before selling. If you have registered for buying, then you are already registered and don't need to do so again to sell. You just use the same details (username and password) as you do for buying.

First of all, decide what you are going to sell and why. There should only be one proper why – to make money. Selling over the Internet is enjoyable and easy but it's also there for a reason. It's a business so treat it accordingly.

Why Should I Sell Anything Over the Internet?

That's a very good question. You could save money by doing so. First of all, there is no stall rent unlike antiques fairs. If you sell your goods at a traditional auction, as stated previously, you have to take their charges into account (lottage, commission and insurance). If you are selling particularly good stock, you might choose to use one of the more established auction houses, maybe one of the main London ones and this could cost you a fair amount in charges – possibly around £20 for lottage alone. Not to forget insurance and commission. The Internet auctions cost considerably less than this. On top of that, you get your money faster – sometimes within 24 hours of the sale – compare that to the usual three to four weeks of most traditional auction houses.

The Internet auctions are a lot cheaper both in terms of lottage (what they often term 'insertion fees') which can be as little as 10p and commission. *Commission rates vary so check the relevant site for details but, at the time of writing, commission fees are considerably less than even the cheapest traditional auction houses – by around 50%!*

And, because you have the goods in your own home, you're not charged insurance. The buyer pays for postage and package so your overheads are minimal and that's just one of the reasons why Internet auctions have such a huge following.

If you are selling via your own website (see Chapter 6), you only have to pay for creating and upkeeping the site. There will be no charge for individual sales as it's like having your own shop. There are specialist antiques sites which are like working antiques centres but on the Internet. To be honest, I've looked at quite a few and have yet to see any which impress me, but the situation changes all the time and we all have different needs so check around for yourself and see if there are any which appeal. Some of these will do all of the work for you, including taking photographs. They can be ideal for the novice seller so speak to other dealers and ask for recommendations. I have yet to see any which I would either use or recommend but new sites crop up every day. My main problem with these sites is that they are often too slow or tend to try to be 'clever' and that's not what you need. You want to click onto a site, be presented with a list of subjects (eg books, Art Deco, Art Nouveau, comics etc) and then be able to see the items pictured on one page or over several pages instead of having to click on individual, often vague, descriptions. At the time of writing, I know of no site which does this which suggests that one of you might want to create the ideal on-line antiques centre because there's definitely a need for it.

What Should I Sell?

It's up to you but there are certain things which are better sold elsewhere for practical reasons. If you are selling over the Internet, you will be reaching an international audience and, unless you specify otherwise (which could lose you money), you could be sending your stock anywhere in the world. The buyer pays for postage but they could be deterred from buying pieces which are too heavy or big to post or ship – unless it's a very specialist area. You'll probably start off by selling fairly neutral goods – i.e. china, small pictures, postcards. These are small, postable items but you might also think about putting dinner services on the Internet. Personally I wouldn't. They can be a nightmare to pack and a single breakage *en route* could cost you the sale, unless the buyer has agreed to pay insurance. If you haven't packed the goods properly, it's down to you. They are also heavy and bulky which can deter some buyers unless they're exceptional. *That is the key to successful Internet selling – exceptional sells and at a premium price.*

You can sell anything over the Internet, even a canoe but you might not get as much as you would at a normal fair. I do sell my special pieces with a few other bits thrown in for good measure. Once you know the market better, you'll be able to decide for yourself what's worth selling over the Internet. Simple things like Wade Whimsies and nursery rhymes which we can find with ease over here are very popular in the US and you often get more money by selling them over the Internet than at fairs or traditional auctions.

> **Useful tip**
> Use Internet auctions to reach a wider market but by selling specific goods – save job lots of tired stock for traditional auctions.

The bottom line is that you can sell anything over the Internet but you might not always get as much as you want. As with traditional auctions, set reserve prices if you are selling via the Internet. There are two ways of doing this. Either:

◆ set a reserve by clicking on the reserve price button and filling in your minimum accepted price, i.e. your reserve. There's a minimal payment for this service but unsold goods can be re-entered and your second listing fee is refunded if the goods are sold second time around.

◆ or start the bidding at your reserve price.

However, the lower your starting price, the more bidders. Why? Because everybody wants a bargain, but don't worry, if you've set a reserve price, your goods cannot be sold for less than that. Meanwhile, you'll have a lot more bidders and the price could far exceed your reserve. As with traditional auctions, set a realistic reserve. You're in business to sell.

If you haven't sold on an on-line auction before, this could all sound rather too complicated to be tempting but it really isn't, as you will see below.

How to Sell on Ebay

Sit in front of your computer (if you have one) and connect to the 'world's largest marketplace' as it calls itself. Ebay (*www.ebay.co.uk* for selling and *www.ebay.com* for buying) has around 34 million users. It's huge. They won't all be interested in the goods you're buying or selling but a decent proportion of them will. Once you're connected, click on the 'sell' button at the top of the screen. Next, click on the 'How to sell tour'. This takes a few minutes and, at times, can be a bit slow but it's worth persevering. It will take you through how to sell step by step – even regular users could benefit from this service.

I'm going to give you a quick tour now. What is true of Ebay is often true of the other Internet auctions, such as *www.qxl.com*. The most important thing to remember is not to be afraid, just take your time and discover why the trade has changed so much since the advent of the Internet.

A Step-by-Step Guide

It's a good idea for you to go through some of this procedure on-line so move over to your computer and connect to the Internet, then click on *www.ebay.co.uk* before reading any further – it's not vital but it could just make things a bit easier for you. If you're used to selling on Ebay, then just read on to see if I mention anything which you don't normally use but could find beneficial.

If you are going to read on in front of your computer, I want you to go through all of the steps but not actually sell anything at this stage. Just go as far as the category listing if you're not registered, or subcategory listing if you are, and then disconnect, but don't worry – you'll still be able to see the screen. Remember, you can get into trouble if you practise for real and list something which you don't have to sell. Just try it out and see if it appeals. It really is remarkably easy. Don't forget to try the 'How to sell tour' which will take you through all of these steps whether you're registered or not – and you'll see exactly how it works.

1. **Click on sell.** This will automatically take you through to another screen – if selling for real, make sure that you're registered before you do this and have your username and password at the ready in case you don't remember them.

2. **Choose category.** Ebay is subdivided into categories, as you would have seen when you connected. Let's say that you're selling a Carlton Ware Walking Ware Big-foot teapot. Carlton Ware is a make of china so click on 'pottery and glass'.

3. **Item info.** Enter your user ID (that's your username) and password, then click on continue. If you're not already registered, you can't go any further without registering at this point.

4. **Sub-category.** This should come up automatically, but it doesn't always so just click on the box which asks you to click on it if the information has failed to be listed. Next, choose your sub-category. You'll notice that Carlton Ware is listed under both porcelain

and pottery. In this case, it's pottery – porcelain is much thinner and more delicate. Click on 'Carlton Ware' in the pottery section. Out of interest, go through these lists so that you can see what other options you have. If you're on-line, disconnect at this point, you can see the rest of the process without needing to be on-line.

5. **Enter a title.** This is what attracts would-be buyers to look at your stock. Don't waste your chances by adding things like 'L@@K' or 'WOW' – you'll look unprofessional but, more importantly, you've got more sellable things to say. Only use the word 'rare' if it is rare. Keep it simple. Say what it is succinctly – you have the description section to give more detail. Some buyers will search title and description but most will only search title so say what it is as soon as possible. In this case 'Carlton Ware Walking Ware Big-foot teapot'. That says it all.

6. **Enter description.** Keep it accurate. You might want to give measurements. This is a good idea so that people know what size to expect, especially if the goods come in more than one size or are not easy to find. Remember that you're selling internationally so use an international, metric measurement – cm sells better than inches but use both if you'd prefer. If you're selling something by a potter such as Basil Matthews, give some information about him. It sounds insensitive but, if the potter is dead, say so – that way, your buyers will know that his products are no longer available or are hard to find. Give colours – you'll probably be using photos but colours do not always come out properly so say so. Let them know that it's attractive without going over the top and avoid words like 'cute' – they just look ridiculous. Keep it simple and accurate. The description's length is up to you but I tend to say about 3-4 lines' worth if the piece needs it. Give the maker's name, the designer's name (if applicable and you know it). Provide dates if you can. Describe the mark if it needs it (this can be used to determine date and desirability of a piece – especially if it's been signed by the designer).

7. **Pictures.** We're going to be looking at this in more detail in the next chapter but pictures increase sales. If you're trying to sell something, show them what it is, especially for rarer or unusual pieces. They're cheap to list – Ebay charge a nominal amount per picture (first picture free if you go for five photos) but do remember that it can take time for photos to load on to the screen and you could have lost a bored buyer before the picture appears – the higher the resolution, the longer it takes to 'develop' on screen. My advice is to use photos when you can. Take a simple, frontal

picture, one from the side (if it needs it) and the base – always show the backstamp when possible. If you are selling damaged pieces, take a photo of the damage, preferably with a ruler next to it so would-be buyers can see it before bidding. Ebay will take you through the steps of loading your pictures onto the screen very carefully so don't worry if you don't know what you're doing. We all have to learn sometime and it is very easy.

8. **Side show.** An all singing, all dancing feature which will make your goods jump about. Oh dear, not for professional dealers but worth doing if you're selling stuff to younger buyers – if you really have to. Personally, I'd save your money.

9. **The Gallery.** This is one of Ebay's most underused features and for a reason. I normally add a picture of my goods to the gallery because it's only 15p[1] but I'm not sure how much use it is to be featured in the gallery proper, especially at almost £10 a go – I'd leave it if I were you but spend the 15p, just in case.

10. **Item location.** This can be useful for seeing where the goods are. Effectively, it's asking where you are. I always list myself as London – I'm not far from it and, for security, I'd rather not give too many details as to where I am. Keep it simple, give a vague sense of the area as it can encourage local bidding – or let those from overseas know which country you're in. Some people make a joke about it (eg The Cold North of England), just keep it simple and not too detailed.

11. **Quantity.** If you're selling more than one example of the same goods, it becomes a Dutch Auction with different fees attached (eg separate listing fees for each item of stock). Be careful, if you're selling a tea service with 21 pieces, you're only selling one item. If you have five identical books which you wish to sell separately, type '5' in the box.

12. **Minimum bid.** This is your starting point. I've already discussed this but the main point is that you have two choices – set it low to attract more buyers or start at your reserve price – it could lose you a sale but you'll save yourself the small reserve fee (30p–£1.20).

[1] Prices are subject to change.

13. **Auction duration.** You have a choice of three, five, seven or ten days. Always try to include a weekend as you'll get more interested parties that way – people browse at weekends when they might not have time during the week. I do ten days to allow myself extra time but it's entirely up to you. Five to seven days are possibly the most popular choices and you could be doing yourself a disservice by only running a very short, 3-day auction, especially if that's all mid-week.

14. **Reserve price.** Worth doing but be realistic. If it doesn't meet the reserve, it's not sold and you will only be charged the 'final value fee' (i.e. commission) if the goods do sell.

15. **Buy it now.** This option allows buyers to buy the goods for a set price which you determine (if you choose to use this feature – it's not compulsory) before the start of the auction. For instance, a laptop computer might have a 'buy it now' facility of £450. If you really, really want it and don't want to miss losing out, then buy it, but you could be paying over the odds – it might have sold for £350 otherwise and you could have saved £100. But that's as a buyer. As a seller, you could end the sale faster, get your money quicker or you could get less than you might have got in the auction itself. It has both merits and negative points and is entirely down to your own needs.

16. **Free counter.** Counters are great ways of determining how many people have looked at your auction. It can give you an idea of how well or badly you're doing with your listing – not everyone will buy but you want to tempt as many people to look as possible. If you have lots of browsers but not many buyers, is there a reason for it? Counters are useful tools and they're free – use them.

17. **Types of payment.** You might choose to have a credit card option which is useful when wanting fast payment and selling overseas. This does cost extra but can be worth it. Either arrange it with a bank (shop around for the best service and cheapest fees) or sign up to Paypal, Ebay's credit/debit card facility – fees are payable but it can be worth it, especially for overseas sales – much faster. If you choose to have your own facilities, check what charges you will incur. If you're only intending to sell a couple of goods a month – or even less – it might not be worth your while. Most card companies will charge you a minimum of £15 a month or expect to receive charges of £15+ a month and charge you for any shortfalls. If you have a shop or take credit cards anyway, this is a good, quick option. Never accept card details by e-mail – it's not

secure. If taking cheques, wait for them to clear before sending out the goods to avoid trouble from bounced or cancelled cheques or play it safe and ask for a banker's draft (a pre-cleared cheque). Other options are cash, but ask for the buyer to send it through registered mail – or any mail which insures it for the value sent – not all services accept cash. It avoids any problems with 'missing' money. You could also accept travellers' cheques but ask the buyer to write your name on them so that you're the only person who can cash them. This is a popular option for overseas buyers who can change money at minimal cost. I use Paypal for all overseas transactions because it is so convenient.

18. **Where you sell.** This is an important one – sell everywhere (i.e. ships worldwide) for maximum sales and prices. But only if you want. If you're not sure, stick to the UK only until you feel happier – it could be all you need.

> **Useful tip**
> Where Ebay is concerned, buy on *www.ebay.com* for maximum number of lots but sell on *www.ebay.co.uk* – that way, all of your charges will be in pounds sterling and your buyers will include those who only buy from England on *ebay.co.uk*.

When the Sale Ends

No matter where you're selling over the Internet, be it via your own website or an Internet auction, good communication is essential. When the sale is over, contact your buyer and let them know that they're the highest bidder or you will be selling your goods to them. Remind them how you like to be paid and, politely, ask for a quick payment. You should hear from them within a day or two. However, after three days chase them up, expressing worry that you have not heard from them and reminding them that they agreed to buy your goods. Give them five to seven days in all. If you have not heard either relist the goods on your website (if not sold on an Internet auction) or write to the Internet auction and explain what has happened. You will not be charged for any sales which have fallen through because a buyer pulled out. However, this is not common so don't worry. If you don't hear, persevere, but it's far more likely that they'll be delighted to be the highest bidder and will reply ASAP.

Ask for their address so you know where to send the goods and give them yours so that they know where to send the money. Always wait for payment, or for the payment to clear, before sending goods and ask them to let you know that the goods have been received safely. Now all you have to do is post them.

Postage and Packing

Always charge your buyers p&p after weighing the goods – never over or undercharge. It's never worth trying to make a little bit extra on the p&p – it only breeds ill-will and can lose you sales.

Packaging is one of the most important aspects of Internet or mail order selling. You can always arrange to meet your buyers at fairs if it's possible but most just want a fast and efficient delivery. Invest in some bubble wrap and always over – as opposed to under-wrap. Find a suitable box or padded envelope depending on what you're selling. Boxes can be bought from packaging firms, stationers and the post office. I even save ones I get when buying books on-line and reuse them to send goods, covering the bookseller's details properly. Polyester bubbles (available from packaging firms) help to protect the goods – save money and reuse them when other people send you pieces. Recycling is cost effective. Make sure that the goods cannot slide or be damaged in any way and Sellotape the box or package profusely. Not just the edges but round and round – it helps to prevent tampering in the post. There was a famous case of goods being removed at a big American airport and only the empty boxes being sent on – this can be prevented by very obvious taping. It also stops any stock from falling out because of inadequate taping – it has been known to happen.

Write your buyer's name and address clearly on the front and fill in any Customs' forms if relevant. They'll ask you for a brief description of the goods – remember that not everyone know what Carlton Ware (or whatever) is, so just write 'china' and then describe the goods. For the Walking Ware, Big-foot teapot, I'd just write 'teapot' – they don't care what type it is. Tick the gift or merchandise box (gifts do not always incur Customs' duties but you're selling goods, so that's merchandise...) and enter the amount it cost. Add airmail stickers (which are free from Post Offices) if you're sending overseas and ask for a receipt for the postage for your records and a proof of postage certificate to prove that you sent the goods in case of any dispute. I always send goods by special delivery to buyers in the UK both to prove and guarantee safe arrival – many items are also insured this way but not all types of goods are covered. Check before sending.

If the buyer wants the goods insured, speak to the Post Office for advice or arrange for a special courier such as DHL (see your local phone directory) – this can be very costly so advise the buyer before signing anything. I always use the Post Office – it's relatively cheap and easy.

Selling over the Internet really is easy and saves you time. Once you get used to it, it's very quick. Careful packing is the most time-consuming part.

You can even sell on the Internet in the morning before you go to work or when you get back from a fair. There are thousands of dealers whose lives have changed because of the Internet, especially Ebay. It's not the only option but it is still the best of the on-line auctions so sign up today and get selling.

CHAPTER FIVE

Photographs on the Internet

As the old saying goes, a picture can say a thousand words – it can also drastically increase your number of buyers. Imagine seeing something saying, 'stamp with the queen's head and a blue background'. Well, what does that really mean? What shade of blue, what did the Queen look like at the time? Is there anything else on the stamp?

Would you bid for a 'Royal Doulton stoneware vase with flowers'? Possibly if they also named the pattern and you knew your patterns but it doesn't mean a thing to you as it is. It's not tempting. However, if they also included a photograph, preferably without you having to click on anything else (like turning a page), then you might be tempted to bid. If you're busy or just unsure of how to use the Internet (or 'surfing the Net' as browsing is better known), you don't want to muck about by having to turn pages or use guesswork. By using a picture, you'll reach a wider audience.

I Don't Have a Lot of Money for a Camera

When you're starting out, be it as a dealer or someone just using the Internet, you don't want to spend a lot of money. What's the point of buying a top of the range camera – even if you can afford it – and then realising that the Internet is not for you?

The good news is that you can buy a digital camera for under £50. The difference between a normal and digital camera is that the latter is designed specifically for use on computers. They don't use film so you can get instant pictures without the expense of developing them, but you can e-mail them away to firms such as Jessops (*www.jessops.com*) to receive 'hard copies', i.e. proper photos for less money than developing traditional film. You even get to choose which photos you actually want developed – or if you want more than one copy, something which you can't do with traditional cameras until they've been developed.

Obviously, the more you're going to be using your camera, the better the camera you'll need but start off small for now. These are the very basics that you'll need to consider:

- **Price** – it will be a major factor in your decision. My first digital camera cost me £50 and paid for itself after my first couple of sales. My next one cost me over £500 but took only two weeks to pay for itself. Start small and build up.

- **Batteries** – some cameras run off normal AA batteries – they're the ones which you can get in any supermarket and are used for clocks, remote controls and digital cameras. The more expensive cameras tend to use rechargeable batteries which can save money but can also run out at the wrong time. Sony are amongst the best for long-term battery charge. While some cameras run out after around 15–20 minutes' use, the properly charged Sony can last over 150 minutes – that's a few weeks' work.

- **Memory** – the cheaper cameras have small memories. In simple terms, you can only take about eight pictures at a time before needing to download them – that's put them on the computer – before you can take any more pictures. Other cameras work with memory sticks or cards which allow for more photos to be stored on the camera. These can be purchased separately and can be costly (£40 + for the larger memories) but they soon pay for themselves. Imagine being able to take 200 or even more photos without having to download them. An easy but often time-consuming job. Buy as much memory as you can, depending on your needs and pocket.

- **Close-ups** – not always in the form of zoom like more traditional cameras, some digitals have buttons which can perform 'macro' – that's very close up work and is very useful when taking photos of 'detail' such as backstamps or small chips. These tend to be better on the more expensive cameras but some of the cheaper cameras perform the job – which is all you need.

- **LCD display** – these are fantastic but not strictly necessary when selling goods over the Internet and many dealers manage without them. An LCD display captures an image, allowing you to see immediately if your photo is in focus or correctly lined up. They are very useful, especially when taking photos which capture a scene or a moment – you can see immediately if you need to take another shot. Just think of how many out-of-focus photos you've paid to have developed – it doesn't happen with an LCD display but they cost more. That said, you can find digital cameras with LCDs for around £100.

Are names important? No, but you can pay for the reputation which the more famous names often justly deserve. My own camera is a Sony and I cannot recommend it highly enough. New models come out all the time – don't be afraid to ask for help in the camera shop. If you are not able to get expert help then go elsewhere – don't waste money but find out exactly what you need. Jessops have branches all over the country (see your local phone directory) with properly trained, knowledgeable staff. Ask for help from a digital camera expert and explain why you need a camera – mention that you need to take close-ups as all cameras are different. More features cost more money and you probably won't use half of them. Flash is useful, especially when taking photos inside or in poorly lit areas – people need to see what they're buying and they can't if your item is in shadow.

Traditional Cameras and Scanners

You can use a traditional camera to sell on the Internet but you'll either need your own scanner or have access to one. A scanner is a simple machine that transfers images or even text off a page onto a computer. The best versions are what are known as 'flatbed scanners'. Think of them as photocopy machines – you just place your photos picture-side down on the flat surface, shut the lid and press the copy button which transfers the image to your computer. It's that easy, but you do have the added cost and delay of developing photos. If you can afford a digital camera, even a £40 one, then it's the better option. When selling printed items such as postcards, ephemera or books, simply scan them in via the scanner – no cameras needed. Great for copying book covers when selling books.

What Happens if I Don't Have a Camera, Scanner or Even a Computer?

That's easy, find someone who has. There are various companies which cater for people like you and some of these are located in antiques centres such as Heanor, Derbyshire (01773 531181). There are firms who will offer to take photos of your stock and sell it on their websites but these might not be suitable for your needs – ask around if you're not sure. Or you could just sell your goods without photos. It can work for more common items, e.g. Wade elephant whimsies. But it's not ideal and could lose you potential buyers – and profit.

Is it Easy to Take Photos for the Internet?

As with all things, keep it simple. There are some tried and tested rules for taking photographs, no matter what the subject or reason.

+ Get as close as you can – background is a waste of space.

+ Be careful not to let the background intrude – place your object against a plain cloth, not too dark or you won't see it and not white as this can reflect the light and distort the image. Avoid patterns as this can detract from the object.

+ Use lighting – don't let it reflect off the object but use lights to keep your goods out of shadows and show your items at their best.

+ Clean your goods before photographing them – it sounds obvious but look at how many unattractively dirty and dusty goods are for sale over the Internet – it puts people off as they don't know what's dirt and what's damage.

+ Never use out of focus pictures – there's no point.

+ Try to focus on the backstamp so buyers can see it and get an idea of the date/ maker/designer/painter and other special features.

+ If the object only has one good angle, take it from there. Other goods, such as a dog ornament, should be photographed from the front and side for increased sales – the more they see, the more they'll want it.

+ Take a close-up of any damage, maybe use a ruler against it if it's substantial – it will save trouble in the long run.

I Have the Photos, What Now?

Click on the photos section of the selling section and follow the instructions – Ebay will lift the photos from your computer with a few simple steps. Decide in advance which photos you want to use.

Photos are an easy way of telling the would-be buyer what you've got.

Long-term, you'll need a decent camera if you intend to use Ebay or any of the other sites, perhaps your own, on a regular basis. My digital camera has changed the way that I work. I don't just use it for selling over the Internet but for illustrating articles. I sell my photos to magazines and newspapers and my digital camera was worth every penny. It's easy to transfer the pictures from the camera to the computer. Like most cameras, it just requires leads but some cameras, such as some of the Fujis, make it even easier for you and use special cradles which transfer the pictures at the touch of a button without needing individual transfers. It takes a couple of minutes to transfer over 100 photos from my Sony camera to my Sony laptop – which is why I bought a Sony laptop and not another make. I also use my camera for personal use and, in an age of e-mails, it's wonderful just being able to send photos to my friends or to dealers who want to see what other stock I have. It's made buying a lot easier as well – I like to see what I'm buying before I spend any money.

There are special courses around which will teach you how to make the most out of your camera, including improving the lighting after the photo has been taken and cropping (cutting out the bits you don't want). These are very useful and also cheap. Ask at your local computer school or college for details. Your camera will come with its own software which will give you some useful extras. It's easy to use without training but you could get more out of it if you have that little extra help – it depends how computer literate you are or what other uses you intend to make out of your camera.

If you are going to use the Internet for selling, you *will* need a camera long-term but £50 (and under) cameras could be perfect for your requirements. You can even go on Ebay or QXL and get a new or secondhand one for even less. I saw a perfectly good one sell for £27 today, still in its original box. You'll get that back in one or two sales and the rest is pure profit (less the small selling fees). Long-term, digital cameras are much easier, more practical and cheaper to run than conventional cameras and a scanner. I highly recommend them.

CHAPTER SIX

Do I need My Own Website?

Most Internet dealers start out on Ebay or QXL. They realise how incredibly successful it is for them and take the next step – they get their own website. But what is a website? It's a 24-hour shop. It really is that easy. Unlike a shop, you don't need to be there, you don't have closing hours and you don't need staff apart from one, very useful one – a website designer. If you have the expertise you could do it yourself, but most people prefer to employ professionals and profit from their ideas.

You will need to tell the designer some of your main requirements – they should be able to point out anything that you've forgotten. It just helps to know in advance what sort of things you expect from them and how simple or complex your requirements are.

Some people have simple websites which have a picture of their business, their address and phone number and that's it. Which is all very well but a hugely wasted opportunity. After all, what does it tell you about their business? The best antiques and retail websites all have the same basic structure of a home page (the first page) and separate departments.

The 'First' Page

Don't be too clever, just get your would-be buyers in the mood with contact details and photos of your better stock. This should be your **home page**. Some dealers use first pages which have pretty pictures or moving scenes, but which don't tell you anything and could deter impatient but genuine buyers who are meant to click on something else before being transferred to the home page. Stick to the basics.

The ideal home page should be like an illustrated index, showing what's on offer.

Let's say that you're a children's books specialist. The wallpaper of your website (that's like a background sheet) could be taken from the front cover illustration of a popular classic such as

Enid Blyton or Biggles, something pretty and evocative of a bygone age. On the right should be your contact details – e-mail address, phone number, business address – but never your home address. Use a Post Office (P.O.) box which is even better if you don't have a business address – ask your local Post Office for details and a form. In the centre, have photos or a quote from a suitable book and, on the left, a list of authors or topics with 'others' listed at the bottom. This listing should be used as a portal (doorway) to the rest of your site, so buyers click on Enid Blyton and get linked to your page selling Enid Blyton books immediately. Each page should have the same listings but with 'home' added. Like a perfect department store, it should be easy to get around with a 'check out' (i.e. till) in every department.

What to Include in Your Website

Websites can be very complex but they needn't be. Surf the Net and see what appeals to you about each site you find. What really annoys you or what do you think is a waste of time? If you want to add a site to your 'favourites' listing, ask yourself why, what appeals to you about that site and can you use something similar on your own website?

◆ If you are also doing fairs or are in a centre, list their details and let the buyers know where they can find you with other stock – this will help sales and could also encourage uncertain collectors who might be happier buying face-to-face or are worried that particularly delicate pieces might be damaged in transit. Millions of people love using the Internet but they don't all feel secure about using it. This way, you give them the best of both worlds – the real and the virtual.

◆ You might also want to have an 'about us' section. This should be a short summary which is used to reassure would-be buyers that you're reputable. It's difficult if you've only just started out but start by saying how long you've been involved in the antiques world. I've been dealing for over 20 years but I've actually been involved in the antiques world for over 25 years – that five years can make a big difference when you're just starting out. I'm not advising you to lie but to make the most of your existing knowledge. You might not realise just how much you actually know about antiques. You might be an expert in one field but know quite a lot about other areas as well. In this game, you pick up a lot of information without even realising it – let the buyers know that you know what you're talking about.

◆ Have a separate 'contact us' page which will link straight through to your e-mail. Use a separate e-mail address to your normal one just to make your life easier and keep your files straight.

◆ Reply to all e-mails as quickly as you can – it encourages buyers and can increase sales.

◆ When you're listing your stock, do it in columns or a clear manner which allows the buyer to find what they want with ease.

◆ Don't go into too much detail about the history of the pieces but give some information if you can – dates are always popular, as are pattern names or publishers (if applicable).

◆ Always use photographs on a website.

◆ Try to update regularly – once a week ideally but at least once a month otherwise. Buyers get bored and stop looking at infrequently updated websites so you could lose business if you don't treat it like a business.

◆ Don't forget to remove stock once it's been sold. That said, if you don't have much stock at the beginning, leave it on but mark it as 'sold' – it will encourage buyers to know that they're not the only ones thinking of buying and will help them to buy faster as they'll realise that they have competition. Too many 'sold' pieces can be frustrating for would-be buyers, though.

Websites cost a few hundred pounds to set up – it depends on your needs and the designer. Go for something which feels good – *a quality site will get visited more often than a scruffy, neglected-looking one.*

I should also add that a website is a shop with fixed prices. It's not an auction (unless you want it to be when you're more established and will have enough regular buyers for that to work), so add the prices by the photos. You can't sell anything if your buyers don't know what to pay. If you can take credit cards, once you're more established, it's worth doing so – especially to attract overseas buyers.

What Should I Call My Website?

Once you know that you want a website and know what you want to include in it, you'll need to give it a name. But, to succeed, it must be a good name. Domain names need to be registered so, if you think that you know what to call it, connect to the Internet and type that in (eg *www.Iwantmyownwebsite.com*). One of three things should happen:

◆ you'll be connected to an existing website which means that someone thought of that name first

◆ you'll be told that there's no such address – try typing it again in case you made a mistake (or press the refresh button)

◆ or you'll be connected to a domain name provider and, like the previous possibility, that's good. What that means is that you can buy that name.

Website names have to be bought (prices vary but expect to pay around £50+) – it's how to register them. Once it's registered, it's yours and, if the design is in place, you're ready to start trading.

What's In a Name?

Let's start backwards. If you use the English '.co.uk' (pronounced dot co dot uk) after your site name, you'll immediately limit your market. America and Japan are two of the largest antiques and collectables buying nations. They don't use .co.uk unless they know that you're there but they will use .com – especially the vast American market. It's also worth registering .net as that's the next step forward once .com is full and you could lose an established name to a better marketer. It's only three letters and it's not much to register most domain names – it's normally around £50. You'll have to renew your website's name every few years but, apart from that, once you've paid for the name and your website design and production, it's all free. It's a shop with no rent.

Now for the tricky bit, what do you call it? Be simple – you can be witty at the same time but stick to the facts. What are you trying to sell?

You need to base your name on what you're offering, not who you are unless you're famous.

Authors name their websites after themselves because what they're selling *is* their name. But you're probably not. Let's say that you sell sporting or nautical goods – 'moneyforoldrope.com' would work – rope is used in yachting and various sports, plus you're selling old stuff, but would it work for everyone? What about the people who go to a search engine and type in 'old nauticalia' (yachting stuff) – would they find you unless you've listed your details and comments in a search engine (see 'How Do I Get Visitors?' below, for details). You need to encapsulate your stock and it doesn't have to be clever, it doesn't have to be long, it just needs to do the job.

Play around and see what works for you. Be practical – you know who you are but does anyone else? If the answer is no, not really, don't use your name. Many of the good names will have gone but not all. It really is a matter of trying it out – ask friends for advice and choose something sensible that you'll be happy repeating to complete strangers – that should get rid of some of your sillier ideas automatically. When it comes to a name, you're not here to have fun but to make money and you can't do that if people can't find you. *A good name will bring you buyers with minimal work.*

How Do I Get Visitors?

Dealers on Ebay use it as a marketing tool, giving would-be buyers the option to look at their website. They also refer their website browsers to their Ebay auctions – it's good business sense. If they do fairs, they have business cards or leaflets on their stall, advertising their site. Some advertise in the antiques magazines and some have links with other specialist sites – it's often free as long as it's reciprocal. You could also sign up to search engines – Google doesn't charge (or guarantee inclusion) and it's easy to do. Simply go to *www.google.com* and click on the 'site inclusion' option. This will take you to a page where you will be asked for your URL (webpage address) including the http:// prefix. You can also add comments or keywords likely to attract buyers.

Depending what you're selling, words like 'vintage' are good for attracting American buyers, (eg 'vintage children's books, Enid Blyton, Biggles, Just William' etc). Stick to names which are famous – note here the use of Just William, the series and not the author name – more people will recognise the series than the author except for the most famous ones e.g. Enid Blyton – but add Noddy as well.

Some search engines will charge so decide how often you use that particular search engine yourself – if it's often, it might be worth doing, depending on cost. You will probably receive mailing from someone offering to add you to their or lots of other search engines. It's up to you. I work for a magazine and I regularly receive this e-mailing (I call it junk mail) from the same company, despite politely refusing to use this service. It's entirely up to you – you need to be listed somewhere as the easier you are to find, the more buyers you'll get. I'm not sure that I would pay to be listed when I can get it for free elsewhere.

CHAPTER SEVEN

Do I Even Need the Internet to Be a Dealer?

The Internet is not compulsory but it can help to expand your business or make you money while you sleep. You can find rare or cheap stock – sometimes both at once. The Internet is not just about buying and selling antiques, you can also:

* find out information about elusive stock
* find fellow collectors or out of print books
* get new books at a fraction of the normal price.

No it isn't essential. But it can open up a whole new world.

The Internet offers so much for so little time and trouble. You can find virtually anything you want from fair and auction information to the best routes to fairs and discovering new centres. I became a full-time journalist and changed from full-time to part-time dealing through answering an ad on it while trying to find the date for an old Royal Doulton Bunnykins figure. That, in turn, led to this book, a radio antiques phone-in and TV work.

The Internet is a useful tool for keeping an eye on the market – which goods have had their day, what's worth what and where to find them. There are sites which tell you what's coming up at auction – I asked about a hard-to-find studio potter and it told me that two of his pieces were in an auction in Derbyshire at 10 o'clock that morning. I would not have known otherwise. It can do the same for you.

By using the Internet you can become a dealer without ever having to leave your office or house – apart from to post your cheques while waiting for the postman to deliver your bargain, Internet-bought stock.

PART FIVE
What to Sell

This part is designed to give you ideas about what type of goods to sell. Think of it as a taster. Chances are you already have a vague or very definite idea about what sort of goods you're going to be selling, but one thing you will learn in this trade is to be flexible. By opening yourself up to new ideas, you'll discover a rich and varied world full of beautiful and curious objects, all waiting for you to learn about and profit from them.

You might start in one direction but be completely won over and end up selling completely different things or adding new ideas to your existing area. This section will help you to discover the sheer variety of antiques and their potential.

You could spend a fortune on books or join expensive classes which will teach you a little about antiques, but let me help you by showing you just some of the areas which you might not have considered. If they appeal, then go out and learn about them. If they don't, why waste any more time or money on them by buying books? Read on and use this as a starting point in your life as a dealer, for nothing ever stays the same and antiques and collectables are everywhere if you know what they are.

CHAPTER ONE

What Is a Collectable?

The antiques trade has changed completely in the last 20 years. Collectables have taken over from genuine antiques with a passion because they sell – buyers love them.

Collectables cover a broad spectrum of goods but basically encapsulate virtually everything which people buy in the 'antiques' world which are less than 100 years old from pop memorabilia to limited edition china – there's a buyer for them all.

Some dealers view collectables as the ruination of the trade and see them as cheap fashion, not quality, but all antiques started life as new and collectables are no different. Some will last to become antiques whilst others are highly profitable but short-term fads. We'll be looking at those in Chapter 21 and they'll either appeal or not. The whole point about dealing in collectables, be they brand new or over 50 years old, is to know when to move on and to know your market.

Collectables can command high prices, but many are affordable and a good way of getting into the trade. If you look around your house, it's virtually guaranteed that you have some collectables and, if you like them, then someone else is bound to as well.

Where there are collectables, there are collectors, and many of the manufacturers have taken advantage of this by starting their own collectors' clubs, often offering limited edition or limited by year pieces.

What's the Difference Between a Limited Edition and a Piece Which is Limited by Year?

A proper limited edition has a set number of pieces. A limited edition of 250 will only have 250 pieces produced – in theory. Some factories are dishonest and produce 275 or even more, with the extras being sold out of the back door. Ideally, the pieces should be numbered individually, but many firms will use certificates which have numbers on them instead of on the goods themselves. I don't like this as certificates get lost very easily and tend to bend and fold which is not attractive. I once had a buyer who tried to tell her children that they shouldn't buy any Wade limited editions unless they had their certificates because they might be fake. I interrupted her (politely) and told her something very important about dealers – we're not always organised. Some of us lose certificates. Even me. If you do buy limited editions, then make sure that you wrap the certificates with the pieces to avoid losing sales.

Are all limited editions worth buying? No, far from it. Look at how many pieces are in each edition. The smaller the edition, the better as they will have more competition. If only 25 pieces are made, then there were only 25 lucky buyers, which makes demand higher than if 25,000 people bought the piece. Opinions vary but limited editions of 2,500 and smaller are worth buying, any higher and you should buy for yourself, not resale unless it's a really good piece.

What Does Limited by Year or People Mean?

Some manufacturers will try to sell goods which they claim to be 'limited editions' but which don't reveal the issue size. That's because they're not 'limited edition' in the acceptable sense of the word. The misleading title appeals to collectors who think that they're getting something special which only a few other people have the chance to buy. Unfortunately, they're being conned. What these manufacturers actually do is accept your order which you made in good faith and then produce as many goods as buyers. The edition size can vary from 500 to 50,000 but they can still call it 'limited' because it's limited to the people who actually ordered it. This is a con.

> **Useful tip**
> Never buy a limited edition piece unless you know how many pieces are being produced. This should be printed on the certificate or on the figure itself.

Limited by year is an acceptable selling device used by some of the top manufacturers such as Royal Doulton and Halcyon Days and many of the collectors' clubs. Edition sizes can be huge but the pieces are only produced in the year of manufacture. A year piece is generally dated on the figure and/or the certificate and can only be bought during that year (except at secondary outlets – that's fairs and centres and from shops which stockpile the goods or don't sell them in time). Royal Doulton produce a special Bunnykins figure each year. These highly collectable, dressed rabbit figurines are often produced in a series which encourages buyers to buy the year pieces for several years to complete the set. With four or five annual figures, this is a canny piece of marketing which allows collectors the chance to build up sets slowly and with dedication. Too many limited editions can be financially crippling as some Wade collectors have discovered but by producing year figures, collectors can spread their investment out over the course of several years.

Are They Sensible Buys?

They can be – certainly anything by Royal Doulton which is even vaguely limited is worth collecting as long as the quality is there. Recent financial problems have seen them commission items from the Far East under the Royal Doulton banner – they are clearly marked as coming from there but the quality is lacking and they're not particularly good investments – from what I've seen so far, anyway. Their British-made year pieces are always worth collecting. Solid factories such as Doulton (dealers rarely use the full name) will always be collectable.

The basic rule – which covers all collectables, whether limited or not – is to stick to quality.

If you like a year piece, buy it but be aware that the limited by year definition is vague and 50,000+ of these pieces might be made but the demand can exceed that within months. The better factories will destroy the mould on 31 December of the year in question so use your own judgement and stick to what appeals – if the quality is there.

Are All Limited Editions Worth Buying?

Sadly, no. I was in the supermarket the other day and I saw 'limited edition' chocolates! Many different types of businesses are cashing in on the collectors' market, not all advisedly. Confectioners have realised that a good way of testing out new products is to introduce them as limited in some way either because of the amount produced (hence 'limited editions') or timewise. It's a good marketing ploy but it's not for you. I have seen limited edition Snowman (Raymond Briggs's popular creation) chocolates in an antiques centre alongside longer lasting Royal Doulton examples, but this showed that the dealer had a sense of humour or was just very naïve. Unless you intend to eat them, don't buy them – it's just a marketing ploy and a waste of money.

The very basic definition of a collectable is something which is collected (excluding furniture). That might seem very obvious but are you aware that people will collect anything? There are teapot collectors, cruet collectors, people who collect fishing reels and old cameras, some collect old cereal boxes, others china shoes – whatever is attractive, quirky or irresistible is collectable but not necessarily a collectable. Old cereal boxes may or may not be collectables, if they sell that is what counts.

Collectables are often seen as goods made specifically for the collectors' market (eg limited editions or anything by established firms such as Royal Doulton or Moorcroft), but collectable items can be even more interesting and often a lot more lucrative than these pieces or even genuine antiques. Stick to what you like but see what else people buy by visiting as many fairs, centres and auctions as you can.

> **Useful tip**
> If you are selling collect_Ables to the US market, call them 'collect_Ibles' – they spell it with an 'i' while we use an 'a' – it confuses a lot of people.

What Makes a Good Collectable?

There are some basic rules for collecting or dealing in collectables. These rules apply whether you're buying brand new goods from shops or existing collectables from the antiques world:

◆ Stick to quality – it will last.

◆ Go for originality – constant harping to the past (eg mock Deco or a reissue of old pieces, maybe with different colours) is faddish and not a good long-term investment. It will also cheapen the rest of your stock.

◆ Figures (goods resembling people – a term also used for animal-shaped goods) and animals outsell all other goods, including plates. They also have a larger market and are a better all-round buy.

♦ Natural colours are generally better than garish ones and too bright colours can have a limited market.

♦ Quality items based on popular children's books (eg Brambly Hedge and Noddy) or classic TV series (eg The Magic Roundabout) are often good, long-term investments but often only if they were produced at the same time as the series – modern Magic Roundabout pieces will not have the same collectability as the original, harder to find pieces which were not produced in such large quantities as modern runs.

♦ Quality goods based on popular adverts/products (eg the Dulux dog or Guinness figures) are good sellers.

What to Avoid

♦ Different colourways – a common marketing ploy to avoid creating new designs.

♦ Limited editions for the sake of it – not always a good investment.

♦ Anything being sold on the back (or inside) of non-antiques magazines as collectable – the quality is rarely there and the issue numbers are often too big to be collectable. They're too easy to get so why should people buy them from you?

♦ Goods which will not last, eg beer or chocolates.

♦ Goods by The Bradford Exchange, Danbury Mint and Franklin Mint are very popular with the public but do not sell well at antiques venues. In my opinion, they do not offer long-term investment.

♦ Too modern goods might age badly – think of future, not just short-term investment – your buyers will.

◆ Reproductions of old designs by the original factories (eg Royal Winton is reissuing their chintz – it's the wrong era so no long-term potential as serious buyers will want the original).

◆ The next Harry Potter book's first edition – we all know about it now and it's just not issued in small enough numbers to be collectable – buy it to read it, not for a profit unless you intend to sell it over the Internet to the overseas market which buys the original, English edition for premium prices (three times or more the cover price within a week of their issue).

◆ Look for scratches across the Royal Doulton mark on the base of RD items – this means that they're seconds. That's when goods are not perfect when leaving the factory but sold off as lower quality.

CHAPTER TWO

What is an Antique?

Like thousands of other people, you might love visiting 'antiques' fairs but don't visit for the genuine antiques. Maybe you found the word 'antique' off-putting. In the last few years, the names of events have been changed from 'antiques' fairs to 'antiques and collectors fairs' to sound more appealing to the modern buyer and reflect the limited amount of true antiques still in circulation.

There is something about the word 'antiques' which is strangely uninviting. It sounds musty or expensive – often the reality, but not always. But what *exactly* is an antique?

Quite simply, anything which was made in excess of 100 years ago is an antique.

And that's a very dull explanation. Antiques are a time-capsule of history, they capture the essence of an era. Admittedly, they can often capture only a certain strata of society because the poor had poorer goods, the pre-Victorian versions of which have rarely withstood the test of time. That said, not all antiques are top quality and not all are worth buying, but some are and they are the ones which will never be out of fashion no matter what fashion dictates. Many of them will have been the height of fashion in their day which appeals to some, but not all, buyers.

Let me tell you a little secret – it doesn't matter if you know what an antique is when you see it, who really cares if you know whether it was Regency or Georgian? The only thing that really matters is whether you love it or not.

You might choose not to deal in antiques and stick to collectables but don't overlook them. They have much to teach, no matter what your choice or level of dealing. Appreciate them for themselves and buy what you can when you can. They'll only go up in value. Unlike some of the collectables.

When is an Antique not an Antique?

When it's a reproduction (repro) or a fake. Repros pay tribute to the great eras of furniture (or whatever). They are not designed to con but to offer a cheaper way of possessing a beautiful object. That's the sincere part. Some dealers will buy repro and sell it as genuine – others will deliberately make copies of antiques and sell them as originals; we call these fakes and it's illegal. There's also a very good chance that, at least once in your career, you'll get caught out.

There are some very basic methods to avoid getting tricked:

♦ Lick your finger (or a tissue) and wipe it over a piece of furniture – under a table is a good place. If someone wants to 'age' a piece of furniture or change the wood from cheap, modern wood to one of the more popular older woods such as rosewood or mahogany, they will dye it. Not all dyes are good ones. If your finger or cloth comes away with a bit of brown (not just dust or dirt), the piece has been aged and very amateurly. Less attention will have been given to the underside of a piece or the side of the drawers than the top so check – either by this method or using your eyes. A table's underside should be approximately the same colour as its top – not always exactly the same because the top will fade in the sun. If it is exactly the same shade, leave it – it hasn't been around long enough to fade but the faker might not have realised this. Don't confuse it with genuine veneer (quality wooden cover over a cheaper wood). This was especially popular in the Deco period but it's easy to differentiate between genuine veneer and modern, faked goods – the originals will have signs of ageing on their underside and they're often dusty and show signs of age.

♦ Look for tea leaves – this sounds strange but tea is a great way of ageing goods and not everyone uses tea bags. It gives pieces a nice, old look but do the wet finger test – bits of it can come away almost as easily as it's applied.

♦ Look for a good old screw – this is one of the age-old mistakes made by lazy or less knowledgeable con artists. They will concentrate on the major details such as the curve of the leg and the colour of the wood but miss out the simple details such as the right screws and hinges. Antiques are old – they shouldn't have clean, shiny, modern screws – check them out.

◆ Dovetailing *vs.* nails – this is possibly overly simplistic but good, old furniture was not knocked together and nailed in place. Instead drawers and other fittings would have been locked together by dovetailings – that's when the wood is carved to resemble the angled tails of doves. They worked like a jigsaw. Nails suggest repro or fakes.

◆ Glue might be useful but should not be seen oozing out of antique furniture – con artists and inferior reproduction firms use it rather a lot – check before buying.

◆ Look for a pattern in any crazing or a too clean base on china goods – these are signs of fakes/repros. Old things get dirty and this becomes ingrained in their fibre – crazing should hold dirt, bases should be grubby where they touch surfaces and real crazing is irregular.

◆ Repro or fake china has brighter colours than the original, generally with crude moulding to match the poor quality paintwork.

◆ And the weight is wrong – too heavy or too light. Real antiques feel 'right' – fakes don't.

CHAPTER THREE

Art Nouveau and Arts and Crafts

There are certain terms which you will be expected to understand when you become a dealer – even buyers are meant to know what they mean. The most famous of these are **Art Nouveau** and **Art Deco**. In this chapter we're going to be looking at Art Nouveau and one of its most sellable predecessors, the **Arts and Crafts** movement which influenced the gentler, more erotic Art Nouveau movement. I'm not going to bore you with history or why the movement sprang up – I'm not going to mention the parallels in literature or art (much as I'd love to) – as a dealer, you don't need to know that and there are far weightier books than this to fulfil your interest. Suffice to say that the Art Nouveau period was amongst one of the most beautiful ever created. You will hear certain names bandied about, such as **William Morris** in relation to Arts and Crafts and **Liberty** for Art Nouveau so get used to them. William Morris was one of the leading exponents (creators and users) of the period and many of the curved symmetrical patterns which we associate with the Arts and Crafts movement are influenced by his work for **Lord Burleigh** – a man who could afford to have such style created for him. Liberty was one of the main retailers of the Arts and Crafts and later, the eternally popular Art Nouveau style.

What is Art Nouveau?

Art Nouveau means 'new art' and was a new way for artists, painters and writers to express themselves by harking back to Medieval times, viewed as a more romantic era. In historical terms, a new century was about to begin and it was not a peaceful era; the seeds of the First World War were being sown and the art world did what everyone in any hardship would love to do – it escaped.

Art Nouveau is very simple but might not always look like it. Its basis is in nature with the tulip and rose being especially prevalent. Lines are clean but sumptuous with **Charles Rennie Mackintosh**, (1868–1928) one of the period's most famous designers, taking lines to a new height by criss-crossing them and producing stylish ladderbacks; simplicity with style. The rose, used in some of his work, is associated with him and is also used in contemporary jewellery influenced by the 'Mackintosh style'. If you are in or near Glasgow, visit the various museums and the Glasgow School of Art to get a sense of Art Nouveau at its finest.

English and Continental Art Nouveau was softer than Mackintosh's. The lines were gentler, more curvaceous, and pewter and silver thrived. On the Continent, **WMF** was the main manufacturer and then, as now, is as sought after as Liberty.

Another name to look for is **Ruskin**, whose gentle blue and green pottery 'stones' (enamelled china plaques) dominated the market, decorating mirrors and vases, worn as brooches and adding colour to the softness of the silver metals. His eggshell thin china is also very desirable.

It was not only silver which came into its own but also the softness of copper, beaten into instantly recognisable patterns of the periods. Unlike today's china and art markets, there was a concerted effort to unite them and the movement changed, in turn, to form Art Deco with its harsher, more geometric shapes.

In terms of dates, we're talking late 19th, early 20th century. For many people, the period is shorter than that and many books will place it over a twenty-year period – 1900–1920 with Arts and Crafts seen as the previous twenty years – but it's not as simplistic as that. In many ways, dates are unimportant: Art Nouveau is an all-encompassing term and its designs are instantly recognisable.

What is Arts and Crafts?

There are some dealers and buyers who find the Art Nouveau movement almost too wishy-washy, who reject its romantic air which was influenced by the Medieval Gothic period (pointed arches, waifish women with long, flowing, Queen Guinevere-type hair). Those dealers either avoid Art Nouveau totally or buy the hardier, almost more macho Arts and Crafts movement. Instead of gentle flowers, the Arts and Crafts movement used cruder shapes, harsh but still stylised tulips, heavy carving and strong shapes beaten into copper. The two movements are compatible and often intertwine – you might choose to sell both. I love the Arts and Crafts movement for its practicality. I'm not afraid to sit on my Arts and Crafts dining chairs because they're sturdy. It's not an expensive movement and some dealers would argue that it shouldn't be considered separately from the Art Nouveau period at all. They could be right but I tend to think of it as His and Hers movements. The

Art Nouveau is willowy, it's often delicate and can be slightly too feminine but Arts and Crafts is heavy, and it's still relatively cheap to start buying now.

Arts and Crafts tulips decoration. The strong lines are typical of the movement and used to decorate everything from furniture and metalwork to jewellery.

Dealing in the Movements

Fashions come and go but Arts and Crafts and, especially, Art Nouveau is above all that. In many ways, it's had its day but is still an essential part of the antiques trade and has its place in specialist fairs and auctions, as well as with general dealers.

It encompasses everything – china, glass, metalwork, wood, furniture, paintings and jewellery. It has mass appeal because it was always dated as it looked back to an era of romance. And, whether you're a romantic or not, there's profit in it. Or you can do what I do: sell some of it and keep the rest at home. The illustration is taken from my dining room chairs – cheaper than most modern chairs but built to last and very, very stylish.

CHAPTER FOUR

Art Deco

Welcome to one of the most popular areas of dealing. Art Deco (decorative art) at its best is stylish, geometric, stunningly decorated and easy to sell and, at its worst is gaudy and orange. And that is about the only problem that you might find – its preferred colours are orange and yellow and not everyone likes them. I took a friend around an antiques fair and was introducing her to the best-selling makes of china. She looked at Burleigh and Clarice Cliff and announced that they looked 'old'. Not old as in attractive and authentic but old as in tired and faded. Not everybody appreciates the soft, honey-coloured background used by some of the potters, not everyone appreciates the sweeping lines of the furniture or its relative heaviness and, above all, not everyone appreciates the price tag that accompanies good Deco, but enough people do to make it worthwhile.

Aesthetically, good Deco is one of the most attractive areas of dealing but it can get too much. You can either specialise or have a few pieces on your stall. This is *your* business, do what you want to but within a realistic budget. If you don't have a lot of money, Deco might not be for you – good quality jugs rarely cost less than £200, many of them sell for over £500–1,500 which is fine if you have it but, otherwise, do what I do and sell Deco when you see good bits at affordable prices. I have sold a lot of Deco in my day

An Art Deco cup and saucer with sweeping lines and geometric patterns which, typically, would have been brightly decorated with vivid yellow and oranges.

and enjoyed having it on my stall but I'm not sure that I'd want any of it in my house. It's almost too stylised for me; I prefer the simplicity of the Arts and Crafts movement but hundreds of dealers disagree.

What is Art Deco?

For a start, never call it Art Deco except on your labels – dealers always call it Deco. It was born out of the Art Nouveau movement, at the 1925 Paris exhibition and spread throughout England, not just in terms of furniture, china and glass but in architecture – more so than the Art Nouveau period. The world was about to have another World War and the movement grew out of the economic and social depression of the 1920s. It is florid, curvaceous, bright and party-like. There is nothing subdued about Deco, but the buildings stand out today and will last in a way which few modern designs will do because the style is modern and dated at the same time. It is flowing, the buildings seem to have movement in their lines, however, we're not here to discuss architecture but what you can buy or sell. I love the dancing figures, with their movement and grace. The jugs and crockery, led by Clarice Cliff (see Chapter 6) are geometric, and the furniture is heavy but geometric from flowing lines to sharp angles. It is a noticeable era.

Go round any antiques fair and, whether you like it or not, Deco will stand out from its leaping deer to crouching panthers.

It is a movement with movement. Art Nouveau had tulips and roses, Deco invented its own flowers with matching petals and free flow. Deco could not be restrained and it is one of the most imaginative periods ever – that's why it has such mass appeal. There is nothing constrained or hemmed in, the colours are demandingly bright and cheerful and the shapes are irresistible.

There are many specialist fairs and auctions. Many of the fairs are datelined to include Deco (c1925–39) and specialist dealers or general ones with better pieces of Deco are welcome at any other fair (obviously excluding early datelined and non-relevant specialist fairs).

I mentioned 'better' Deco. That is because not all Deco is good Deco and the lesser but more affordable pieces can demean the rest of your stock because they lack the originality of the rest. Top makes include:

- Clarice Cliff
- Charlotte Rhead
- Susie Cooper
- Goldscheider
- Shelley
- Burleigh
- Grays
- Royal Winton or any of the other Grimswade factory names
- Carlton Ware
- Crown Devon
- Wade and Wadeheath.

Other than china, top collectables include:

- lights
- figures
- clocks
- furniture – especially cabinets and dining sets (tables, chairs and cocktail cabinets)
- jewellery – especially Cartier
- costume jewellery – Chanel, Schiaparelli etc
- metalwork
- radios
- Bakelite.

When is Deco not Deco?

There are two answers to this – when it's a fake and when it's mock Deco. Fake Deco is rougher than the original, the colours tend to be wrong (much lighter or darker) and looks very new. The paintwork is often crude and too thick, whilst the base is too clean. Once you've seen it against the original, you won't get caught out. Look for clumsy moulding and too many of the same pieces on the same stand – a clumsy but easy-to-spot mistake made by bad fakes dealers.

Mock Deco is another matter. It's very contentious within the trade with many organisers refusing to accept it at their fairs, even if it isn't a datelined event. To many dealers, mock Deco is wrong. Not only does it affect real Deco prices (people can afford the recent 'copies' but not the originals so, instead of saving up, they buy the cheaper pieces instead) but it is unoriginal. This is the 21st century and we should be looking forwards, not backwards. Potters and designers should be thinking for themselves, not ripping off old ideas – which is exactly how it is viewed by many of the trade. There is profit in it, but at a price, and dealers should not be caught up in the game which ruins the trade. In 70 years' time will people be buying mock Deco, believing that it reflects our era or, worse still, will mock Deco replace originality of thought? Art Deco was an era but mock Deco is just a copy – and a bad copy at that.

With few exceptions (eg Brian Wood), mock Deco is not worth buying. Lorna Bailey's pieces are everywhere and, in my opinion, are not worth buying unless you reaaly like them. I am listing them under fads (Chapter 21) because I honestly believe that they are short-term investments only and a lot of people are going to get caught out and lose thousands – money better invested in real Deco.

You might have noticed that I said mock Deco is a profitable area so why am I not recommending it in its own right? I'm not a purist but what really annoys me is the lack of quality and originality of many of the mockers. Lorna Bailey started the trend with some of the best marketing ever seen in the collectables business. But marketing alone cannot sustain a business. Her early shapes were mainly created from original moulds by Shorter and Wadeheath. Charlotte Rhead, one of the best of the Deco designers, used other potteries to create the base for her stunning designs, but her work was highly original. Lorna Bailey is becoming more original but her early work is based too much on the ideas and even original moulds of others. The Art Deco period grew out of the Art Nouveau period but with originality. Modern designers need to design for their own era, maybe hark back to a creative time such as Deco but with a modern slant. The mockers do not do that and it is this lack of originality which makes them bad buys.

Stick to originality and quality – Deco had it all.

CHAPTER FIVE

Furniture

Furniture dealers are as different from each other as china dealers are. A chest of drawers is not just a single design from a single era – it would be like assuming that all vases are the same because they're all designed to hold flowers.

Everybody needs furniture; some want large pieces, others small, some modern, others antiques. You will have two basic customers:

- those buying for themselves with specific needs
- and the trade, most of whom know what sells.

Unlike the collectable aspects of dealing, you will be selling practical goods. Delicate chairs can be very attractive but they are often seen as too fragile for most users and will generally appeal to trade, not public, buyers. If you are working in an area which caters mainly for the public, buy accordingly. Remember, other dealers will do this and they'll buy from you, but only if you have the right stock.

What Sells?

Furniture dealing is unlike any other form of dealing. What sells depends on what people need, but within reason. There are some stalwarts of the furniture trade and these are:

- chairs – especially children's chairs
- chests of drawers
- tables – from corner tables to full-sized dining room ones
- bedside cabinets
- washstands
- bookcases
- cabinets – designed for china collections etc

- sideboards
- desks/bureaux/davenports
- stools/footstools.

Most furniture is self-explanatory. For chests of drawers, check sides and bottoms of drawers before buying for signs of damage or fakes/repros and always look at the accessories (locks, handles etc) – they're an easy way of checking for less well-made fakes and forgeries. Just as importantly, the more interesting and attractive accessories can be the deciding factor in a sale. Some buyers want very simple furniture but others want added extras such as carved columns or moulded frontages. If you have the space, try to accommodate them all, otherwise stick to the better examples according to your budget.

Chairs

Everybody needs a chair, but there are various uses and dozens of types of chairs with some which sell better than others. People who buy dining tables tend to want matching **dining chairs** – four being the minimum, with some needing a dozen, sometimes more, but this is not normal so try to buy sets of either four or six chairs. Those who are buying in sets tend to want four matching chairs with two matching (or similar) **carvers**. Carvers also sell individually, as well as in pairs, for people who want comfortable chairs in their homes.

> **Keyword**
> **Carver – a heavy dining chair with arms.**

Not everybody will buy in sets but you should expect to cater for the people who do if you have the room. A set constitutes chairs of the same design but some buyers want a similar feel, if they can't get exactness. If you buy chairs of a similar age and style, you might want to get them reupholstered with the same material to give the effect of a set with a difference, but take the extra cost of reupholstery into account.

> **Useful tip**
> Reupholstering is a way to freshen up scruffy chairs and repair saggy bottoms at relatively minimal cost. A good reupholster will pay for itself but be careful about the material you choose. Go for period designs, if not authentic material (a pricier option but it can be worth it) and try to use hard-wearing materials. Ask your upholsterer for details but also remember the needs of your modern buyers – stripes might have been popular in Regency England but times have changed and they don't appeal to everyone – you might be limiting the number of buyers.

Windsor chairs

One of the most popular styles of chair is a **Windsor chair**. Designed for use in a hall or inn, this hard-looking chair is often crudely designed with a straight back and without arms. They are very good sellers but, as with all chairs, turn them over before buying them and make sure that each leg is firmly inserted and not loose or cracked. Unless you know a good restorer or are skilled yourself, avoid any chair with loose or broken legs – they don't sell for maximum profits. If at all.

> **Useful tip**
> Woodworm can ruin furniture and many buyers won't buy any pieces with those telltale holes. Old woodworm is not a problem and can actually add 'character' to furniture as long as it isn't too regular – another fakester's trick – or too prolific, but new woodworm will need treating. I would advise any newcomer against buying furniture with active (i.e. living) woodworm as it can take time to treat and some experts argue that only costly special heating treatment can kill the woodworm (debatable). How can you tell if it's active? Turn the furniture with holes facing downwards and gently tap it – if 'dust' (looks like sawdust caused by the woodworm's gnawing) falls out, then it's active. If not, it's old and not a problem. You can try treating woodworm yourself by buying over the counter remedies from a DIY shop (along with suitable safety precautions, including gloves and goggles) but it's debatable how effective it is. Save your money and don't buy goods with active woodworm until you're more established – if then.

Children's Chairs and Prams

Children's chairs are very good sellers – if you can find them. These small, often beautifully made chairs are bought by people not just for their children but to display dolls and, as such, are highly in demand. From the trade's point of view, they are very easy to store and transport because of their size and are light enough to be carried by everyone. One thing to watch is that normal-sized chairs have not had their legs cut down to capitalise on the demand. Check that everything is in proportion and that the legs are not only even but also suitably scuffed or dirty on their tips.

Some children's chairs and **prams** (very popular for displaying flowers, not just dolls) are made of cane. Reeds and similar materials are carefully bound using set patterns to create attractive but strong patterns, some of which have been used for centuries. These materials wear out and need to be replaced. You can either sell the chair as it is or go to a restorer who will replace the scruffy wickerwork or rush. This is a highly skilled job using specially treated material (often picked in The Netherlands) and there are relatively few specialists. Look up weavers or basketmakers in your local phone directory or speak to other dealers for their recommendations.

Armchairs and Rocking Chairs

In terms of comfort, few chairs can match **armchairs** or **rocking chairs**. As with all chairs, test them out for comfort – if they're not comfortable, don't buy them. Check the rocking of rockers and turn them over to check for damage, wear or potential problems. Reupholstering will firm up chairs or make them more attractive, but such costs have to be taken into account. Ask around before using any restorer or reupholsterer – like building work, it pays to use recommended firms. Check basic elements such as the backs – are they too high or too low? Are you short or tall? All of that has a bearing to a certain extent, especially if you are only buying for yourself and then it's vital but, if you're buying to sell, buyers, like dealers, come in all shapes and sizes and a good chair will sell to anyone.

Special Chairs

Special chairs such as **lambing chairs, monks' benches** or **cardinals' chairs** are hugely appealing but don't fit into all houses. They are too 'heavy' looking for some modern houses but they are also irresistible to those with suitable surroundings. Whilst out of place in ultra-modern homes or airy flats, these wonderfully rich chairs with their dark woods and heavy carvings belong in any home with character.

The lambing chairs are huge, wide enough for the biggest farmer to feed his lambs in front of a fire, with a compartment under the seat to store relevant materials from bottles of milk to bottles of whisky. They're not cheap (expect to pay £300+, depending on quality and age) but they are an asset to any antiques business – they draw people in and even if they don't buy the chair, they'll end up with something else.

Monks' benches are also heavy-looking and even more practical than the lambing chairs. The compartment under the long seat is just one facet to this practical bench, the back also rolls over to form a table top – that's a good selling point.

Cardinal's chairs, like best-selling **church pews**, were originally designed for use in churches. As befitting a cardinal's status, they are grand, often intricately decorated and very comfortable. Some of them even fold and all are very good sellers.

Be careful when buying church pews as there are many modern examples about, not always sold as such. Look to see if modern screws are used or the underside of the bench isn't as 'aged' looking as the seat or back. Modern ones do sell but you don't want to mix antiques and repro/fakes in your business – it will make the rest of your stock seem questionable and *will* lose you custom.

Other Types of Chairs

Don't just look for types of chairs but also look for special features such as a **ladderback** (it looks like it sounds), **shepherd's crook arms** on chairs (which resemble the curved line of a shepherd's crook) and **balloon backs** which balloon out like squashed ovals and support backs. **Hepplewhite** is one of the most highly sought-after designers, alongside **Chippendale**. Some would argue that Chippendale is better but I prefer Hepplewhite who revolutionised chairs – so much so that his shield-back designs are amongst the most copied and you'll see them in virtually all modern furniture shops which sell chairs. Don't buy any 'Hepplewhite' until you know exactly what you're doing – unless it's from one of the reputable auction houses. There are a lot of fakes about to trap the unwary. Never buy Hepplewhite or Chippendale without a provenance (a history showing its authenticity) – you might not be able to sell them otherwise.

Shaker Furniture

Shaker furniture is amongst the most sought after because of its naïve simplicity. There is a lot of fake Shaker furniture about (often made in Eastern Europe) so be careful when buying it. Designs should be simple and almost crude. The original Shakers were a branch of the Quakers in America and didn't have modern tools but modern fakers do. Beware.

Bureaux, Davenports and Desks

I love **bureaux**, they remind me of my great-grandparents who had a beautiful example. Even though I don't sell much furniture, I always look at them when I'm on buying trips and at auctions because I know that they sell. They are not just practical and full of history but they're attractive. They hide your papers and become a tidy way of storing your stockbooks and can always be sold on if you feel like a change or need the money. When you work at an antique desk or a bureau, it never quite feels like work and they have character which modern computer desks lack. Computer desks can be changed as needs expand, bureaux are there to be cherished which makes them best sellers. Look for ones with inner drawers and areas to hold pens, as these are the most popular. If you're thinking about buying **roll-top desks**, check that the tops roll back easily – if they don't then avoid them, they'll be hard to sell.

Even more sought after than bureaux by those in the know are **davenports** (always with a lower case d, never a capital letter). They are scaled down versions of bureaux and are named after the man for whom the first one was originally designed, Captain Davenport, who needed something smaller than a bureau. Davenports often have drawers running down one side and are sometimes very simple but can also be highly ornate. Some have delicate rails like balconies along their tops and, like bureaux and desks, they sell extremely well. Ideal for laptop users.

Tables

You won't just deal in one item of furniture because everyone wants different things and it's easy for a member of the public to buy everything that they need from one business. Tables are amongst the most varied pieces of furniture. They come in all shapes and sizes (but avoid any with uneven tops – they need to be practical). People need different types of tables for different needs and these include:

- **Dining tables** – look for ones with extra 'leaves' (i.e. sections) for easy expansion without taking up too much room when not needed.

- **Refectory tables** – for the larger house or even kitchen. These long, heavy-looking tables need space so avoid them if you don't have it – or if you're selling in an area with smaller houses.

- **Corner tables** – often ornate and easy to store.

- **Nests of tables and occasional tables** – small but practical and great sellers.

- **Side tables.**

- **Card tables** – like anything connected to gambling, good examples – i.e. good quality, either simple or ornate and in good condition – are very popular and reach good prices (a good Georgian version can fetch £1,200 +).

- **Bedside tables and cabinets.**

Avoid any which are too wobbly and insert a folded card under any with a slight wobble. As with all furniture, wrap tables in blankets or thick cloths when transporting to avoid scratches or bumps and invest in some 'antique furniture' polish – it's like moisturiser. You might also want to invest in some dry flower displays/baskets as these help to sell what is, after all, a fairly large, flat surface. If you can, buy dinner services or tea services and lay the table to show potential buyers just how attractive they are, especially when entertaining guests or your family in style. Vases or epergnes (elaborate vases often made of Vaseline glass – that's translucent yellow-green glass – held in place by a silver stand) offer stylish accessories, as do candelabra with good quality matching candles.

Larger Items

Wardrobes are slightly more problematic sellers as size is important. If you have the space, you might want to think about the huge, often French, versions which are good sellers, but not as good as the 'average' sized ones which can fit into any modern home. Wardrobes are practical so check that the rails are strong by lightly tugging on them – or even just looking. Scratch marks will reveal if there is a frequent problem with a faulty rail. Check that the doors shut and look for ones with keys – locked doors sell. Pine, oak (darker than pine, often with the richness of mahogany) and mahogany (rich, dark-coloured wood) are the best sellers as they are hard-wearing and fit into most houses.

Like wardrobes, **sideboards and dressers** can be too large for most houses. They are also not essential items of furniture, unlike tables and chairs, but they are attractive and can be used for displaying sets of plates and dining services until the sideboard is sold. There is a demand for them but it is fairly limited so buy accordingly.

Collectors love displaying their delicate finds in **cabinets** and dealers moving into units or shops always need cabinets to protect their pricier goods. They are relatively easy to find, especially the late Art Nouveau, Art Deco versions with their decorated glass sides. The Deco versions often have beautifully curved sides but might be too large for the average house. Because they are so easy to find, stick to nicer examples and avoid any which don't have keys – the whole point of a cabinet is to keep things safe, be it from children or chance theft. They can often be bought very cheaply at auctions.

Stools, piano stools and **footstools** always sell well because they are practical.

◆ Stools are useful for eating at breakfast bars in the kitchen or when sitting at a dressing table or in front of a mirror. Ones with only three legs cannot be sold at auction because of Health and Safety rules.

◆ Piano stools are not only used by pianists and other musicians but as an extra chair at a dining table. The rotating ones (they rotate to increase or decrease in height, depending on the sitter's needs) are especially popular and have wooden or cushioned seats.

◆ There are two types of footstools. The traditional ones are the best sellers and appeal to a broad spectrum of buyers – I have several in my house which I use daily as I find them comfortable to use because I'm short and they're also the perfect height for reaching into the kitchen cupboards. Then there are **gout stools**. As the name suggests, these were originally intended to lift the legs to help ease the pain and discomfort of gout sufferers. They are still used for this purpose but their rocking form (think of an open V) also appeals to healthy people but only those willing to try them. If you are selling chairs, position the footstools or gout stools in such a way that buyers settle into or onto them when testing the chairs for comfort – they'll sell faster that way.

The best-selling type of furniture is the type which virtually everyone needs, such as **bookcases** which are freestanding or designed to be screwed into the walls. Some have glass doors, others are open. They're not always used for books, many people use them to display china or glass. They don't have to be attractive to sell but, as with all things, the more attractive they are, the more you can charge.

Not everybody needs them, in fact few people do, but **washstands** are very popular at the moment. I use mine as a drinks' cupboard whilst other people use theirs in the kitchen to store crockery. The most attractive ones are Edwardian (1901-1910) and have tiled backs, often Art Nouveau ones. A washstand, as the name suggests, was intended for washing. They are like sturdy tables, sometimes with a cupboard, and are now often used by people who don't have the room or money for large sideboards. They sometimes have at least one towel rail or perhaps one on either side (which some people use to hold oven gloves) and normally have a decorative back which would either be tall or short but was aimed at catching the drips from washing. They would originally have been used to hold large washing jugs and bowls but are now more likely to be used for plants or glasses. They are practical but not often used as originally intended. Some have marble tops (great for pastry making), others wood. Some are simple, others highly decorative and there are modern copies about (often sold as original). Look for unrealistically dyed wood, modern screws, bright, chrome rails and a too clean appearance showing lack of age.

Other Easy-to-Sell Furniture Includes . . .

♦ **Fireplaces, fire surrounds** and **firedogs** (tools for maintaining a fire – poker, tongs, brush and pan, best bought and sold on a stand. Decorative versions sell best). Large fire surrounds are attractive but can be too large to sell.
♦ **Plant stands.**
♦ **Musical instruments** (also sold by specialists) pianos and violins are the best sellers.

Whatever you buy, clean it and keep it at its best by regular polishing for fast sales at the best price. Determining the age of furniture takes time and experience but buy some books and take the time to speak to other dealers and handle furniture – it's the best way to learn. To a certain extent, quality dictates price but look at the turn of a leg and the curve of a chair for extra sellability. To confuse you further, simplicity is as much in demand as decoration but stick to quality and you won't have any problems.

CHAPTER SIX

China

This is probably the most important chapter in this section. This section is not a definitive guide to dealing but aims to show you different areas of collecting and dealing. A quick look round an average antiques fair will show you that the majority of dealers sell china. Even furniture dealers will sell the odd piece of china or are regular sellers of dinner services which complement their tables and sideboards.

China is not just practical but decorative, and even practical examples such as plates and vases should be decorative as well. Simple objects sell but look at them more carefully, study their curves and lines and you'll find that their simplicity is deceptive. What sells is style – it's not always good quality but it should be. Some dealers go for fast profits regardless of style and quality and so can you. I'm not condemning it but I would advise you to think of one, simple fact – you're the person who sees your stock the most so buy something which you'd enjoying seeing for more than a few seconds. Maybe even something which you want for yourself.

I've already discussed whether damaged pieces are worth buying and, on the whole, I'm in favour of buying a few imperfect examples of better goods. At this stage in your career, stick to perfect examples if you can and spend time handling goods, you'll get a better feel for antiques in general that way – it's also a good way of spotting damage – let your fingers do the work for you.

There are thousands of makes of china; from major factories to small, studio potters. Some are better than others, and names should not mean everything, but they often do in this trade. *Follow your own judgement but be aware that unsigned pieces, no matter how wonderful and how well made, are far harder to sell than known names.* This chapter will examine, in very basic details, some of the best and some of the most popular makes of china – they're not always the same thing.

If you want to deal in china, one book is compulsory. It's the china dealers' bible and will help you to maximise both your profit and your knowledge: *Encyclopaedia of British Pottery and Porcelain Marks*, Geoffrey A. Godden (Barrie & Jenkins, London, ISBN 0 257 65782 7). Known as Godden's in the trade – save money and buy it from an antiques fair.

You might also want to invest in the European version, *Directory of European Porcelain*, Ludwig Danckert (NAG Press, an imprint of Robert Hale Ltd, London, ISBN 07198 0013 7). Both of these books contain the marks of most of the major and some minor pottery companies, along with their dates. They are the essential reference books for dealers, especially for identifying and dating china.

Royal Doulton

Royal Doulton is one of the stalwarts of the antiques world. It is very rare to have a single general fair without a piece of this quality china but it takes on many different forms and you might choose to specialise in certain areas or just sell what you like. Previously known as Doulton & Co (and various other names), the company has been in existence since the 19th century (1858 in Lambeth and 1882 in Burslem) and has several, best-selling lines:

♦ **Lambeth Ware and stoneware.** Light-coloured stoneware. Practical pieces such as vases and flagons with detailed moulding and attractive painting – normally in a blue-green colour. It's a strong market but does not appeal to everyone. The Dickens pieces are highly sought after.

♦ **Chine** was created by decorating the pottery through lace to create a tapestried effect, the lace was burnt off in the kiln to create beautifully decorated pieces. Currently under-rated (especially by auctioneers), these are a sound investment but avoid pieces with clumsy moulding or too bright colours – these could be fakes.

♦ **Figures.** Doulton's figures are in demand throughout the world with many still made today. The original Deco figures are the most highly desired with prices to match. Check limbs and heads for signs of repair and look for the more decorative figures with movement, such as dancers, as these are very popular. Child figures sell very well and the limited edition figures such as the royals sell easily. People buy figures in sets so try to build them up to make it easier, but avoid any which are dull or with one colour (eg the Images series) as these are much harder to sell, despite their clean lines.

♦ **Bunnykins.** The dressed rabbit figures have a huge, international market and rightly so. Some of the recent figures lack the attraction of their older counterparts but they are still worth buying – if you like them. Avoid any with out-of-proportion arms as these are not as easy to sell, but stick with tried and tested favourites such as uniformed Bunnykins, girly versions (eg bedtime and ballerinas), any limited by edition or number and any which you like – that's the way to buy them. Hardest to find are the early pieces and these have prices to match but are worth it – look for the teapot, jug and sugar in the shape of rabbits. They're lovely and have hundreds, if not thousands, of potential buyers. Sell them at specialist auction sales via Bonham's (speak to Mark Oliver on 020 7629 6602) for best prices or go to the sale to see the best of the rest. There is a market for the crockery (especially those by Barbara Vernon, a nun and the creator of Bunnykins) but not as strong as that for the figures.

◆ **Brambly Hedge**. Based on the books by Jill Barklem, these dressed mice have a period feel which makes them very appealing – and that's what sells. Encompassing both figures and practical items such as powder pots, teapots and thimbles, the entire range is worth buying – even new from the shops because this market has yet to come into its own but the prices are rising steeply so buy it while you can.

◆ **Character jugs.** These have a fairly ageing market (with apologies) with famous characters and any connected to the antiques business (eg The Auctioneer) or transport (eg The Train Driver) amongst the best sellers. Be careful if selling the miniature versions which are easily 'palmed' (stolen by being fitted into the palm of a hand) – possibly because of the high prices they command.

With the possible exception of some of their recent, Far East made pieces such as the houses (poor quality and design), anything by Doulton is collectable.

◆ Other ranges to consider include:
  – animals – dressed or otherwise
  – birds
  – the Snowman (based on the book by Raymond Briggs) figures and crockery
  – flambé (rich, red-coloured pieces)
  – Disney and Winnie the Pooh
  – dolls – yet to come into their own so buy now while they're still relatively cheap
  – but avoid dinner services as these are hard to sell, even with the Doulton name.

Beswick

Pronounced Bez-ick (the 'w' is silent), this pottery, now closed, was owned by the Royal Doulton Group since 1969 but, even before that, Doulton dealers often sold Beswick as well because the quality and collectors are similar. The Beswick range is vast but stick to best-sellers such as animals and birds, especially ducks (or anything connected to Peter Scott). Humorous animals, such as those by David Hands, command high prices. Other ranges to consider include:

- Beatrix Potter figures (the Royal Albert versions sell but not as well). Best buy is the early Duchess model which didn't sell as well originally because it looked like a black lump. Later demand pushed the price up in excess of £1,500.

- Kitty McBride – crudely detailed dressed mice.

- Winnie the Pooh and other children's book characters, including Alice in Wonderland and Rupert the Bear.

- Face masks (animals and humans) and the wall-mounted floral displays are all good buys.

Royal Worcester

It is not simple to define Royal Worcester. The factory has produced a vast range including blush (cream-pink delicate china in the form of vases and dishes), beautifully-moulded figures, birds and figural candle-snuffers (but ignore the recent ones which lack the design and gentle colouring of the earlier pieces – they're too garish). There is far more to Worcester (pronounced Woo-ster) than just these ranges but these are the best. It is not a cheap make but the quality is outstanding and pieces are getting harder to buy – get them while you can and stick to perfect pieces where possible. Check them carefully, as they are very delicate and damage easily.

Clarice Cliff

One of the most sought-after makes of china is Clarice Cliff which, for many, personifies the Art Deco movement. Originally made as cheap, usable pottery for Woolworth's, it's surprising how many people still use their Clarice – but they shouldn't. This is one of the priciest makes on the market with a coffee can (small cup) and saucer selling for £250 +, depending on the pattern and that is the key to Clarice – the name is not enough, it is the patterns which sell. Stick to the brightly coloured ones in the stylish, geometric designs. Avoid trumpet vases – they look wonderful, but can be hard to sell. The moulded creamy pieces lack the best-selling decorations of the pricier pieces but they still have their market. Ignore plain plates or scarcely decorated meat platters, these don't sell as well and take up a lot of room. Like everything, don't depend on a name but go for originality of design and colour. Clarice sells – even having one piece can get you past a fair's waiting list.

Charlotte Rhead

This stylish designer was Clarice's contemporary. Famed for her tubular (thick, tube-like lines of paint) decoration, she worked with a variety of potteries – hers was the decoration, not the pottery itself. Her pieces are getting increasingly hard to find but are worth buying. She stands for everything a dealer should want – quality, style and originality. Unlike Clarice, her work was not cheap fodder for the masses and, in my opinion, is far superior and a much better buy.

Susie Cooper

Susie Cooper is probably the third ranking of these three designers. Her work was mainly practical and she's most notable for her tea sets and dinner services, but it's her art pottery that is the most interesting with even leading auctioneers not always able to recognise it. Her prices have dipped recently but demand is set to return so buy it while you can – stick to the more stylish and appealing pieces and leave anything too mundane. If you're at home, raid your own kitchen cupboards, you might even have a few bits in there.

Burleigh

Burgess and Leigh combined to produce Burleigh, a highly original range of pottery whose jugs and Art Deco tea and dinner services are highly sought after. The cups often have decorative moulding in the handles and are gorgeous designs. They were everywhere when I was growing up in the business but they're hard to find now. The factory was restarted in the 1990s and, unfortunately, their reproduction jugs were adopted as 'genuine' by some unscrupulous dealers before the factory realised (thanks to an article I wrote in *The Dealer*) and changed the mark to prevent this from happening again – in theory, at least. If you're not sure what you're doing, speak to a specialist dealer and ask for their advice. The colours of the modern jugs are different but only if you know what the originals were. Avoid any with questionable paintwork – they've probably been repainted to look genuine. Don't be afraid to buy genuine Burleigh, you'll get used to spotting fakes very easily and the originals are worth it.

Shelley

English china at its best. Shelley is renowned for its tea sets, with trios (cup, saucer and tea plate) commanding high prices. One of the best of the Deco firms, stick to the stylish and you'll sell well. Best buys are the Mabel Lucie Attwell figures and tea services. Like Burleigh, their children's china sells very well. Shelley dealers find that Burleigh complements their existing stock and, if you can't afford or don't want to sell a lot of Deco, you might want to consider just combining Shelley with Burleigh – if you like them.

Goldscheider

One of the most popular of the Continental potteries, Goldscheider is not cheap but offers stunning pieces from figures to wallmasks from the Deco period, as well as distinctive terracotta facemasks. Their animals are very good sellers and the whole range is worth buying, whether you're a Deco specialist or a general dealer. The pieces are so eye-catching that a single piece is enough to offset any stall, no matter what you sell. Several pieces can be too overpowering but they have a very good following and their comical animals are superb if the figures are too much for your taste.

Royal Copenhagen

The Danish pottery has a strong market, not just for the trademark blue and white china but its animals with their distinctive, slightly blurry glaze (lending them a gentle look) and harder to find studio pottery. Copenhagen offers very good quality (seconds are marked and sold as such – except by dishonest or ignorant dealers – look for marks on the bases) and simple but attractive designs, whilst the studio pottery takes on many forms but retains both the quality and originality of their main output. There are specialist dealers, suggesting that the market is strong enough. Don't be afraid to specialise because you'll not only attract the Copenhagen collectors and dealers but people who collect particular animals – their dogs are especially popular.

Poole

Poole is a strange make, almost schizophrenic in design but highly collectable. Most people think of Poole in its 1960's style, white-cream matt china with swirling decorations in pastel colours in the form of deer and bluebirds, but it's much more than that. From matt-coloured, heavy-looking, pastelly animals, to heavy-set tiles and brightly coloured studio pieces, to fairly bland animals in matt-brown or a blue-green glaze, the pottery has done it all and turned back in on itself. Modern Poole has returned to its studio pottery days but using modern colours, bright reds and yellows, instead of the original bright orange and lime green. The work is vibrant and worth buying now and selling later – stockpile what you can now. Poole is easy to find but not always worth buying. Avoid damaged pieces and the mundane – bigger can be better but style is everything.

Goebel and Hummel

Produced at the same factory, Goebel and Hummel are the best of the continental firms to have become fully integrated into British collecting. This could be because of the humorous side to their designs, as well as their obvious quality.

Goebel pieces are glazed, often marked with a bee or a 'V' sign (if it isn't actually marked Goebel) and very distinctive because of the humour. They mix well with many types of china, including Poole, Sylvac, Carlton Ware, Beswick and Wade, and occupy the novelty side of dealing, even their ornaments are novelties. Look for the monks and monkeys, long-term favourites in the collecting world.

Hummel, by comparison, is sedate and nostalgic. The matt figures based on the work of the nun, Sister Maria Innocentia Hummel, depict young children from a bygone age of innocence, even the chimney sweep is adorable. The market is strong and Hummel is not as ubiquitous as it once was but it's a good, fun market whichever name you pick.

Sylvac

You will have seen lots of Sylvac at fairs, even if you don't realise it. They are famed for their matt-finished (i.e. not glossy) animals, especially rabbits and Scotties. There are a lot of fakes around, which depressed the market for a while, but the fakes are easy to avoid – if you know what to spot. Go for detailed moulding, dull-looking colours and smooth signatures – the fakes are either shiny or too new-looking, they're often a bit jerky as well, especially where the signatures are concerned. Don't avoid Sylvac but avoid its fakes. Best buys are the animals, face pots (designed to hold condiments and jams) and some of the prettier vases – avoid anything too mundane unless you know the market well.

> **Useful tip**
> Dogs are good sellers regardless of make or material, be it china, glass or jewellery but stick to the top three sellers if you're not sure of your market – Scotties, poodles and Dalmatians are the top dogs.

Wade and Wadeheath

Wadeheath is often regarded as the least important part of Wade but, in many ways, they produced superior goods including Disney figurals, tea services and stunning Deco jugs as well as matt animals which are often mistaken for Sylvac (the rabbit, often found unmarked, has the code 509). Virtually everybody over 25 has owned a piece of Wade sometime in their life. Most people think of Wade as the Whimsey-producing pottery.

Whimsies, pocket money animals, were huge business, but don't reflect the true extent of the factory which produced everything from tiles for space shuttles to toilet accessories – but most dealers ignore those and stick to the established favourites of:

♦ Animals – Whimsies, drumboxes (a band), dogs, horses – everything, really.

♦ Disney – hatboxes and their larger counterparts, blow-ups, various animals and jugs and Snow White figures (two sets).

♦ TV and book favourites – including TV pets (dogs and a cat) and the Noddy set.

♦ Irish Wade – green-blue coloured china and a range of elves – highly underrated so buy while you can.

♦ Houses – still affordable but prices rising fast. The smaller figures sell best but storage jars, teapots, milk and sugar are also worth considering.

♦ Practical stuff – vases, jugs, ashtrays, musical jugs, plates, bowls, dinner and tea services etc. Prices rising but not as good as the animals unless they're Deco.

♦ Teapots – figural ones (such as the ducks) are the best sellers.

♦ Advertising – figurals are the best but the rest sell as well, even old pub ashtrays.

♦ Art Deco ladies – the paint peels (except for the hard to find, extremely pricey and very pretty glazed versions) but are still worth buying. Check that arms, legs and hands are original – they tend to damage easily and restoration is not always mentioned. Dogs were also made using the same materials, all but the Alsatians are hard to find.

♦ Large, glazed animals by Faust Lang (and others), often on a green-blue base – the best of Wade's output, in my opinion – get them if you see them as they're hard to find. Check the stag's antlers – the originals were bones which were just inserted into the holes and most of them have been lost but dealers have been known to 'add' versions – it can reduce their value.

◆ Face masks – four in all, rare but perfect Deco buys.

◆ Modern limited editions – everything from The Magic Roundabout's Dougal to Betty Boop.

These are just a few examples. Wade is one of the best of the collectables around but quality is often lacking. Be careful when buying and selling the modern, limited editions – the quality is often poor with the paintwork uneven and the moulding haphazard. There are almost too many of them to be viable – avoid if you can, unless you really like them. Just remember that the collectors can buy them from the same place as you – and for the same price. Recognisable limited edition pieces such as Yogi Bear and the Clangers sell but non-recognisable characters can suffer.

Be very careful when using the Wade price guides – prices are often completely wrong – far too high or far too low but do contain useful information about pieces, with photographs – ideal for spotting unsigned items.

Szeiler

Currently going through a revival, Szeiler dealers often sell Wade as well – some of the pieces are very similar and both sets of dealers can find themselves picking up the wrong make by mistake. The animals are often comical with a distinctive brown-blue-grey colouring (similar to some of the Wade pieces from the 1950-60s). Prices are rising fast but animals sell so they're a sound buy.

Carlton Ware

Carlton has a wide range of goods with collectors for all but the dullest pieces (of which there are many). I sell a lot of it because it's fun and certain areas are still very affordable. You might choose to sell across the board or stick to one or two specialist areas, thinking of other types of collectors (such as teapots). Best buys are:

◆ Floral embossed – practical pieces (eg teapots, toastracks, cruets etc), such as buttercups and anemones moulded to resemble flowers.

- Art Deco – jazzy, geometric designs.
- Rouge royale and similar – hand-decorated artistic works, with richly coloured bases (rouge royale is a rich red with gold trimmings).
- Teapots – amongst the best of the novelty makers.
- Cruets – novelty and ornate.
- Toastracks – novelty and stylish.
- Animals – practical and ornamental from sheep biscuit barrels to ribbed dogs.
- Blush.
- Figures and powder bowls.
- Advertising – especially Guinness figures but be wary of the brightly coloured, badly-moulded fakes.
- Tea services – generally stylish sellers.
- Walking ware – various legs and feet in a variety of practical applications from teapots to napkin rings – fun and easy to sell.
- Alice in Wonderland.

There are a lot of fakes about, especially of the Guinness pieces, but they're easy to spot – colours are too bright, the moulding too clumsy. Other fakes include:

- golfers
- Hitler
- tortoise cruets
- liner (as in ship)
- tank.

Crown Devon

Sharing many of the same designers, potters and paintresses as Carlton Ware, Crown Devon has yet to come fully into its own which makes it a good investment or specialist area. It covers a huge range, including some beautifully painted pieces very similar to those produced by the Carlton Ware factory (not surprising since they had the same designers). Other best buys include the figures (very similar to Wade's cellulose-painted ones but with thicker paint – be careful that you don't get caught out buying the wrong make) and dogs' heads. Vases are good, especially the more elaborately designed ones. Stick to good designs and you can't go wrong.

Royal Winton

Winton is a very good make of china which came out of the Grimwades factory and is often sold by dealers selling Carlton Ware's floral embossed range. There is Winton and Winton but its chintz (floral) designs are amongst the most popular, especially the pattern, 'Julia'. Winton is currently reproducing some of its more distinctive ranges but with a special backstamp – be careful as these can be altered with relative ease so check that all backstamps and bases are smooth before buying any of the chintz. Best buys are the chintz and petunia (in pink or yellow) pieces.

Maling

Famous for its lustrous glazes in pinks and bright greens (amongst others), Maling influenced other potters such as Arthur Woods, but remained the best and is highly sought after but pricey. It's very distinctive once you know it – and complements the Winton range very well (and vice versa).

Masons

A good quality firm which appeals to the 'serious' dealer. Whilst it is often hard to determine the age of this highly decorated pottery with its white/cream background because the same mark was used for decades, look for signs of age in the quality of the patterning and the creaminess of the surround. Lovely pieces designed for use from jam pots to dinner services. A good, solid market.

Midwinter

If you got married in the 1950–60s, chances are that your dinner service was by Midwinter and that's what makes it such a good seller. Not only are people buying replacement cups and dinner services but they're also buying nostalgia; dinner services which depict an era. Quality of design with quality of china, opt for the most stylish and sellable pieces from the 1950-60s – Riviera and Cannes, France at its best with its yachts, umbrellas and outdoor cafés designed by Sir Hugh Casson. Firm favourites and not just yet more plates.

Blue and White

The name says it all. Blue and white china has been the favourite colouring for factories such as Spode since 1790, and some dealers and buyers specialise in the dinner services, jugs and bowls which they and other potteries produced. Serving platters, toastracks and tureens are good sellers but avoid it if you want more colour in your life. That said, it's a strong market with more buyers than you might expect.

Wedgwood

Particularly popular with American buyers, Wedgwood is renowned for its Jaspar Ware – white cameos, most famously on a blue base. Other colours sell, especially black, but the blue is the perennial favourite. Wedgwood also did biscuit (rough, matt finish) figures but they are not as good sellers.

Moorcroft

There is a lot of Moorcroft on the market at the moment, much of it modern. Some might argue that there's enough and could advise you to avoid it, but there *is* a market for it. Go to the specialist sales to get an idea of just how good the factory is at its best but try to avoid just dealing in Modern Moorcroft – you might not be allowed into all fairs and centres with it.

Moorland is a division of the Moorcroft factory and has yet to come into its own so be careful if buying it at the moment. **Cobridge** is another part of the pottery and has a following but is not quite there – keep an eye on it because it could develop its own, separate identity soon. It needs to.

The Rye Potters

A small town on the Kent-Sussex borders has produced several factories whose staff have often swapped over, lending the potteries a sameness – it doesn't mean that they're unoriginal but they have the same, basic feeling – with a touch of originality. Still a growing area, it's worth checking out and doing what I've done – stockpiling until the market comes into its own. The potteries include:

- Rye (the most established of them all)
- David Sharp (the best of the four at the moment – especially his animals and moneyboxes)
- Iden
- Cinque Ports (based at the Monastery, Rye).

Wemyss and Plichta

Pronounced Wee-mm-zz and Plick-tah, they are virtually the same pottery but aimed at different types of people. To put it tactfully, Plichta (with its trademark thistles, spots or bubble-type decoration) is the cheaper version and renowned for its animals and animal cruets. The most famous collector of Wemyss was the Queen Mother. There are two basic forms of Wemyss – animals or practical goods such as plant pots with their trademark roses (hence the Queen Mother's interest) and the smaller, practical and more affordable range with its trademark chicken. Try to stick to animals for easy sales and avoid Plichta's white, bubbly-type pieces – they're not attractive and hard to sell. Pigs are the best sellers and range from the small and sweet, through to practical ones (such as pomanders) to the grotesquely huge with matching prices. Cats are the next best sellers.

Denby

I always have the odd bit of Denby on my stall, from electric blue vases to their famous, hollowed-out eyed lambs. Denby's vast range is not always marked but the animals are very distinctive with their almost chalky finish. Avoid the later tea and dinner services as they're very heavy and not great sellers and stick to the animals, figural hot water bottles (penguin, hare etc), moulded vases (eg chalky-type effect with pastel-coloured fish, flowers and insects), electric blue designs and the big vases, jugs and pot plants from the 1950–70s by the likes of Glynn Colledge. Denby is notable for its heavy-set pottery, which can make it heavy to carry and the larger pieces take up a lot of room but they are worth it. I think that Denby is still one of the most underrated of the potteries (along with Langley Pottery Ltd which united with Denby in 1976) and the unmarked animals offer huge profit potential for those with the necessary – and very easy to learn – knowledge.

Studio Pottery

Studio pottery can take on many forms. It doesn't have to be brown, but often is, it doesn't have to be clumsily moulded but can be and, annoyingly, it isn't always signed. It can be practical or ornate and is made by a single potter or a small pottery. Studio pottery covers a vast area but some dealers concentrate on one area alone – Devon. Devonware is huge business and some of the best potters were based there, including Brannam and Baron – two of my own favourites, especially their pieces which include fish, animals or lizards. It's impossible for a guide of this size to list all of the studio potters but a few of the best include:

- **Bernard Leach** – brown but a best-seller.
- **Bernard Rooke** – animals and dragonflies sell well but try to hang on to them for a while if you can until the market is firmly established.
- **Brannam** – trademark rich blue or green finish. Animal figures are a good buy as are their fish vases but try to avoid harder-to-sell yellow.
- **Baron** – especially the lizard and animal ranges.
- **Basil Matthews** – stick to the 1950s, flowery animal range if you can find it or his dogs.

There are a lot more studio potters than this but I have tried to give you a taster. You might not want the best-selling but very dull brown pieces or, for a change, the dull green pieces, but there is a market for them. I stuck to the more attractive figural ones which have mass appeal and don't need knowledge to sell – I have it but my buyers don't and that can make selling difficult if prices are high for no obvious aesthetic reason (i.e. they're not very pretty).

Other Makes

This chapter is designed to give you a guide to what's out there. I have tried to include the best-sellers but am aware that not everyone is mentioned – space is a factor but so is availability. There are a lot of other good factories such as Minton with its Majolica ware (heavy-looking, brown-blue pieces with a Continental feel), Spode, Grays, Satsuma (Japanese pieces with distinctive decoration) and Radford but I hope that I have given you a feel of what is out there. You don't have to read books but they are worth buying or getting free from your local library (ask them to order them in – they'll charge you a small fee but it will save you money in the long run) if only to look at the pictures. One of the best of the reference books dealers is Bobby's Books who offer a mail order service (01474 823388 or *Bobbysbooks@aol.com*) and attends many of the larger fairs and they'll know which books are worth reading and which aren't.

Collectables magazines will give you further ideas, but take care as they are often focused on modern pieces and you can't sell brand new pieces at all the fairs and rightly so – why should people pay to get into antiques fairs when they can go into their local china shop for free? *Try to buy good quality pieces with original designs, something which appeals to you or other people when you feel more confident.*

I should say that I have deliberately not mentioned Staffordshire – they made the famous fireside dogs (vaguely spaniels) which many people's parents or grandparents had at home, possibly even on their mantelpieces. Staffordshire is being faked hugely and I don't want you to get caught out. There are some ways of spotting the worst fakes easily (shiny, white bases, crudely moulded and painted, overly even crazing) but the better ones could catch you out and some so-called reputable dealers are even selling the fakes with guarantees – because they think that they can get away with it. Unless it's your passion or you know exactly what you're doing, avoid it – otherwise you could lose a lot of money and your reputation by selling on fake goods.

What sells?

So you want to sell china or just a few pieces of it. What should you be buying, regardless of make?

- figures – especially ones based on famous people or with 'movement' such as dancers or nymphs
- animals – dressed or otherwise, serious or comical
- jugs – better sellers than vases as they can be hung up for attractive displays
- trios (cups, saucers and plates) but not tea sets unless they're very stylised or by good makes (eg Burleigh, Shelley or Susie Cooper)
- coffee cans – they're small coffee cups with saucers
- wall masks, hangings or pockets (wall pockets are vases which are designed to be hung flat against a wall)
- candle-snuffers
- toastracks
- teapots
- cruets
- biscuit barrels
- candlesticks (attractive or figural ones only)
- sugar shakers (can be mistaken for hatpin stands)
- hatpin stands
- napkin rings – especially figural versions
- bells – unusual ones only.

What not to buy

- dinner services – notoriously hard to sell and take up a lot of room both in your car and on your stall. One broken piece and your profit's gone
- anything big, heavy or which takes up a lot of room – this can included Denby, unfortunately – it's up to you
- tea services – unless they're special
- incomplete dinner or tea service – unless they're special
- damaged pieces – again, unless they're special (but I sell them with ease – it's your choice).

CHAPTER SEVEN

Glass

A fast-developing specialist area which now has specialist glass fairs, you might want to concentrate on glass or just sell a few pieces. Either way, they sell best if well-lit so invest in some lights and, if you only have a few pieces, think about displaying them on the top of your shelves where they will attract the most light – and the most attention.

Minor chips can be smoothed out but avoid decanters without stoppers – these are very hard to sell and an obviously wrong stopper will decrease its value.

Specialist dealers will know what they're selling whilst general dealers might only have a vague idea – allowing your superior knowledge to profit from them. Do be careful as some of the types of glass are still produced today and it can be hard-to-impossible to tell the difference.

If you thought glass was only Murano clowns, read on, it's much more than that – but only if you take the time to learn. There are many makes and types of glass – I say types because several firms produce the same 'type' of glass such as slag glass (made when the slag from iron smeltworks is added to glass to produce streaks).

Baccarat

One of the best of the glass makes and often sold by Lalique dealers, the heavy glass combines style and originality. Expensive but worth it. Decanter and glass backstamp.

Caithness

Caithness is famous for its paperweights but offers more than that. Rich colours and good designs combine to create one of Scotland's best exports loved by the royal family and the public (and dealers) alike.

Carnival Glass

This iridescent glass with its slightly oily-looking finish comes in a variety of colours with orange (marigold) or purple being the most popular. Once given away as prizes at carnivals, it has recently become sellable again after its height 20 years ago. Avoid any with too heavy mould marks. Bowls are fairly common but sell well – vases and punch bowls with matching cups are good sellers.

Cloud Glass

This attractive colourful glass has a swirly cloudy finish, hence the name, and is popular with the public because it is relatively cheap and pretty.

Daum

Pronounced Dome, this stunning glass was one of the most important art glass makers of the Art Nouveau and is still highly desirable. Instantly recognisable for its trademark, iridescent finish, its pieces range from practical cups and vases to stylish animals. Modern Daum is as inventive as its predecessor – and can be just as expensive, especially when produced in small editions.

Gallé

Pronounced Gal-lay (a short a, like Gallic, not garlic), this is possibly the best of the glass firms. Famous for its 'return to nature', Gallé is fantastic – they used acid-etching or delicate paintings to create trees and flowers in the glass, producing layers of colours in a top-quality design. My favourite of all of the glass makers.

Lalique

This translucent make of glass with its distinctive, iridescent blue-ish finish is one of the best firms on the market. Their range of car mascots, designed for the bonnets of cars, are late Art Nouveau, early Deco in design and are highly sought after. Anything by Lalique sells if the price is right – the quality is always there and even their later pieces such as colourful, one-inch fish have a market. Quality of workmanship and style – buy what you can when you can – older pieces fetch huge sums, especially from the Art Nouveau and Deco periods – so be prepared to spend good money buying them.

Mary Gregory Style

Possibly not as old as it looks, Mary Gregory style's distinctive glass with its charming cameos of children at play is still made today. The colours of the glass are rich – reds and greens – with the painted white children added to create both nostalgia and something for the future. Not seen as often as it should be, this is definitely an area you should consider. It's the name of a style, made by several makes.

Monart and Vasart

Linked by the same designers but at different glassworks, Monart and Vasart are Scotland's best and most famous glassmakers – apart from Caithness. Very similar in design, Vasart is usually marked while Monart has a smudge within a circle on its base, once hidden by a paper label. The pale bases give way to coloured tops with Vasart having more pastelly colours than Monart and often coloured, central swirls. Collectors want both of the makes so try to stock both if you can find them.

Murano

One of the best-known of the glass names, Murano is actually not the name of a glass factory but is an Italian island with several glassworks, producing the famous, brightly-coloured (dare I say garish?) glass clowns and sweets. Colours are bright and quality is often lacking but there's a solid market and it's a good seller. One warning, though, it can look very cheap next to better quality glass.

Night Lights

The most famous maker of night lights (aka fairy lights) is Price's. An old dealer's trick is to feel the bottom of the base's interior – the breasts on the namesake Price fairy stick up – it's an easy way of confirming the make without having to read anything. Straightforward night lights are domes on bases and are colourless. More popular versions come in colours but the best-selling ones are the shapes. Most sought after are Queen Victoria or the baby's head. The owl sells well as do the flowers which, with their delicate china tops are good sellers but prone to damage, especially the rose. Avoid damaged versions and go for the more unusual ones but expect to pay – they're very popular at the moment. Night lights were designed to keep candles safe when burning at night – very popular for keeping children safe and the dark at bay.

Vaseline Glass

Vaseline glass has a thick, translucent, yellow-green appearance like Vaseline. It sells particularly well to the American market and comes in a variety of uses, most popular of which is the epergne, special vases arranged in silver stands and very good sellers.

Whitefriars

To some dealers, Whitefriars is synonymous with the bark-like vases which they made in rich, bright colours such as red, green and amber. Others think of it in terms of the richly coloured glass with bubbles, used in practical pieces such as ashtrays and also in animals with the penguin being the most sought after – and worth buying damaged just to have an example. Whitefriars offers a full range, often distinctive just for the richness of its colouring but all worth buying and selling – or even collecting. Most of the pieces are still affordable but prices are climbing fast

One of the most avid collectors was a friend of mine, Brian Chopping, whose wife, Jean, bought him an Art Nouveau piece of Whitefriars (a sage-green basket, completely different from the better known ranges) on Carlton Television's *It's a Gift*. I am honoured to say that I now own a piece of Whitefriars from Brian's own collection which Jean very kindly gave me shortly after his premature death. This section has been written with them both in mind.

Best Pieces and Colours

Glass comes in different shapes and colours. Some pieces sell better than others and some colours will sell well, no matter what they are. The easiest to sell pieces are:

♦ **Decanters** – but only with their original stoppers, avoid topless decanters.

♦ **Vases** – more so than jugs.

♦ **Paperweights** – a huge market. John Ditchfield with his distinctive, iridescent glass is one of the most popular but his pieces might not be a long-lasting trend – be careful, prices have risen since they were hyped on a television show and might come crashing down soon.

♦ **Glasses** – Georgian glasses have a huge market but not many general dealers would recognise them. Buy stylish examples, no matter what you're buying.

♦ **Witches balls** – hollow balls of glass intended to trap witches trying to break into houses.

♦ **Figures** – especially fish – and clowns.

Best colours are:

♦ cranberry – pink-red like the fruit
♦ red

- ◆ amethyst – hold it up to the light to distinguish it from black
- ◆ green
- ◆ turquoise
- ◆ iridescent purple-green
- ◆ clear
- ◆ orange
- ◆ amber – but not brown, often a very subtle difference.

To a specialist, glass is not just glass and there are certain countries which excel at it – France and Scotland produced very different but collectable glass whilst Bohemia is much underrated. Rumanian fish – so popular at Bingo halls in the 1970s – have a devoted following (but try not to give in to it). As with all things, go for design. Georgian glasses have their own specialists so learn from them. If you see something that you like on someone's stall, ask them for advice if they're not busy. Glass is a strange area, it's a relatively recent mass-specialist area and there is still a lot to learn so take advantage of this and buy what you like. If you live in or near London, take the time to visit the antiques centres which have several specialists. I'd suggest Grays (020 7629 7034), Alfies (020 7723 6066) and Antiquarius (020 7351 5353) – they have more specialist dealers than most other centres I know, with a good selection of all of the above mentioned glass makes and types as well as other makes such as Mdina and easy-to-sell crystal.

CHAPTER EIGHT

Gold and Silver

When I first started dealing, gold and silver were bought for the metal; they would be sold according to weight, not usage or design and then melted down. I saw dozens of exquisite Georgian pieces change hands knowing that they would be destroyed and their history melted away. It probably still happens but people now buy for beauty and design.

> **Useful tip**
> You have got to buy a hallmark book if you wish to be a gold, silver or jewellery dealer. This is not a suggestion but the law dictates that there should be hallmark guides present when such goods are being sold so make sure that you have a copy with you to avoid trouble. They're available from bookshops and at fairs from antiques bookdealers. The best of the lot is the classic and recently revised *Bradbury's Book of Hallmarks* by Frederick Bradbury (Robert Hale, London). Unlike the others, it encompasses gold and platinum hallmarks as well as silver and silver plate.

Learn the most common hallmarks (eg Birmingham's anchor) and as much as you can without having to resort to the book. Some dealers will change the age of a piece, using an authentic hallmark on a later piece (known as a marriage) – by knowing what you're doing, you'll avoid a costly mistake. This change does not happen often but always check that bases are original and don't have tell-tale lumps at the side where they've been replaced.

Just because something is silver or gold, it does not automatically make it sellable. Go for well-designed or stylish pieces – bigger is not necessarily more expensive and some of the smaller pieces such as silver (or pewter) snuffboxes sell exceptionally well.

There are established favourites which are always worth considering. These include:

◆ teapots and coffee-pots – sometimes found with matching milk and sugar
◆ toastracks – especially stylish ones such as those by Liberty
◆ tankards

- small boxes such as pillboxes or snuffboxes
- candlesticks
- bowls, including punchbowls and rosebowls – but sometimes not as good as some of the other pieces
- platters or large plates
- display stands for preserve jars
- salt cellars
- pepper pots – often found in figural form eg a kangaroo or a chick
- mustard pots
- cruets
- vestas – match boxes, often found in figural form eg dice or a gun
- photo frames
- cigarette cases – often used for business cards
- business card cases
- tie-pins
- scissors
- knives – including letter openers.

Buy a gold tester (sold at the larger fairs) for non-hallmarked or more costly pieces.

Attractive displays and clean goods increase sales but rinse carefully after cleaning to remove unsightly residue. See Section Three, Chapter Nine (page 159) for more details on careful cleaning.

If dealing in smaller objects such as vestas, invest in a jewellery case. Safety precautions (see the next chapter) should also be followed, especially as you will be carrying a lot of cash in this often costly market. You'll also need suitable packaging material such as bubble wrap, jewellery bags and quality carrier bags for your quality stock.

CHAPTER NINE

Jewellery

The practicalities:

- If you are going to sell jewellery, invest in some cabinets which can be locked.
- Never leave a cabinet unlocked or you could lose everything.
- Never leave your jewellery in your car or stop for a drink near a fair with your jewellery in your car – it could be stolen.

Right, that's the annoying part. Jewellery dealers can get targeted but common sense and being careful can avoid some of the opportunistic problems. For the multiple-day fairs, never leave your stock at the fair like other dealers – the security is good but there could be problems with late-leaving or early-arriving dealers. Be sensible and you shouldn't have any problems.

As well as locked jewellery cabinets, you will need jewellery bags, ring boxes, display stands, special jewellery labels, glass polish, jewellery pliers, jewellery scales and a special jewellery magnifying glass (a loupe). No matter how good you might think your eyes are, a loupe will help you see that bit better – essential when buying and selling quality stones. If dealing in diamonds, you will also need a diamond tester which you can buy at larger fairs.

There are different grades of jewellery dealers. Work out what you can afford and buy within that framework. You might find it easier to buy at auction but check out all of the stones and fittings before you buy anything to ensure that they are all as described.

A quick glance at fairs will show you that gold is the preferred metal, although silver, white gold and platinum have their own market. Plain gold is fine but stones also sell well. Depending on your market, you will need different types and grades of stones with different cuts from cabochon (domed) to faceted (cut to reflect the light – facet means face). Get to learn your stones by speaking to jewellers and handling jewellery at auctions as well as reading books. You need to handle jewellery to get a sense of it.

One of the tricks for selling jewellery for gifts or impulse buys is to display a chart or carefully written sign with birth stones, emphasising their meaning. It's cheap to do but helps sales. You might even do a focused display on the stone of the month – eg May

(Taurus) is emerald.

Always clean your jewellery or have it professionally cleaned before trying to sell it. Clean your cabinets on a regular basis as they smear when people touch them to look at, or point out, their contents.

What Sells Best?

Rings, earrings and brooches are the best-selling types of jewellery, with necklaces and lockets coming next and bracelet sales falling recently as fewer people wear them. Buy a ring sizer from jewellery accessory supply outlets (see your local telephone directory or visit suppliers at fairs). This means that you can tell people what size ring finger they have and sell rings to people who want surprise presents – it's a cheap but efficient way of increasing sales. You might also want to sell watches and maybe even some clocks – they often go to the same type of buyers.

The best stones are the most obvious ones. Buy as high and as good quality as you can afford – diamonds, rubies, sapphires and emeralds if you can, topaz, amber, garnet, amethyst and peridot if not – or combine them all. Always stock pearls as these have a very strong market, especially in the summer when weddings increase. Get different lengths from chokers to ropes and, for the 16–18 inch necklaces (the best-sellers), go for plain and graduated pearls as both are in demand.

> **Useful tip**
> Graduated pearls use different sizes of pearls, starting small with larger ones towards the centre. Pearls are damaged by water, hairspray and perfume so tell your non-trade customers to keep their necklaces/earrings away from them. Pearls come in different colours with the creamy ones selling the best, followed by the pink-cream ones with grey/black pearls generally selling to older, more sophisticated women. Check that pearls are real by rubbing them against each other – they'll feel slightly abrasive. Fake pearls will feel smooth. Pearls improve their lustre if worn regularly so don't be afraid to wear your stock – or lend them to someone who will.

You might find that more traditional goods sell the best so buy accordingly – start off small, get to know your market and expand.

Costume Jewellery

This is a much neglected area except by specialists, but it is surprisingly easy to find good buys with very good profit potential – and that's one of the reason why you want to become a dealer.

Let me tell you something very basic about dealing in costume jewellery – *if it's not signed, they won't buy it.* Some dealers will take the risk, and most of the public don't know any better for the simple reason that most dealers don't know anything about this area so they're not used to seeing signed pieces and won't understand why most of the pieces, however exquisite, cost more than £5, but specialist dealers will and *they won't buy unsigned pieces.*

The costume jewellery market is picking up from a real low. I used to specialise in it but got out to open a shop when the market started to dip. It crashed shortly after, but some dealers stuck at it and it's now reached an acceptable point, but prices are still depressed from their peak in the mid 1990s. One of the reasons for this is that the main buyers are not around – the Italians who used to buy costume jewellery by the armful.

The costume jewellery world is very small and everyone knows each other so I'll let you into one of our secrets – never, ever do 'sale or return' (which is when you give someone the goods on the understanding that they'll pay you when they sell the goods or return what they can't sell – a very bad way of doing business, whatever you sell). Not all dealers are honest and some will ask for goods on credit – and you'll never see them – or a penny – again. Most of the dealers are lovely and happy to give advice. Just be careful – there are some questionable dealers in the trade.

Costume jewellery is wonderful, you have the appearance of real gemstones without either the security worries or the cost, but that does not mean that it's all cheap – you can still expect to pay £250+ for good brooches by some of the top names such as Chanel and Miriam Haskell.

What many people don't realise about this area is that names count, some of the top designers owned or worked for fashion houses or real jewellers and it shows.

Makes like Ciner started out making real jewellery and used these techniques in their range of costume jewellery. Crystal stones are kept in place in the same way as real gems, the only difference is in the materials used. The quality is superb.

What's in a name?

Profit. You see, the right name can add pounds to the price of a piece of costume jewellery and the wrong name can lose you a sale. Some of the designers, such as Trifari, have ranges comparable to the best and most extensive of the china companies. Trifari can sell for a few pounds for a gold-coloured brooch to a few hundred for a 'jelly belly' – that's a clear 'stone' which looks like jelly. You could even end up paying more for Miriam Haskell's fake pearls than real ones – it's all in a name. And the names are:

- **Chanel** – possibly more for the name than the designs.

- **Miriam Haskell** – famous for her pearls but did a whole range of other jewellery as well.

- **Trifari** – huge range but a very good seller. Stick to the quirky or attractive, wearable pieces for fast sales.

- **Sherman** – the Canadian equivalent of Trifari. Good quality but harder to sell as not everyone knows who it is.

- **Schiaparelli** – Chanel's main competitor combines style with *je ne sais quoi*. Wearable if you dare.

- **Joseff** – the man who designed jewellery for 90% of the movies in 1930–40s Hollywood, including *Gone with the Wind*. His special dye created an 'old gold' finish which did not reflect on camera. Clients included Ginger Rogers and Joan Crawford. It's a very good seller, not just because of the movie connection (he also did a retail range which is what you'll be selling) but because of the designs – they're fabulous – I even wear some of them myself and that's a good way to sell your costume jewellery. I've even sold pieces which I've been wearing.

◆ **Hattie Carnegie** and **Nettie Rosenstein** – contemporaries and competitors. Carnegie (named after the famous hall) comes out the clear winner where jewellery is concerned – they were also milliners and dress designers. Best buys are her African series, made in coral and turquoise or green and coral plastic – quirky and well-made with a surprisingly contemporary feel.

◆ **Coro** – a mixed range, some good, some bad but most of it sells. Go for their 'duettes' range – two brooches held together on a single frame (eg owls or horses) which can also be worn separately – try to find them with matching earrings if you can. Also look for their figural watches (the watch face is often hidden behind part of the brooch such as the centre of a flower) and tremblers – designed to wobble when worn. Coro combined style with originality at surprisingly good prices.

◆ **Ciner** – not always marked so look for their trademark repeating circles on the back. Best buys are their fantasy brooches and more 'important' pieces such as the unicorns.

◆ **Har** – leaders of quirkiness and must-haves for costume jewellery buffs. Look for the dragon or snake series for fast, profitable sellers.

◆ **Robert** – fun, quality designs – look for his musical-themed brooches with matching earrings, the banjos are great fun and easy to sell.

◆ **Christian Dior** – various designers worked for Dior's costume jewellery range, but one of the best was **Mitchel Maer** who combined style with originality with must-have parures (sets of necklaces, earrings, bracelets and often brooches as well). Dior outsells all of the main fashion houses except for Chanel.

◆ **Weiss** – famous for its 'black diamond' a smoky-grey crystal. The butterfly brooches are best-buys as are **Regency's**.

◆ **Florenza** – one of the quirkiest of the designers whose 'Victorian' range is a best-seller.

◆ **Eisenberg** – famous for its 'Ice' range – the best of the fake diamonds and worn by those who had the real ones but didn't want to wear them.

♦ **Lea Stein** – French designer of stylish, plastic animal brooches and less stylish (but very easy to sell) unsigned bangles and rings. Avoid the earrings which use unfinished cat and fox heads and are modern in usage, but Lea Stein sells – stick to the cats and foxes for best sales and choose the colours with care, people buy them to wear so think in terms of wearability. Collectors go for the more unusual designs such as face-on elephant, Elvis, John Travolta and Joan Crawford (a design also known as Carmen Miranda). One of the easiest to sell of the costume jewellers, I've sold dozens of pieces – by keeping my profits low and turnover high. That's the best way to sell the cheaper jewellery.

♦ **Pavone** – highly influenced by Lea Stein, Pavone used galalith, an early, thick form of plastic which is extremely good quality. Working in the 1970s, her animal brooches sell very well, especially to collectors and dealers of Lea Stein. The cat bangles are never signed and are harder to sell – possibly just because they're about twice the price (or more) of the brooches.

It doesn't matter what you sell, just sound enthusiastic about it and take care over your displays – invest in some necklace or earring stands if you're selling them. Keep the pricier stock in locked cabinets or display cases for safety and wrap them individually at the end of the fair – they'll scratch otherwise.

Avoid any brooches with broken pins, although rubbed 'pearls' can always be repearlised. Learn some basic facts as this can help to sell your jewellery to uncertain buyers – most of the crystals before and after the war were Austrian, made by Swarovski crystal and any brooch from the 1930–40s just marked 'Austria' uses Swarovski – a very good selling point.

Lights

Lights have increased drastically in popularity as people decorate their houses in keeping with their period. 1930s lights are very popular and dealers specialise in them. Be prepared to change the wiring to update it safely and buy attractive, spare shades when you see them – some lights are sold without any at all. People love redecorating their houses and one of the cheapest ways to do this is with the lights and light fittings. Buy period, Bakelite (plastic from the 1930-40s) light switches and spare lamp shades for your stall – even general dealers sell lights as they add height, as well as light, to their stalls.

Avoid the mass-produced, repro Tiffany (coloured-glass shades in Art Nouveau style) lamps and stick to authentic lights instead. Best-sellers are table lamps whilst standard lights do sell but have to fit into cars (the buyer's, as well as your own) and you might not be able to display them at all fairs (fire regulations can prevent goods being placed in front of stalls).

Most centres have lamps and lamp/light shades so shop around and buy the most stylish or practical – remember, style is not everyone's taste and sometimes simplicity is better. Try to hang light shades from your stall to show people how they'll look and always have a modern lamp which you can shine through any shades to catch those difficult sales.

Figural bronze lamps in the shape of snake charmers and birds are good sellers but replace any unsuitable shades as these could deter potential sales.

Useful tip
Remove any old wiring and plugs from lamps – you'll breach Health and Safety regulations otherwise.

Books and Ephemera

Selling Ephemera

It is not compulsory to sell books and ephemera together but many dealers do. Ephemera (paper or cardboard items which many people would just throw away) comprises:

◆ old cereal or soap powder boxes
◆ letters and postcards
◆ diaries
◆ and autographs.

It's a fascinating market.

Some dealers specialise in autographs. Sometimes, these come in the form of letters, but they can have different prices for the same famous person. If a famous general has written a letter to his wife, discussing mundane household matters, the letter would not be worth as much as one in which he'd written about a military campaign but, for social and not military historians, it could be viewed as more important – for dealers, it's not.

Keep letters and autographs in special, clear bags (available from larger fairs and the specialist ephemera fairs) – this will allow people to see them without damaging them accidentally. The same goes for **postcards** which are sold better if arranged by county or subject matter – people get bored quickly if they have to look too hard for what they want.

Selling Books

Being a book dealer does not mean that you have to sell old books, but you can. Some dealers specialise in modern, first editions with others tightening that speciality to just crime or some other genre such as children's books. The profits can be vast. A first edition, e.g. Minette Walters *The Ice House* (1992), currently fetches £450+. The modern first editions are very easy to find – you can pick them up from your local charity shop or do what the dealers do and buy them straight from bookshops, stockpiling them until they go up in value. Newcomer Sarah Diamond's *The Beach Road* was worth £120 on the secondary market while it was still in the shops for £16.99. Increase the books' values by asking the authors to sign them either at special author events at the larger bookshops (join their mailing lists to find out who will be in and when) or write to the publishers. Don't get them signed to anyone in particular as this will limit their appeal. 'Best wishes from . . .' is fine.

You can be a general book dealer, selling everything or you can specialise. There are various specialist areas and these include:

◆ children's books
◆ military books
◆ literature
◆ poetry
◆ crime
◆ nature – especially beautifully illustrated plates which some dealers will remove and frame for maximum profits
◆ scientific books
◆ erotica – to avoid complaints be careful not to let children handle them
◆ books with maps – which some dealers will remove and frame for easy profits
◆ modern first editions.

There are rules for handling books, especially older ones. Don't ever bend them back at the spine – it's surprising how many of your readers will. What you will quickly discover is that you will be used as a library. I've had people read my books from cover to cover and then walk away, either without saying a word, or complaining that they're not first editions. If this happens, ask them if they are intending to buy the book and offer to wrap it – all but the thickest skinned will get the hint and buy it or move on. If they are thick skinned, either let them read it or ask them to move on. They are the type of people who will bend the spines or crease the pages and this will decrease the value of your book. They rarely buy.

Lightly price the books inside on the first page that people see in pencil – never use a pen or a sticky label as these tend to rip pages and pen marks cannot be eradicated –

you'll lose sales that way. You might prefer to price your goods using a thin sheet of paper rather like a bookmark. This can work but the piece of paper often gets lost – along with your price. Book buyers expect a 10–20% discount so allow that in the price (eg price a £20 book at £22–24, depending on what sized discount you intend to give).

There are various types of people who buy books – trade, collectors and readers. Some people buy books by certain authors (eg Charles Dickens) and some people buy books because of their covers or illustrations. Think about all of these considerations when buying and don't forget to visit your local auction where you should be able to pick up two or three boxes of books for £5 – or less. Take what you want and leave the rest in there for the next sale.

If you have books with gold edges (either all the way round or only on one edge), you should handle them extra carefully as the gold edging is prone to wear – some dealers use cotton gloves when handling goods to prevent them from being damaged by their sweat or natural body secretions. This is also true for very old or frail books. Unless you know what you're doing, use specialist bookbinders or repairers for damaged books – never use sticky tape as it causes damage.

Childhood Favourites

You might choose to specialise in childhood favourites, including children's books and annuals such as Noddy or Rupert the Bear. This is a great area either as a specialist or as a general dealer. There is money in nostalgia as people spend to recapture their childhood memories. There is an annoying side as well – they want to play with your stock. That's fine if you're selling goods less than £10 but worrying if your stock is £500 + . Because some of the buyers had the same pieces when they were young, they don't rate them. Some of them will have them at home and will take great delight in telling you so – it doesn't matter. They're not your customers and the people who are will fast become regulars.

What is a childhood favourite? They're what you knew when you grew up – whether you're 8 or 80. They could be characters from your favourite books, films, cartoons, comic strip characters or TV favourites and there are some firm favourites who are definitely worth stocking:

* The Magic Roundabout – huge market
* Noddy (and friends) – huge, international market
* Rupert – huge, international market
* Alice in Wonderland – huge, international market
* Beatrix Potter – a classic favourite
* Winnie the Pooh (original and Disney) – very good market
* Mabel Lucy Attwell – a timeless classic with a huge, devoted following
* Bonzo – one of the earliest of the childhood favourites who has attracted a much younger audience
* Disney – especially Mickey Mouse, Snow White and the Seven Dwarfs, Bambi, Lady and the Tramp, Dumbo, Pluto and Donald Duck. Massive, international market, especially in the US and Japan
* Muffin the Mule
* Pinky and Perky
* Snoopy – huge, international market
* Sooty – huge, especially for the Japanese market

- Wind in the Willows/Toad of Toad Hall – look for the illustrated books as well as the figurals
- Barbie – not accepted at some fairs but old Barbies are hot and have specialist auctions, their clothes reflect the fashion of their era – and yours
- The Snowman – based on the book by Raymond Briggs
- Thomas the Tank Engine – the only train service which will always be popular
- Paddington – but definitely not Postman Pat
- Andy Pandy – but not as much as some of the others
- Brambly Hedge
- The Owl and the Pussycat – in all shapes and forms
- Kate Greenaway – famed for her Victorian/Edwardian figures of children
- Noah's Ark – from the crudely made old wooden versions to stylish modern enamels
- Chitty Chitty Bang Bang – and other children's films
- Spiderman – comic classic with a cult following
- Superman
- Batman etc
- Beano
- Thunderbirds – and anything by Gerry Anderson, the greatest thing to happen to puppets since, well, string
- Star Wars
- Star Trek
- Dr Who – and anything sci-fi.

A quick look around the shops will tell you that the 30-something generation is the latest to benefit from nostalgia. Mr Ben is back, Bagpuss is ubiquitous and the Clangers are...well, they're my favourites but are they here to stay? I don't think so but I could be wrong. The real children's favourites are those made at the time which capture the innocence of our childhood. We played with them. The modern, purpose-built childhood favourites are almost hitting the wrong market, successful though they are at the moment. I love Bagpuss but I'm too old to wear him now and that's part of the problem with rejuvenating classics for the ageing child – too mass-produced and too late.

If you want to concentrate on the childhood favourites of the future, buy what they're watching now – The Hoobs, Tweenies etc, but be careful. Unlike when you were growing up, these goods are mass-produced. Teletubbies have taken over. Those in the know are buying what was, not what will be – remember, you've got at least 20 years before today's babies get nostalgic.

When you're dealing in this area, on whatever level, you have to remember that these goods were designed for children to use. You're relatively unlikely to get mint (perfect) examples – for which you'd be expected to pay and charge extra – but avoid any which are too scruffy as they'll be hard to sell.

Further Reading: *The Encyclopaedia of Cult Children's TV* by Richard Lewis (Allison and Busby, London, 2001). It's the essential guide for spotting those must-buy childhood favourites. Recognise the easy-to-sell characters from Camberwick Green and Trumpton with this easy-read guide.

Toys

In many ways dealers in toys and childhood favourites will interlink. However there are specialist fields within specialist fields and, in the case of toys, these include teddy bear or doll dealers, both of whom have their own specialist fairs and auctions. Some of the doll dealers will also specialise in dolls' houses or just dolls' house furniture – the smaller the better and a surprisingly imaginative but costly area. Look around carefully before buying to avoid buying repro by mistake and to get an idea of the prices – they might be a lot higher than you'd expect.

Teddy Bears and Dolls

The teddy bear is an institution – most of us had one when we were growing up and you might still have one. Some teddies are worth thousands, some are just worth their memories. This is down to several key factors – make, colour, material, condition, age, rarity. The top teddy maker is **Steiff**, with its trademark button in the ear – Steiff stands for quality and collectability and its whole range is worth buying.

Merrythought is also a firm favourite with **Dean's** being another good buy. Go for character of face – extras such as growls, glass eyes and articulation (movement of arms, head and legs) help raise interest.

Dolls are very sellable, as are the dolls' heads – the top half of dolls which were designed to slip into powder puffs or stylish dresses. For full dolls, china ones are amongst the most popular but plastic ones sell as well, especially by famous names such as **Sascha** and characters such as **Barbie** – but stick to the better quality, traditional ones if you want to succeed in the competitive dolls' market.

Naked dolls sell but they look rather sad, so clean them up (use soapy water and dry them immediately apart from the bisque ones which should never be submerged). Dress them up in period clothes if you can find them or linen Christening gowns – make them as appealing as possible, they sell to members of the public not just expert buyers, because they're attractive. The same goes for all toys – make them as appealing as possible without altering their original structure – unless they need it. There are specialist toy and teddy hospitals – speak to the specialist dealers and ask for their recommendations.

Puppets

One of the strongest areas of toy collecting besides teddy bears and dolls is puppets – or marionettes to give the most popular versions – the stringed ones – their proper name. Top of these is **Pelham**. Alice in Wonderland and friends, such as the White Rabbit, are amongst the most highly sought after of this popular make. Don't worry about tangled strings – the expert buyers know exactly how to cope with those. In fact, don't be surprised if they tell you a thing or two that you don't know – they're amongst the sweetest and most enthusiastic of the dealers. So much so that many of them make their own clothes for the puppets and will even reprimand you if your Rupert the Bear is wearing dirty clothes or your Thunderbird is too scruffy to go.

And that's another thing. Pelham crosses several markets including Childhood Favourites – many of us grew up with them and many more of us grew up with some of their more famous, licensed characters such as Pinky and Perky (I have several of their records – another collectable area) and Donald Duck. If you are going to specialise in Pelham, think about getting a special stand to display them properly – it's one way of stopping browsers from tangling the strings. Make your own or speak to a carpenter or shopfitter and have one made to order. *The right display is worth every penny – it will quickly pay for itself in increased sales.*

Other Best Buys

The toy area is a large one but it is not all worth selling. Think practicalities – what fits on your stall or with the rest of your stock if you're not intending to specialise but just sell one or two choice items? What is still usable or nostalgic enough for today's buyers? Other best buys include:

- **Train sets** – some might argue that they're not toys but they're sold at toy fairs. Go for top makes such as Hornby but avoid cheap-looking trains such as those by Tri-ang – they don't sell.

- **Dinky and Corgi** – top makes for top vehicles.

- **Meccano** – but not Lego which has never quite made it to the antiques circuit.

- **Board games** pre 1960s – Such as those by Glevum, Waddingtons and Chad Valley. Boxed is best.

- **Jigsaws** – wooden ones by Victory are the best, especially if they have cut-outs of animals, as well as standard jigsaw shapes.

- Other **cuddly toys** – Steiff and Merrythought are amongst the best but stick to quality ones in good condition. Makes like Golden Bear, which do so well on the primary market with their licensed goods (eg The Magic Roundabout and Rainbow), do not do so well on the secondary market so be careful – go for the classics produced when the series first came out.

- **Family games** such as croquet and boules sell – the older, the better.

- **Tin toys** – look for makes such as Schuco for top sales.

If you have the time, visit Pollock's Toy Museum in London (41 Whitfield Street near Goodge Street tube station, 020 7636 3452). For dealers, it's like looking at stock – it's a useful guide for what to buy.

Film Merchandise and Pop Memorabilia

This is a relatively new area of dealing and, to a certain extent, can cross over with childhood favourites and even toys, but it's not just about the gimmicks produced to hype films. There are two main types of goods which dealers want when it comes to films, three if you include autographs – **posters** and **props**.

> Props from one of the most hyped films ever, Harry Potter, were stolen with the intention of selling them on to collectors and dealers because props sell.

People will pay tens, hundreds or even thousands over the odds to get close to their favourite stars or capture an essence of their favourite films and the market is huge – as is the range of goods on offer. The same is true of sporting memorabilia. But be practical, stick to what you can sell and what fits into your selling outlet, be it a stall at a fair or a shop. Even if you are reaching a wider audience by selling over the Internet, think about the practicalities of postage – sorry to be mundane but, if you want to be a dealer, you need to think ahead. Or consider specialist auctions.

If people are going to spend hundreds of pounds or more on film props or pop memorabilia (that's something connected to pop stars such as clothes, posters, instruments, photos etc), they need proof that it's genuine – they need what is called a provenance – effectively, a birth certificate for the goods saying where they came from. Ideally, you also need a photo of the star with them – or a still from the movie showing the prop *in situ*.

> **Useful tip**
> Use authentic photographs to show the stars holding their props or wearing the costume that you're selling.

Some pop memorabilia and film props are best sold at specialist auctions where they will reach a wider audience and, hopefully, realise higher prices. Realistically, they will also be able to display the goods better and the provenance will be more believable.

I once saw a programme where the 'expert' was trying to sell a pop star's signed drum at a car boot sale for £250 – that's not the right market. Of course, it didn't sell – one potential buyer didn't even believe that it was authentic but I bet there were a lot more doubters than that. At a specialist auction, it would probably have sold with ease and for far more than £250. This business is all about knowing what sells where – and a car boot isn't it the right place for an antiques dealer to sell anything other than cheap junk, tired stock or old clothes.

Selling Posters

A good display can sell your stock without you having to open your mouth. This is so true where posters are concerned. We're not just talking film and pop but all types of posters from old travel posters to advertising – hang them up in a nice frame with no creases and they'll sell. Roll them up on your stall and they won't. Unless you know what you're doing, take them to a professional frame shop and get them to frame them in a simple frame – preferably cardboard frame with perspex cover or just a glass mount. This will keep the poster as the centre of attention and not deter buyers with limited imagination who might not be able to look beyond the wrong frame – it's not their fault but yours if this happens. Be prepared to change unsuitable frames and take this into account when working out potential profit margins before you buy any unframed or badly framed posters.

There are some simple rules about posters:

- Avoid any which are too creased, torn, faded (unless they're exceptional) or pornographic – unless you have the right outlet.
- People like to look at posters, they like to browse and they don't want anything which is going to unsettle them so stick to arty, not nasty, ones.

> **Useful tip**
> Where possible, try to get a star to sign an original poster or sign something (eg provenance or picture of themselves) which can be sold with any film prop or pop memorabilia – even pop stars' or politicians' underpants! If it's the right person, anything sells.

Pop Classics (Probably Not What You're Thinking)

This is nothing to do with pop singers but classics of their era. Think Mary Quant or Biba, think of trend-setting designer 1950s furniture and 1960s clothes – these are the Pop Classics that you might want to sell.

The past is trendy and people want to return to it. Retro is huge.

They want the authentic furniture and fittings of their favourite era. The plastic chairs of the 1950–60s, the swivel chairs, the miniskirts and the high boots – they want what you (or your parents) probably just gave away.

It's a fun area of dealing but it's also attractive. Think beyond the obvious and accessorise – stock the right glass to match the rest of your stock, buy the flying ducks which were once so out of fashion to go with the real Pop Classics, top designs from the top, fashion-creating designers of the collectable era. Some call it Pop Classics, others, less knowledgeably kitsch, but there's a market in it. At least, there is for now – it might not last, so be sensible and stick to quality – because that's never out of fashion.

Look for designs by top designers such as Charles and Ray Eames, Joe Colombo, Robin Day, Lucienne Day or Arne Jacobsen who combined innovative style and quality to be the trend-setters of their – and later – generations.

Tins

Like ephemera, many people threw their tins away – you probably still do. Think about what's in the shops at Christmas time, confectioners and biscuit producers are competing with each other to get you to buy their goods. How do they do this? Not by reducing prices (well, some might) but by creating attractive packaging, often in the form of tins and they've been doing this for years.

There is a very strong market in tins but it's bypassed many dealers, possibly because it is almost too specialist. Tins sell but generally to those in the know. You can try to be a general dealer with tins but I'm not sure that it would work. On the other hand, you could make a good living (or just decent money) out of being a specialist tin dealer.

You need to buy the more unusual tins and you don't have to know a huge amount to realise what constitutes unusual. I'm talking about figurals from carriages to clocks, animals to yachts. It's almost all down to the shape. Sadly, it's also down to the condition and some of these tins have rusted beyond repair and are best avoided.

One of the best modern buys is not figural at all but a simple, round tin with a questionable decoration. Someone at **Huntley and Palmer** (one of the most famous of the biscuit firms whose tins are amongst the most collectable – the older and more unusual, the better) saw the proposed decoration for the tin and passed it because all they saw were the pretty, nostalgic, **Kate Greenaway** figures (an artist famed for her innocent depiction of pretty, Victorian/Edwardian-looking children). What they missed is what makes the tin so collectable today – look hard enough and you'll see various figures in the background being, well, lewd! It sells.

Useful tip

If you're thinking about dealing in tins, invest in some plasters and antiseptic lotion – those tins can be sharp and are not always clean, so take care.

Commemoratives

This is a very popular area but I'm tempted to argue that it might have had its day soon. The commemorative market is a celebration of various important events, especially royal occasions such as coronations, jubilees and weddings. And that is why it is limited at the moment – because far too many people are not interested enough in the royal family to spend any money celebrating their achievements. Don't even think about wasting your money on anything that's been produced since 1937 – not many people will buy it from you. The 1977 Jubilee was a huge success but it's hard-to-impossible to sell the vast majority of commemoratives from that era and manufacturers noticeably produced very little for the Queen's 2002 Jubilee – compare that with the celebrations produced for Queen Victoria in 1887. It's a different era and it will seriously affect the commemorative market.

There are exceptions – there are still collectors. There will still be collectors for the older pieces, especially commemorating Queen Victoria and earlier. And some pieces will always sell, no matter what – Doulton figures have a strong market and collectors will buy pieces for the maker's name, not the subject matter.

Commemoratives do not have to be about the royal family. They can mark other events such as sporting victories (especially horse racing for some reason, whilst football programmes – more ephemera than commemoratives – have their own market). And they can mark tragedies – such as the sinking of the *Titanic*.

If you like history, this could be the market for you, but think backwards and don't waste your time or money by stockpiling today's commemoratives – because too few people care any more. Today's politicians cannot compare with Churchill who is probably the best-selling of all politicians when it comes to the commemorative market. This is a stronger area than royals when it comes to modern collectables but be careful – politicians are forgotten as soon as they're out of power and this will affect the prices of their memorabilia. Today's market is humorous, with Carlton Ware's Spitting Image series one of the best-selling modern commemoratives especially the Margaret Thatcher teapot. These white pieces are not marked Carlton Ware, look for the 'Fluck and Law' name instead. When dealing in political goods, stick to the more memorable politicians, such as Disraeli or Kennedy, whatever your political beliefs.

If this is an area that you wish to develop, stick to the best buys – these will still sell, especially if they're by good makes such as Doulton, Paragon and pre-1960s Wade (apart from their later whisky bells for Bells Whisky which have a strong, whisky collectors' market, commanding higher prices than those of Wade collectors):

- figures
- loving cups – double-handled shaped tankards, sometimes musical
- enamels – especially by Halcyon Days
- plates
- teapots
- ephemera (eg pamphlets, coronation or funeral orders etc)
- boxes – preferably metalwork or good quality wood such as Mauchline Ware with its inlaid pictures of special places or events.

Novelties

This is one of my favourite areas. It's fun but can also be practical and stylish. A novelty is something different, but it can also be very ordinary such as a **teapot** or **cruet** (salt, pepper and, sometimes, a mustard pot). It is these two areas on which I wish to focus, together with **moneyboxes** – all three of which are huge areas and intermingle very well. They also fit in comfortably with other goods and, as such, are perfect for general dealers as well as specialists.

What Makes a Good Novelty?

Design and quality. A good novelty should make you smile, be it a teapot shaped like a Liquorice Allsort or a cruet of babies in a pram. Moneyboxes should be figural (shaped) or well decorated – or both.

Are There Any Particular Makes For Which I Should Be Looking?

These goods are generally china, but not always.

> **Useful tip**
> What makes many moneyboxes collectable, regardless of make, is that they did not always have stoppers and thousands were destroyed by people smashing them open to recoup their investment – at a higher cost than they realised.

There are many popular makes for novelties but it should be noted that not all of the cruets were marked – either they were not by certain makes or they were marked on the base of the cruet stand, which is not always found with the unmarked cruets. But there are some top novelty manufacturers which also have their own collectors, these include:

* Carlton Ware – possibly the best all-rounder when it comes to novelties.
* Goebel – the 'ah' factor at its best – one of the best for moneyboxes and cruets.
* Beswick – great teapots, cruets and also biscuit barrels, another novelty.
* Wade and Wadeheath – especially for teapots.
* Royal Doulton – especially in ranges such as Bunnykins and Brambly Hedge. They also made mobiles (the ones designed to hang above a baby's crib) – easily broken so highly collectable.
* David Sharp – good range of moneyboxes.
* Silver Crane – especially their highly sought-after teapots.
* Sylvac – good teapots and cruets.
* Cardew – famed for their teapots both old and new.
* Tony Carter – modern teapots and future classics.

Useful tip

If you wish to buy or sell in the American market, note that cruets are called shakers.

Teapots

The teapot market is huge and ranges from several pounds to several thousand pounds. If you wish to deal in teapots, even if you're just selling one, be careful of the lids. Buyers are not always the most sensible of people and some won't be careful when handling your stock – often at the expense of teapot lids. You can take a chance and not take any precautions. Offer to pass teapots to interested buyers if you're worried or you could take precautions. Either Sellotape the lid to the rest of the teapot and be prepared for people to remove it with or without permission (to check for damage such as a chipped lid or rim) or display them separately. Carry spare Sellotape with you as it can get worn out quickly, but don't use it on pieces where the paint or transfer is already flaking, as it will cause further damage.

It's worth buying spare lids when you get the chance – some of them can change hands for £20+ – and you might as well be the one cashing in.

Cruets

Some dealers will only buy complete cruets but the clever ones buy single ones and empty bases. Why? Because they can either build up the sets themselves or profit from those who need the spare pieces because their own sets are either damaged or incomplete. I sell a lot of bases and single cruets and always buy affordable ones when I can – especially by Carlton Ware.

The better-selling cruets are interesting, they're attractive and it doesn't matter if they're practical or not – they sell. As with all things, think in terms of different types of collectors. Monkey cruets by Goebel sell to cruet, Goebel and monkey collectors – as well as people who just like them – that's four different types of buyers, not forgetting the trade who just want good stock.

Moneyboxes

Moneyboxes are also good sellers. They're often given to babies as alternative Christening or birth presents – mine was a Goebel duck. It's a huge market but don't worry if you see ones without stoppers, you can find spare ones around, and serious collectors and the trade will buy them regardless. If you deal in Carlton Ware's flat-shaped moneyboxes with transfers (eg in the flat-sided shape of Noah's Ark, a train, a cat etc), buy as many different colour variations as you can – the collectors know what they're doing and they want them all.

What Other Types of Novelties Are There?

There are loads but the other main areas are:

◆ toastracks
◆ jam pots
◆ eggcups – huge market but the collectors are often not willing to spend much
◆ paperweights
◆ napkin rings
◆ candlesnuffers
◆ Toby jugs (figural character mugs and jugs)
◆ cheese and butter dishes – often plain-shaped but sometimes fun – especially by

Carlton Ware and Wade
- clocks
- menu holders.

The basic key to novelties is not just to buy good quality but also good designs – advertising and animals are some of the best buys.

Other Popular Areas

The antiques and collectables world is huge. I've tried to highlight some of the most popular or best areas in the previous chapters but there are many other areas which you might wish to consider. There are probably too many to mention but I'm going to give a very brief summary of some of the best of the rest.

Ancient and Oriental

Often sold together, these cover ancient goods from Roman times and even earlier. Egyptian artefacts are very popular with the right buyers. Check into import and export licences unless you are intending to sell them exclusively in Britain. Old Chinese goods are not all Ming but often have the same richness and quality of the famous dynasty. A rich area, not just in terms of profit but history. Be careful where you're selling it as it doesn't always appeal to the masses. Bath is known for its ancient and Oriental goods, as are the London antiques centres, but don't expect to be able to sell with ease if you live deep in the country with a small, local market – but I could be wrong.

Animals

Some dealers sell goods based on animals, with some going further and just selling dog collectables or anything related to cats from pictures to jewellery. There's a very good market but be careful not to specialise yourself out of customers.

Bakelite and Plastics

Purists would argue that Bakelite is a thick 'plastic' available in brown only. The rest of us think of it as a wondrous material which comes in a variety of colours such as a rich orange-red or green which has been moulded into a variety of uses from working radio sets to jewellery. Great general or specialist areas but avoid mixing it with modern reproductions (AKA fakes) which could lose you sales and demean the rest of your stock. Think about selling plastic jewellery and accessories such as Lucite (clear plastic) handbags as well.

Boxes

Many old, wooden boxes have been converted to modern use, such as old knife boxes changed to decanter holders or stationery boxes, which is a shame. Stick to good quality boxes, preferably with their original usage. Look for a beautiful patina (sheen), extra detailing and stylish locks for best-buy, desirable pieces and polish them gently until they shine.

Breweriania

The pub market. Not just popular with theme pubs, but advertising collectors and those who love pubs or collect certain makes. Carlton Ware, Beswick and Wade produced goods for pubs, not just the jugs and ashtrays in Wade's case but also the figures which stood on the bars. Collectors even buy old pub signs. If it's been near alcohol, it will sell. Whiskey and Guinness are the most collectable.

Cigarette Cards

The market is not as good as it once was because of the negative aspect of smoking (it kills) but the old cigarette cards still have a firm following and are sold framed or loose, in sets or singly. Sets are the best but sell what you can and keep them safe in special ephemera bags to avoid becoming bent or dirty. Go for popular themes such as film stars for easy sellers.

Clocks and Watches

A beautiful, practical area with specialist fairs which appeal to the public as well as collectors and trade – because we all need to know the time. From wrist to pocket watches, these are in demand with those from the First World War having their own specialist market. It can be a costly area but turnover is often high and specialists are in demand in antiques centres. Clock restorers are very popular, something which you might want to consider doing as well if you have the relevant skills. Clocks and watches with guarantees sell more easily than those without, especially the more expensive ones such as old Rolexes – another specialist area within a specialist area.

Corkscrews

A specialist market which some general dealers also do on a small scale. Go for figurative ones such as dogs, the practical or the stylish and learn what you're doing – some corkscrews are worth thousands but only the specialists know which ones.

Costume and Textiles

Period dress, theatrical costumes and textiles (curtains and cushions). These can include accessories such as **handbags** and **compacts** – also popular with **costume jewellery** dealers. Top compact makes are Schuco (animal-chaped versions), Kigu, Stratton and Pygmalion with their fabulous, figural designs.

Crested Ware

Plain, white china by makes such as **Goss** and **Carlton** with crests of places and people. These can be figural and sometimes have cats on them, sometimes based on the work by famous cat artist, **Louis Wain** – appeals to Louis Wain and cat dealers as well. If you can, try to buy crested ware for the county in which you're selling, eg Clacton on Sea when you're selling in Essex – it increases sales. Stick to the figurals, such as cenotaphs and cannons, and avoid plates which are hard-to-impossible to sell.

Enamels

Beautifully decorated boxes or attractive figurals, this is an attractive area that has the added benefit of being small and light. Top modern make is **Halcyon Days** with **Moorcroft** a new (but overpriced) contender. **Staffordshire Enamels**, **Royal Stratford** (once called **House of Ashley**) and **Crummles English Enamels** also have their collectors, with Royal Stratford being the best. Original eighteenth century designs are very desirable but often damaged. Go for quality and originality of design (the figurative ones such as birdcages and carousels are very good) and also good 'clunks' on closing – cheaper versions sound cheap. This is a relatively new area (except for those of us who have been buying them for years and the hard to find Georgian versions) and works well with small, quality wooden objects such as **treen** or **mother of pearl** goods.

Linen

An attractive area for specialist dealers. Christening gowns and old-fashioned nightdresses sell alongside simple but beautiful tablecloths. Think of cleaning costs and ironing time in all sales and invest in wooden clothes dryers for attractive displays. Beware sticky fingers – some of your stock will have to be washed after every fair but it's a beautiful area for the right dealer. If, like me, you don't iron, forget it. Linen dealers can also sell tapestries (framed or otherwise) and old curtains – people need them.

Luggage

This is a fascinating area varying from trunks made for Atlantic cruises in the stylish 1920–30s to matching leather suitcases and any other case with some history. This is a different but attractive area with a good market. Invest in some good, special leather polish and be prepared to air musty cases and hatboxes.

Militaria

Anything to do with war and the men and weapons of war – and peace. From uniforms to medals and everything imaginable (and then some) in between.

Pens and Pencils

This area of expertise also includes pen rests and inkwells – which can both double up as novelties. It's a good area, though you'll need to learn what's what to capitalise on those must-buy pieces, but pens have a strong market and buyers will travel far if they know that you're a specialist as there are not that many such dealers around, despite demand.

Photography and Photographic Equipment

A fascinating and often very beautiful area. The old **Kodak** Brownies are not always good buys but can decorate your stall beautifully, attracting customers, while **Leicas** are more in demand. Daguerreotypes are good sellers but go for attractive subjects – and the same goes for old photographs with erotica being a firm favourite – not for the shy.

Radios and Televisions

A fast-growing market, which has seen the renovation of old radios and televisions (especially radios) with Bakelite and the old wooden sets from the 1930–50s being the most popular. Go for style, not just use. Some dealers only sell radios, others just have a few – do what suits you and find a good restorer if you can't do it yourself. It's an entertaining market and you can even listen to the modern radio on a 60-year old set. Good for nostalgia and those restoring old homes with period fittings.

Scientific Instruments

With specialist fairs, this is one for the intellectuals or the imaginative amongst you. It's also a very good way to get past a general fair's waiting list as it's relatively unusual (compared to china dealers, that is). Expect to have to explain the usage of the some of the more obscure goods (or use detailed labelling), and revel in the past and its dreams and limitations. Most obvious buys are the telescope and globe, but medical instruments and even old maths sets have their place in this fascinating world.

Sporting Memorabilia and Equipment

From football programmes to old, leather footballs and old cricket bats as well as signed photos of the best from Don Bradman to George Best – there's a market for it. Fishing reels are a firm favourite,whilst saddles and whips change hands outside the more expected arenas – think in terms not just of collectors and dealers but themed pubs and restaurants. Nostalgia sells, so combine your love of sport with love of money for good sales. If going to matches, get the players to sign your programme after the game for maximum profit, especially for more important sporting fixtures.

Wood

Wood is beautiful. Not just for what it can become but for itself. It has different colours and tones (hues), even imperfections such as knots add something to its quality whilst woodworm, strangely, can add character – but too much should be avoided. Wood is not always just wood, it can become different things under different conditions or makers. **Treen** is a rich wood with a special sheen that has been gently carved into practical usage such as boxes and goblets, while Scotland's **Mauchline Ware** is recognisable for the pictures which decorate its lightly coloured surface and commemorates places with practical pieces such as thimbles and boxes.

Fads

Beware the bad, long-term investment. Some collectables are short-term buys only. We call these fads. They're not there to be stockpiled but they offer fast profits – as long as you know when to get in and when to get out – fast. These are the areas which will trap the unwary and one thing that I've learnt as a dealer is to spot trends. Some trends are great and will last and last – others are fads so learn the difference fast – or you'll lose money. Fads do not affect the antiques world, just its collectables area. They often have one, common factor – *lack of quality* – and that's why they don't last.

This is a strange area and there are bound to be differences of opinion between dealers, but most of them will agree with me (and those who don't will be selling what I'm advising you to treat with care). Fads can be profitable – but only if you treat them accordingly.

Fast-Fading Fads

Okay, they don't all fade immediately and some of them are still limping on, but these are some of the most notorious – or controversial – fads:

- Cabbage Patch Dolls – costly must-buys of the 1980s which have recently re-emerged on to the collectors' market but at considerably less than their original value – buyers were burnt.

- Ty beanies – fantastic marketing but prices plummeted. It still has a market but they're not accepted at many fairs and the specialist fairs often have overpriced stalls and are struggling to survive – they're great fun for kids but not good investments. Unless you're lucky.

- Furbies – remember them? The must-buys are must-dies.

- Lorna Bailey – arguable but I'm not sure that she'll survive and buyers risk losing their investment. Quality and originality are questionable, marketing is first-rate.

- Harry Potter – too much, too soon. Expect prices to plummet soon – if they even rose. Recommended Retail Prices (RRPs) for 'collectables' will be as high as they get for most of the pieces – Royal Doulton's figures are possibly the only good buys apart from first editions of the first three books.

- Pokemon cards – out of sight, out of mind – out of pocket.

Fads are like shares, spot what's coming before everyone else does and get out before they do. But how do you spot a trend? Sometimes, it's instinct. Fads are not trends. Trends start and fade in the secondary market – you'll suddenly start noticing particular things. At the time of writing, it's Carnival glass which was last in style almost 20 years ago, but it's back and starting to materialise in more and more places – possibly from dealers delighted to get rid of 20-year old stock.

A fad starts on the primary market – that's shops. That said, it's often not just shops but children's playgrounds or the collectors' magazines. I probably shouldn't say this as I'm a journalist but not everything you read in the press should be believed (unless I write it, of course!). Why? Because sometimes there's an ulterior motive. Do you remember what I said about price guides – that they're sometimes written by people selling their own collections? The same can be true of some articles. Not just one or two but a batch. If you read a publication on a regular basis, see if they're hyping a particular product – does this reflect what you see or are they trying to create a market? That's good PR, constantly mentioning something gives it attention, attention creates interest, creates buyers, creates articles (no longer PR as such) about buyers, creates more buyers. And so on until people suddenly realise that what they're buying is not good quality, it's not original – everyone has it. Just like those Japanese pocket pets and the latest mobile phones. People move on to the next must-buy area and the market collapses. The fad is out of fashion – and you've lost your money.

PART SIX
Business Basics

This part will cover the negative aspect of dealing – the paperwork and the payback. There are many dealers out there who ignore several of these chapters and there are many who once did – to their cost. The bottom line is do it properly and you'll have nothing to fear. All of the main authorities will visit fairs at some time or other – the taxman, Mr VAT and even the DSS. If you're earning money, you have to pay for it so do it properly and read on.

CHAPTER ONE

Tax

I'm not going to go into too much detail but you *must* register your business with the taxman within your first three months of trading or face a fine. Even if it's just a hobby, they need to know. I've seen what happens when the taxman goes to fairs and centres – dealers run. Literally. Some never return and just leave their stock there and that could be you.

Just play by the rules and you won't have to worry.

The first thing that you must do is to ring your local tax office – the number's in your local phone directory under Government Offices and then under its correct name, Inland Revenue. Don't be scared. They like it when you ring up as it saves them time and money because you're one less person they'll need to find and prosecute for non-registration. If that sounds like scare tactics, it isn't. There are horrible tales in the trade of tax and VAT dodgers who have been caught out and had to sell their own collections, as well as their stock. It's extreme but it does happen.

All you have to do is explain that you're about to or have just become self-employed and that you want to register. You could also ring the Helpline for the Newly Self-employed on 08459 15 45 15 seven days a week, 8am-8pm (or 08457 660 830 Mon-Fri if you wish to speak to someone in Welsh). They're very helpful and friendly and will not only send you a booklet called *Thinking of Working for Yourself*, which contains forms for you to register as self-employed, but will also give you the option of registering over the phone. This will save you time and is a convenient way to register and have some of your questions answered at the same time.

Register to become self-employed

You can either fill in a simple form or register over the phone which takes around five minutes. You will need to give your:

- name
- National Insurance number
- date of birth – in figures eg 09/05/1971
- address and postcode
- home or mobile phone number
- tax reference number (if known)
- start date of your business
- your business name and address, if applicable, eg you have a shop or are working in a centre, but don't give this address unless you're certain that you'll be staying there long-term – you have to remember to tell them that you've moved, otherwise
- your business or mobile phone number
- your business fax number, if you have one
- your business e-mail address, if you have one
- your position in the business, eg proprietor
- what sort of self-employed work you will do, eg antiques dealer

The leaflet and form will mention National Insurance which can be paid by direct debit. A form is attached for this or will be sent to you – you can even do it all over the phone.

What is National Insurance?

NI, as it's called on the forms and by tax offices, is your way of paying for your future. Your NI contributions, as a self-employed person, are known as Class 2 NI contributions. In simple parlance, they're £2 a week – at the time of writing. People earning £4,029 or less are exempt from NI payments.

- **But what are they?** They're your pension, amongst other things.

- **Do I have to pay them?** That depends. If you are what is classified as a 'small earner' (i.e. earning below a set sum – around £4,615 at the time of writing but check as this is liable to change with every tax year – that's April to April), you could be exempt. There are various exceptions so speak to the Self-employed Helpline for advice.

- **This is just a part-time job and I already pay NI contributions and tax with my main**

job, why should I pay them again? Because you must. Whether you're a full-timer, a part-timer or a hobby dealer, you have got to pay tax if you earn over your personal allowance limit – that's £4,615 at the moment. Regardless of that, you still have to register – *you'll get fined £100 (subject to appeal) if you don't register within the first three months of trading* from the end of your first month's trading (i.e. three months from the end of May if you start dealing in May). Speak to your accountant, local tax office or the Self-employed Helpline about your NI contributions if you have another job as well – the rules will change with every tax year but there are certain exemptions so ask when you register – you don't want to overpay.

What Else Can the Self-employed Helpline Offer Me?

When I started dealing and, later on when I opened my shop, there was nothing like this. With so many people opting out of conventional employment, working for themselves when retired or having their own business alongside a job, there became a need to help them – to help you – to do it properly. The helpline offers so many things, not just an easy way to register and useful advice but:

- A video about being self-employed and how to cope financially (i.e. tax).

- Booklets and leaflets.

- Workshops – one-to-one and group workshops in your own tax area, learning from each other. It's important not to feel overawed or alone when you start out and these sessions are open not only to the registered but those thinking about becoming self-employed.

- A guide for cutting through the red tape. This is a hefty guide and, because it costs so much to produce and send, is only available to the registered self-employed.

Do I Really Have to Register for Tax, It's Only a Hobby?

It's not worth the penalties if you don't register, but the good news is that you might not actually have to pay any tax if you don't earn enough. If your earnings (that's profit after expenses such as stall rent and stock) do not exceed your personal allowance (currently £4,615), you might not have to pay tax – it depends what else you do. Register and speak to your accountant or local tax office to find out how much tax you have to pay at the end of the tax year.

Do I Need an Accountant?

No, many dealers prefer to save money and do their own accounts, but that's assuming that their business is a simple one and they have time. You might feel safer using an accountant or just happier – it's up to you. Not all accountants will understand the antiques business, especially if you're not earning huge amounts of money doing it, so shop around until you find one who does – or speak to a friendly dealer for their recommendations once you've known them for a while. Not all dealers are happy to talk about any financial matters and, with so many still not registered for tax (and liable to be heavily fined when caught out – at best), some will clam up if you even mention accountants.

An accountant is there to help you but only if you make it easy for them by accurate record keeping.

Record Keeping – That Sounds Like Hard Work

It is until you get the hang of it. You are so lucky to be starting out now because you can start as you mean to go on and then it's really easy. I've already made many of these points but you might not have thought of them as record keeping so I'm just going to list what you need for good record keeping:

◆ Buy a file or series of files and write their subject matters on them – receipts for stock, receipts for rent, misc. That's the fun file – all those other expenses such as petrol (if applicable), food, stationery – including the cost of those files – business phone calls, mobile phone and the hundreds of other business expenses which cut into your taxable profits.

♦ Keep receipts – this is the main one. When you buy stock, get a receipt for it – how else are you going to prove that you didn't make more profit if asked?

♦ Bank records – you are required by the Inland Revenue to keep a copy of all of your relevant bank accounts (i.e. any which are even remotely business related). Keep them in a file to keep them all together.

How Long Do I Have to Keep These Records?

Five years. If you don't keep accurate records, you could face fines of up to £3,000 (subject to appeal). On the plus side, good records enable you not just to file easy and accurate tax returns but to see for yourself how well your business is progressing. Good dealers will even do their accounts on the same day as a fair to keep up to date, or first thing the following morning, so they always know how much they have to spend on stock and how successful each fair has – or has not – been.

Record keeping is not enjoyable and can be seen as a waste of time but it isn't. You have to do it for tax reasons but also do it for yourself. It's your business, so keep control of it and watch it grow.

Your Tax Bill

Paying tax should not be seen as a necessity (although it is) but as a way of seeing how successful you have been. The more you have to pay, the better your business, but can you afford to pay it? The ideal is to keep a separate account containing enough money to pay the tax bill when you get it, but few dealers are that well organised. What many dealers do is sell special stock, even part of their own collections, to pay off their tax bill and that's a shame. By being organised, the tax bill becomes an annoyance, not a problem, so try to keep enough aside to pay the bill when it comes.

You're not an employee any more so you don't get your tax sorted out for you. Instead, you will be sent a self-employment supplement with your tax form but ask for one if it is not sent automatically with your tax form. It's easy to fill in with step-by-step instructions. If you have an accountant, they will do it for you and you can even do it over the Internet (*www.inlandrevenue.gov.uk/e-tax/index.htm*) but register early to ensure that your password arrives in time for you to file your return on-line. Don't forget to keep a copy for your own records.

When Do I Have to Send In My Tax Return?

Whilst there is no set date, there are two cut-off points. Ideally, return your form as soon as possible to make your life easier and so that it's done. As long as you have accurate records and a calculator, filing tax returns is as quick and easy as making beans on toast. And both are unpleasant. If you see advertisements on the television or wherever reminding you to return your tax return, and you have not yet got one, phone the tax office immediately. They can make mistakes and fail to send them out but it is you, and not they, who will end up paying the £100 penalty for a late return if you do not arrange to get one in time. The majority of people receive their forms in plenty of time so this should not be a problem.

There are two basic dates by which forms should or must be returned.

If you send your form by the end of September, the Inland Revenue will calculate your tax for you and you have until January to pay.

However, if, like millions of people, you delay it until the end of January, you not only have to calculate your own tax (not as difficult as it sounds but time-consuming, especially if maths is not your strong point) but pay it by the end of January as well, or face paying interest until it is paid in full.

And if you don't send your form by January? You get a Late Penalty Notice – better known as a £100 fine with another £100 if you still don't send it. Do what I do and send your form by registered delivery, no matter when you send it. That way, you have proof that it was not only sent but arrived on time – just in case.

And Then There's VAT – Or Is There?

If you are not earning £56,000 or more (VAT threshold at the time of writing), then you do not need to be VAT registered. But what does 'earning £56,000 or more' actually mean? We're not talking profits, but overall takings, regardless of profit margins. If you earn £56,000 or over as a dealer, you have to be VAT registered. If you have a job paying you £50,000 pa (or whatever), and you become a dealer in your spare time and take £6,000 or more over the course of the tax year, you've earned enough money to cross the VAT threshold. If in doubt, ring your local VAT office (listed under Government Offices in your local phone directory). In real terms, this means that you:

- need an accountant
- need to keep very accurate records
- have extra paperwork to do
- need to list your VAT number on all of your receipts or business paperwork
- need to be able to afford to pay your VAT bills regularly
- can claim VAT back on everything from petrol to stock from other VAT registered dealers
- should be delighted – you're a success.

Everyone hopes to avoid paying VAT, not just because it eats 17.5% of your takings, but also because of the paperwork. Yet there is something almost enviable about those who do earn that much – because they've made it.

Further Help

The government has produced a variety of leaflets which explain all of these points in more detail or contain registration forms. If you have access to the Internet, their website (*www.hmce.gov.uk*) is superb and can offer up-to-date information regarding VAT and its rules – amongst other things. The majority of their leaflets and forms are reproduced on this site. I have also found the VAT helpline (0845 101 9000) very useful, and manned by friendly and efficient staff who know the system very well – if in doubt, ask.

CHAPTER TWO

Customs and Excise

This is as much fun as tax, but it needn't be. First, if you have no intention of buying or selling abroad, this does not concern you. However, if, like me, you've become addicted to the Internet and know that the rest of the world, in particular America, is one big, round profit, then you need to read on. Why? Because I'm about to save you some money. And it's all perfectly legal.

When you're sending goods overseas, it's up to the buyer to pay the Customs Duties for that country. There are certain things which are not permissible or difficult to send abroad, such as Works of Art classified as 'national treasures' or firearms (amongst others). This probably won't concern you but it needed to be said. If in any doubt, contact the Department of Trade and Industry (020 7215 5000) and ask about exporting goods.

However, if you're importing goods either by post or bringing them back into the country with you from a buying trip (often a good way to combine a holiday with a stock-buying excursion – Canada is perfect for this), then you might need to know about Customs Duties. Note, I said 'might'. If you are living in an EU country such as Great Britain and buying from another EU country such as France with its fabulous antiques fairs and markets, then you don't need to pay Duty. Why? Because it's classified as **Free Trade** – there are no Customs barriers between such countries, so no charges.

But there are charges for buying from other countries and these depend on what you're purchasing. Some of these charges can seem a bit confusing but they shouldn't be. I just have goods sent to me and pay the relevant amount when they arrive, but that might not be as easy as it sounds. You could end up paying too much.

Let's simplify this before we all get bogged down. *Goods are classified, that means put into different sections, according to Customs and Excise. The Classification Helpline (01702 366077) is there to help you know which category your goods should be in.*

Simple enough – most dealers don't even bother with that. If you're buying goods from overseas with tight profit margins, Customs Duties can not only eat the profit but end up making the item too expensive to sell on. It's important to know what charges to expect. There are too many types of goods and charges for me to list here so call the National Advice Service for help (0845 010 9000) and ask about specific charges. Three of the more popular ones are listed here:

♦ antiques – for goods over 100 years old, there is no duty but a reduced VAT charge of 5%
♦ collectables – no duty but a reduced VAT charge of 5%
♦ jewellery – 2–4% of the item's cost + VAT (17.5%) on the Duty (i.e. the 2–4%).

You'll probably be buying collectables at some time in your career but, if you import them, you could be charged the full rate for china (or whatever), which will include the full VAT of 17.5%. This can make your bargain buy no longer profitable or even sellable. Don't worry, if it's collectable you can pay the reduced rate.

How Do I Prove Something's Collectable to Get the Reduced Rate?

When I asked Customs for a definition of collectable, I was told that it must be something which people collect. Not always easy to explain, but make it easier for everyone and take a magazine or book proving that your piece has a collectors' market. The name and contact details of a collectors' club could also help. They just need to see that it's collectable to reduce the rate, if it isn't done already – articles in magazines are perfect for that or even books such as this one can help to save you money.

How and Where Do I Pay?

You'll probably receive a note through your door asking you to collect your package or parcel to pay Customs Duties. Depending on its size, this could be your local Post Office's delivery office or a regional one. Go prepared, have a piece of paper with the classification details (if applicable) and Duty rate (most larger libraries contain the Customs and Excise Duties book in their reference section or just ring the Helpline) and, if applicable, something proving that your goods are collectable. If the rate which they're charging is correct, pay in cash or a cheque (accepted up to the card limit only in most cases). If not, appeal. You might not be able to collect your parcel at the time if you appeal so decide if it's worth it – how much would you lose if you're being overcharged and how quickly do you need the goods? Most appeals can be sorted out immediately, whilst others take a few days. Offer to speak to the Customs officer over the phone if necessary and speak calmly – you have nothing to hide and it's only a small annoyance.

Customs Duties are annoying but necessary, unfortunately. Yes, you can smuggle goods into the country from trips abroad. You might get away with it but you might not.

> One dealer thought that he was being very clever. He sent some of his goods home in one post clearly marked as 'gift' (i.e. he was trying to avoid Duty by not admitting that his goods were merchandise – despite him being a VAT registered dealer). In another post, he sent a letter to himself listing how much he'd paid for everything – he didn't even try to disguise his writing or send it to a friend. Customs intercepted both the parcel and the letter. They then visited his house and removed a huge amount of stock – for back taxes and unpaid Customs Duties.

You might be able to get away with not declaring goods or you might not – that dealer probably wishes that he had declared the goods. It would have been much cheaper.

Useful tip

I have friends who work for Customs – they're antiques dealers as well and love listening to fellow dealers boasting how much stock they've smuggled in. So be careful.

When I go through Customs at the airport on my way home from an overseas buying trip, I go prepared. I have a list of what I've bought and how much I've paid for it in my handbag. I carry all of my stock in a separate bag so that I can produce it with minimum inconvenience and I calmly wait until I'm called when walking through the red channel. I never try to hide anything, just pay what I owe and, when it's all over, I repack my goods and go home – then I add the Customs Duties onto the price of my stock. On one trip, together with the cost of my flight, hotel and food, I only had to add £3 to the cost of each item. It was definitely worth it for my peace of mind. Customs Duties are not fun, they do cut into your profit but it's much easier to pay them and pass the cost on to your customers than risk getting caught or to go to the other extreme and just not buy from overseas at all – you'll miss out on some good stock if you do that.

CHAPTER THREE

Insurance

Have you ever wondered about the crashes you hear at fairs? You probably just assume that the dealer will take such losses out of their insurance, but they probably won't because *the vast majority of dealers are not insured*. Before we go to a fair, we have to agree to the organisers' rules. One of the rules, used by most organisers, is not to charge them in the event of an accident – even if it's their fault. We agree to it almost without thought, but what happens if a dealer has a large vase which is knocked over on top of someone's head and injures them? Chances are, they won't be insured and the injured party will have to sue them in the hope that the dealer can actually afford to pay compensation. While most, if not all, shops will have indemnity insurance for such reasons, most dealers won't. Why? Because they can't afford it.

What Is Insurance?

Insurance is there to protect you from loss or injury – even both. If your entire stock is broken or stolen and you're not insured, you lose it all. It seems sensible, when you hear this, to take out insurance. Well, it does and it doesn't for the simple reason that specialist insurance can be too costly to be viable, especially in such a high turnover business. It's entirely up to you. I would suggest that you at least look into it, you might decide that you'd rather not risk being without it. There are not many antiques insurers around but try Anthony Wakefield and Co in Dorking (0800 28 18 04). If you have pricier stock, or a large collection worth a minimum of £125,000, it might be worth speaking to AXA (020 7265 4600). As well as protecting your business, you should also think about your household insurance – if you have good antiques or a collection at home, think about insuring them. It will cost extra but so does peace of mind. When I had a china collection, I insured it – the idea of losing a lifetime's worth of costly collecting in a single fire was appeased by a small fee. Shop around and see who offers you the best deal.

You should also register as a part-time or full-time antiques dealer on your car insurance if you use it for business use. Just remember to add the extra cost onto your stock and budget accordingly. You can get fined if not.

Insurance is the price that you pay for a good night's sleep. I've written articles about people who've lost £40,000 + worth of stock which was uninsured because they didn't take sensible precautions. Some of the best insurance needn't cost you a penny – because it's basic common sense:

- Empty your car immediately after a fair, never leave the goods in the car overnight – and load it with stock on the morning of the fair, not the night before.

- Avoid telling people where you live and don't invite strangers into your home.

- Hide antiques or expensive items when you have workmen/estate agents in the house. If you are trying to sell your house, remove your better items from show.

- Buy an ultraviolet pen from your local police station or at fairs and mark expensive or personal items with your postcode – remember to re-mark them if you move. This is a very good way of helping police to recover your goods. Do not use on stock – you'll be telling people where you live and the goods are only yours for the short-term.

- Never leave goods in an insecure building such as an unlocked garden shed or garage.

- Cover up stock if it can be seen from the outside.

- Don't leave expensive items out overnight at fairs, even if the buildings are going to be locked. Take them with you or wrap them and hide in a box under your stall.

- Always check that your table and clamped shelves are up properly at fairs before putting stock on them to avoid those costly crashes.

- Ask antiques centres about security before agreeing to move in.

- Instal an alarm which connects straight to the police station if you have a shop.

- Increase your security at home, add locks to windows and top quality door locks if you don't already have them – add the extra cost to your stock.

Conclusion

Do you still want to become a dealer after reading this far? I hope so, because dealing can offer you not just a career but a whole new lifestyle. You will be your own boss, there are no goals to achieve apart from those which you have set yourself, there is no pressure. Everything you do is your own choice. Dealing offers an enviable freedom. It can also offer hardships but it needn't. Dealing is as much about you as antiques. The market can dip and soar, just keep going and don't be at the mercy of fashion or your own fears. Take the leap and do it well. *Start slowly, start small and build up. Who knows, you might even be stalling next to me soon. Good luck.*

I'm going to finish with a list of dos and don'ts. Please remember what I've said and take as much as you can from this book. Just follow these few, simple guides and you'll be a successful dealer:

Do

◆ Enjoy it – this is your business and you have no one telling you what to do so what's not to enjoy?

◆ Smile – a cheap and easy way to increase sales.

◆ Learn – I've been doing this for 20 years and I'm still learning. With knowledge comes profit and you'll never get bored.

◆ Be honest – it will increase your sales and keep you enjoying what you do.

◆ Take extra clothing – those halls and outdoor pitches get cold, even in the summer. Layer up and strip down when necessary.

◆ Book early if you want to do a fair – you'll get in and might even get an early-booking discount.

◆ Replace your stock regularly – to increase sales and interest.

◆ Communicate – to increase sales, even before you've bought the goods.

◆ Make friends – it's a strange business, your neighbours at fairs might leave without saying goodbye when you've spent a whole day chatting but you will also make some good friends, some of them might even be your customers.

◆ Buy what you like or enjoy the profits – not always the same thing.

◆ Arrange your goods attractively – it will increase sales.

◆ Go to auctions on a regular basis (if you can afford it) – good stock for cheap prices and a good way of catching up on local trading news.

◆ Try to do regular fairs if you want – a good way to build up regular customers.

◆ Buy your own food – you never know what's on offer, especially if you're travelling around.

◆ Arrive early, no matter what you're doing – good parking goes quickly.

◆ Carry cash when you can – makes life easier.

◆ Make a profit.

Don't

◆ Go back on your trade prices.

◆ Give a 'better price' on an 'NT' (no trade) item.

- Have 'sales' – it makes you look not only cheap but as though you normally over-charge. Sales have no place in the antiques business. That's what trade prices are for.

- Get stuck in a rut – if you get bored change your stock, not your way of life.

- Take it to heart – some customers are just rude, don't take it personally.

- Answer back – no matter how much they deserve it. Just rise above it.

- Use price guides.

- Book a fair if you have problems with the organiser.

- Sell fakes – even if you were caught out and just want your money back.

- Waste your time doing valuations for free.

- Take the same old stock to the same old fair – auction off tired stock and use the money to buy new stock.

- Try to get a sale when it's clear that you're not going to – don't waste your time.

- Be impatient – just relax and enjoy it.

And that's the most important thing – enjoy it. I wouldn't still be dealing – or have written this book – if it weren't an enjoyable way of life. Enjoy!

Useful Publications

Antiques and Collectables Magazine, Merricks Media Ltd, Cambridge House South, Henry Street, Bath BA1 1JT. Tel: (01225) 786814. Monthly, £2.95. Interesting articles.

Antique and Collectors Trader, P.O. Box 2034, Hockley, Essex SS5 5YW. Tel: (01702) 207400. Monthly, free at some fairs. Fair listings, some fair news.

Antique Dealer Newspaper, 115 Shaftesbury Avenue, London WC2H 8AD. Tel: (020) 7420 6680. Monthly, free or £1.50 (depending where seen). Good for fair news, reviews and listings.

Antique Trade Calendar, G.P. London, 32 Fredericks Place, North Finchley, London N12 8QE. Tel: (020) 8446 3604. Every three months, £1.50. The best of the fair-listing guides because of its convenient, three-monthly format.

Antiques Diary, P.O. Box 30, Twyford, Reading RG10 8DQ. Tel: (0118) 940 2165. Bimonthly, £1.50. Listings guide. Formerly divided into areas (eg London and southern) which was inconvenient to most dealers, the publication has now united to produce one, nationwide listings guide – much better.

Antiques Info, P.O. Box 93, Broadstairs, Kent CT10 3YR. Tel: (01843) 862069. Bimonthly, £2.70. Good for auction and fair listings, especially for providing auction information in two-monthly slots.

Antiques Trade Gazette, 115 Shaftesbury Avenue, London WC2H 8AD. Tel: (020) 7420 6601. Weekly, £1.80. Good for auction and fair news and listings, the dealer's must-buy newspaper.

Collect it!, Unit 11, Weller Drive, Hogwood Lane Industrial Estate, Finchampstead, Berks RG40 4QZ. Tel: (0118) 973 7888. Monthly, £2.80. Good for collectables information and articles.

The Carboot and Market Calendar, P.O. Box 277, Hereford HR2 9AY. Tel: (01981) 251633. Bimonthly £1.50. Listings of car boot sales with useful contact numbers.

Index

For more detailed listings, please refer to the Contents section at the beginning of the book. This includes individual listings of types of furniture, makes of china, glass etc.